Narrative Craft

Lucy Calkins and Alexandra Marron

Photography by Peter Cunningham

HEINEMANN ◆ PORTSMOUTH, NH

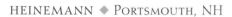

This book is dedicated to Mom, my best friend and greatest confidant.
—Ali

This book is dedicated to the memory of Donald Murray, who taught me to write.
—Lucy

firsthand
An imprint of Heinemann
361 Hanover Street
Portsmouth, NH 03801-3912
www.heinemann.com

Offices and agents throughout the world

© 2013 by Lucy Calkins and Alexandra Marron

The authors and publisher wish to thank those who have generously given permission to reprint borrowed material:

Excerpts from "Eleven" from *Woman Hollering Creek*. Copyright © 1991 by Sandra Cisneros. Published by Vintage Books, a division of Random House Inc., and originally in hardcover by Random House Inc. By permission of Susan Bergholz Literary Services, New York, NY and Lamy, NM and by permission of Bloomsbury Publishing Plc. All rights reserved.

"Papa Who Wakes Up Tired in the Dark" from *The House on Mango Street*. Copyright © 1984 by Sandra Cisneros. Published by Vintage Books, a division of Random House, Inc., and in hardcover by Alfred A. Knopf in 1994. By permission of Susan Bergholz Literary Services, New York, NY and Lamy, NM and by permission of Bloomsbury Publishing Plc. All rights reserved.

Excerpt from *Stevie* by John Steptoe. Copyright © 1969 by John L. Steptoe. Use licensed by the John Steptoe Literary Trust and HarperCollins Publishers. Used by permission of HarperCollins Publishers with the approval of the Estate of John Steptoe.

Cataloging-in-Publication data is on file with the Library of Congress.

ISBN-13: 978-0-325-04740-9
ISBN-10: 0-325-04740-5

Production: Elizabeth Valway, David Stirling, and Abigail Heim
Cover and interior designs: Jenny Jensen Greenleaf
Series photographs by Peter Cunningham, Nadine Baldasare, and Elizabeth Dunford
Composition: Publishers' Design and Production Services, Inc.
Manufacturing: Steve Bernier

Printed in the United States of America on acid-free paper
17 16 15 14 13 ML 3 4 5

Acknowledgments

WE OFTEN TELL CHILDREN that it takes courage to take your best ideas and to say, "These aren't good enough. I can do better," and then to stand on the shoulders of that draft, reaching to do more, to be more. That's what it felt like to the two of us when we tackled this project. It's not as if we had problems with the ideas in *Raising the Quality of Narrative Writing* from the original Units of Study for Teaching Writing, Grades 3–5. We just knew that after teaching narrative writing for all these many years, in classrooms that dot the entire globe, we've learned a lot, and we could, if we tried, create a new book, a new unit, that was worlds better. That is what we have aimed to do.

We're grateful, most of all, to each other, that the other was willing to take a turn asking, "Wait, is that the best we can do?" But it hasn't been just the two of us. We're grateful to Kate Montgomery, who has a special knack for finding the simplest way to say something, for making sure that what we say has all the integrity and complexity in the world.

Hareem Atif Khan, our colleague who lives in Pakistan and is helping to bring literacy to that corner of the world, flew to New York City and put on the yoke of this book, helping us to move it along. Hareem's help is especially evident in the story of Luka and in some of the reading-writing connection work in the final moments of the unit. Bless you, Hareem. Julia Mooney, Kelly Boland, Anna Gratz, and Audra Robb have been sources of support and companionship, and we are grateful to them.

The book benefits from the Teachers College Reading and Writing Project's decades of work developing the methods of teaching and curriculum development that inform everything we have designed. We're grateful to the long list of heroes in the field of writing that have informed the Project's work over all these years: to Pulitzer Prize–winning writer the late Donald Murray, who opened this field to us, to the late Donald Graves, who helped the world understand the power of teaching children writing, to some of the earliest staff members of the TCRWP who have gone on to become nationally known including Randy and Katherine Bomer, Georgia Heard, Katie Ray, Ralph Fletcher, and Nick Flynn and writers such as Katherine Paterson, Patti MacLachlen, Jim Howe, Eloise Greenfield, Naomi Shihab Nye, Kate DiCamillo, and so many others who have helped us and our students learn to write and to want to write.

We're grateful to the entire team at Heinemann. The whole organization has devoted itself to the effort of making these books the best they can be, working with energy and the highest of aspirations. Thanks to Roberta Lew, who has conducted many year-long negotiations with publishers, agents, and authors to secure permissions to use excerpts and images throughout these series, without which these units could contain none of the children's literature and mentor texts that give it such depth. She has even convinced publishers to reissue out-of-print books and, in some cases, print entirely new books especially for the teachers of this series. A special nod also to Elizabeth Valway and Jean Lawler and the rest of the production editors who have entered changes to every page in all the many drafts of this book and others, taking the time to think through the implications of those changes and following up on them. We are more thankful than we can say. Thanks also to lead editor Teva Blair, who has shepherded this project along from the outset and done a graceful job of perfecting and polishing manuscripts.

As in all the units in this series, the class described in this unit is a composite class, with children and partnerships of children gleaned from classrooms in very different contexts, then put together here. We wrote the units this way to bring you both a wide array of wonderful, quirky, various children and also to illustrate for you the predictable (and unpredictable) situations and responses this unit has created in classrooms across the nation and world.

Contents

BEND III   Learning from Mentor Texts

Welcome to the Unit

ALTHOUGH THIS UNIT IS TITLED *NARRATIVE CRAFT*, the real goal is to improve the quality of all writing—and the lasting knowledge and skill of the *writers*. In this first unit of study, you'll strive toward independence and toward dramatic growth in the level of your students' writing, leading them (and you) to leave this one unit expecting that their writing will continue to improve in obvious, dramatic ways as each new unit unfolds. Independence and growth are utterly interrelated, because you'll need to organize a writing workshop within which students work with great investment toward clear goals and within clear structures. This will allow students to hum along, drawing on their growing repertoire of strategies and working with independence. Clear goals and strong samples of mentor texts will play an integral role. Throughout the unit, it will be important to illuminate for students what it is that they are trying to accomplish. It is definitely not enough for them to aim to "tell what I did." Students need to understand they are writing narratives, stories, and need to draw on all they know about narrative writing to craft effective stories. But even that goal—writing effective stories—is not clear enough. What does it mean to write a "great story"? What is a great story? In this unit, you help students crystallize their images of strong narratives, self-assess using student-facing rubrics, and set goals that accelerate their achievement.

The unit described here provides you with an opportunity to teach a class of students the work called for in the Common Core State Standards for Narrative Writing. Expect that some of your students may need more than this one narrative unit before they can reach the ambitious Common Core State Standards skill levels for fifth grade. Because the skills required for narrative writing align with the skills required for opinion and informational writing, this unit can bring your class of writers a long distance toward developing not only the skills needed for narrative writing but also those needed for fifth-grade writing across all genres. That is, in fifth grade, writers need to elaborate more. Narrative writers use detail and description; informational writers use quotations and concrete details. But writers of both kinds of texts need to travel more slowly over the terrain of a topic, grounding their writing in a wealth of specificity, and they need to reread to check for elaboration, returning to important sections to stretch those out by telling them in a more bit-by-bit way. This is just one of the many skills called for in narrative writing, and it can be transferred and adapted to other genres of writing.

It will be especially important for you to be mindful of the overarching ways the CCSS raise the ante for fifth-graders. By fifth grade, writers are expected to use a variety of narrative techniques to develop their stories and, more specifically, their characters. Fifth-graders must learn to manage not only the story (conveying experiences and events precisely and vividly), but also the pacing of events. The Common Core expects that fifth-graders come to writing workshop with years' worth of strategies, allowing these young people to draw on those strategies with increasing independence and facility. To make choices, fifth-graders need to bring their interpretation skills to bear on their own emerging drafts. Just as they read fiction and nonfiction texts, thinking about the shared ideas that are forwarded in those texts and thinking also about the ways authorial decisions have been inspired by the author's intended messages, so too, fifth-graders now need to reread their own emerging drafts, making sure that they are highlighting the central ideas that they want readers to draw from their texts. This means it is especially important for your students to be clear why they are telling a story so they make craft decisions with purposes in mind. The experience of angling their own stories to highlight themes will help students as they work to read interpretively, not only thinking about the central meanings in a text but also noticing how two authors may address the same theme differently.

The expectations embedded in the Common Core State Standards are especially high for narrative writing. Look at the narrative that is included in Appendix C for grade 5, and it will be clear to you that before all your students can meet these ambitious levels, they'll need to invest a lot of time and energy developing their skills. You'll want to communicate to students that it is not practice alone that leads to perfection. The saying should be "Perfect practice makes perfect." That is, for students' skill levels to increase dramatically, they need to be engaged in a cycle of goal-setting, strategic work, self-assessment, and feedback. This cycle will alter students' writing processes so they use their notebooks more as workbenches to try, try, try to achieve specific goals. Research is clear that nothing you can do will have a greater effect than this combination: giving students clear goals, opportunities for engaged work, feedback, and a rallying cry to progress in worthy, significant, concrete ways.

OVERVIEW OF THE UNIT

You will begin the unit by telling your students that they will be revisiting narrative writing. The important message that you'll convey is that this means they will be expected to draw on all they know from prior years of work with narrative writing. This is a perfect opportunity to teach your students that writers carry with them and draw on a repertoire of strategies. For starters, instead of launching your year by teaching a few new strategies for generating narrative writing, you'll want to remind students to draw on the repertoire of strategies they have already learned for generating narrative writing, and this time to aim to use those strategies really well, like professional writers do. For example, instead of jotting any possible topic onto a list, pros generate ideas and dismiss most of them, recording only the best possible candidates. To do this, pros draw on all they know about what makes for a powerful story idea. In this sort of way, your teaching revisits familiar ground in ways that aim for depth.

One of the reasons that it is so important to teach for transfer, helping writers to draw on all they have already learned about good writing, is that this allows writers to be decision makers. During each day's writing workshop, writers need to assess their work, review their options, and make decisions about the work that needs to be done. As they do this, they draw on their complete repertoire of tools and strategies as well as on that day's minilesson. But your emphasis on writing instruction cumulating is a way to also emphasize that the work that writers do each day is certainly not determined merely by that day's minilesson.

That is, you will want to approach the unit anticipating that in all ways, you'll be traveling familiar ground in hopes of raising the level of student work. You can raise the level of work by emphasizing what it means to do any strategy really well and by emphasizing that writers must make decisions based on their plans for a piece of writing, their assessment of the draft, and their full knowledge. But you will also raise the quality of writing by emphasizing the importance of meaning, of significance.

Fifth-graders want to do work that feels important. They've had years of writing little vignettes about getting lost in Macy's or about scoring the winning goal at the soccer game. You'll raise the level of the entire unit if you can rally students to tackle stories of personal significance. Early in the unit, you will find yourself saying something like this to your children: "Your 'I made a soccer goal' story could be anyone's story. James Merrill said, 'The stories you write first are anybody's stories. You have to make them your own.' What is your story of this soccer game? What was going on for you that wasn't going on for anybody else? Where's the real story here?" In an effort to help students write stories that carry significance and that are shaped like true stories, not like chronicles, you'll teach some new strategies for generating personal narrative writing as well as reminding students of strategies they already know. For example, you may teach your students that when a writer wants to write a powerful personal narrative, it can sometimes work to write about the first (or last) time they did something, or about a time they learned something, or to take a topic of personal interest, say, "competition with my brother," and to think about a turning-point story related to that.

Once the unit is well underway, and you've emphasized that writers draw on all they know as they begin a new cycle of writing work, it will be important to find ways to immediately lift the quality of students' work. Pulitzer Prize–winning writer Donald Murray, credited as the father of the writing process, has often said that the single most important quality of all narrative writing is show, don't tell. In effective narrative writing, the entire story is shown, it is dramatized, instead of summarized. As Mark Twain said, "Don't say the old lady screamed. Bring her on and let her scream." The implication of this is that perhaps the one most important way to lift the level of work in this unit is by helping children dream the dream of their stories, reexperiencing an event as they put pen to paper. At the start of the unit, then, you devote a sequence of days to helping students learn to step inside the shoes of the character (in this case, themselves at a different time and place!) and write in the point of view and with the details that are true to the unfolding story.

Throughout this unit, you'll also be supporting new levels of productivity, as is fitting for students who are on the brink of entering middle school. The first bend of this unit is also the start of the school year, and you'll want to go to some lengths to convey your high expectations for productivity. In this bend, you'll expect students to write at least a long (one and a half– or two-page) entry each day, and more for homework.

In Bend II, the second part of the unit, students will choose a seed idea to take through the writing process. You'll help students draw on all the narrative crafting techniques they have ever learned, and your emphasis will be on teaching students that craft and revision are always driven by an effort to communicate meaning. Deciding on a good lead, for example, requires the writer to think, "What is my story really about?" "What am I *really* wanting to say about this event?" As part of this, you will help students learn that the same story can be told differently, depending on the theme the writer wants to bring out. An episode about falling from the monkey bars could be written to show that the writer was afraid but conquered her fears or to show that peer pressure goaded the writer to take reckless risks. By the end of Bend II, students will have written two entire drafts (and been reminded that it usually helps to draft quickly, letting velocity help to create cohesion and to bring voice to the piece) and will have revised their best draft extensively.

In Bend III, the last part of the unit, students will begin anew with a third personal narrative. This time, you'll help them draw on all they learned earlier to progress with more independence. You'll encourage them also to learn from close reading of a mentor text, the narrative section of Cisneros's "Eleven." You will remind them of the power of asking, "What did Sandra Cisneros do to write her story that I, too, could try?" Students will then develop their skills at analyzing and annotating mentor texts and emulating the craft moves of a published author. As they do this, you will return to the work that you taught earlier in the unit—reminding children of the importance of dramatizing a scene to capture the unfolding experience on the page. You'll again help writers relive the event to recapture the truth of the experience. Children will

have much to draw on from their first round of writing and will continue to self-evaluate and set goals as they move forward.

ASSESSMENT

Before you start this unit, we recommend that you take just a bit of time to establish a baseline understanding of your students' skills as narrative writers. This assessment is crucial. We'll provide you with instruments—learning progressions, rubrics, checklists, and a set of exemplar texts written by students—that will help you to see where, in the trajectory of writing development, each of your students lies. The assessment system will help you and your students see next steps. Then, too, this initial assessment is necessary for you to track each individual's progress—and to help your students see themselves improving. The improvement will be palpable. At your first parent-teacher conferences, you'll be able to say, "This is what your child's writing was like at the very start of the year. And look, *this* is what she can do now!"

For this initial assessment to provide accurate baseline data on your writers' narrative skills, be careful not to scaffold your students' work during the assessment. You'll want to simply remind students of the basic qualities you'd expect in a piece of narrative writing, then step back and leave them to their own devices. We recommend that you give students this prompt to start them off (you can find this prompt and more explanation about our assessment system in the *Writing Pathways: Performance Assessments and Learning Progressions, K–5* book that comes with this series):

"I'm really eager to understand what you can do as writers of narratives, of stories, so today, will you please write the best personal narrative, the best Small Moment story, that you can write? Make this be the story of one time in your life. You might focus on just a scene or two. You'll have only forty-five minutes to write this true story, so you'll need to plan, draft, revise, and edit in one sitting. Write in a way that allows you to show off all you know about narrative writing. In your writing, make sure you:

- "Write a beginning for your story

- Use transition words to tell what happened in order

- Elaborate to help readers picture your story

- Show what your story is really about

- Write an ending for your story"

If you worry that saying, "Welcome to a new year. I want to begin by evaluating you," might seem harsh, you might soften this by saying that you can't wait until the end of September before having some of your students' writing to display on bulletin boards. Or perhaps you can make this on-demand writing feel celebratory by saying that you realized from things they've said that many of them are entering your classroom already knowing a lot about writing, and you want to give them all a chance to show off. Just be careful that you don't find yourself being so chatty about this whole endeavor that you end up teaching them a quick course on narrative writing prior to the assessment, unless your whole school has agreed to do that. You will want the various classrooms in a grade to do this on-demand assessment in ways that are consistent across the classrooms.

We suggest that when you tell students the prompt and tell them (or show them the chart of) bulleted suggestions, your students are already at their regular writing seats. Be sure your students have familiar paper to write on and a supply of additional pages if they want them.

We encourage you to duplicate your students' on-demand narratives and to give one copy to each student, asking each writer to tape his on-demand writing into the first page of his writer's notebook, where it can serve as a reminder to the writer and to you that this is the level of work that the writer was able to do at the very start of the year. By keeping the on-demand writing close on hand, you can help writers hold themselves to the job of making sure all their subsequent writing is progressively better. As students collect narrative entries in the days ahead, ask them to look back frequently at their on-demand piece, making sure that they are getting palpably stronger in comparison.

You will also need to assess where each writer falls in the Narrative Writing Learning Progression and to note where the bulk of your class falls, letting that information inform your teaching in the upcoming unit of study. To do this, we suggest you read each student's writing, comparing it to the exemplar texts provided at each level, and then read the specific descriptors to hone in on the specific ways that a student can improve. No text will match a level in its entirety, so don't be knocked off kilter if a piece of writing seems to be generally one level, but there a few criteria it does not meet. The descriptors of the criteria will be particularly useful as you help writers know concrete steps they can take to make their writing better. That is, if a writer's narrative writing is level 5, you and that writer can look at the descriptors of, say, character development for level 5 and note whether the writing adheres to those. If so,

tell that child—or your whole class, if this is broadly applicable—"You used to develop the people in your stories by . . . ," and read the descriptors from the prior level, "but now you are . . . ," and read the level 5 descriptor. "Can I give you a pointer about a way to make your writing even better? Try . . . ," and read from the level 6 descriptor. You can even say, "Let me show you an example," and to do so, you can cite a section of the level 6 benchmark text.

One final word. The baseline assessment is not assessing you. It is assessing the background your children have when they enter your classroom. But when this unit ends, you'll repeat this assessment exactly, and when you collect the student writing and look between the first on-demand and the second, the progress that you see will allow for an assessment not only of your students but also of your teaching and of this curriculum, too. At the end of the *Shaping Texts* unit, you will again conduct an assessment, because that unit's instruction will promote both narrative and essay writing skills. We have found that when you teach knowing that judgment will not revolve around the published texts that writers produced with your input (and ours) but will, instead, revolve around what writers do without any input, in an on-demand situation, this serves as a reminder to you. It reminds you that the goal of any writing instruction is not to produce strong writing. It is to produce strong writers. If we teach in ways that lift the level of today's piece of writing but that does not leave writers able to do better work another day, on another piece, then that teaching is for naught. The good news is that will not be the case. You'll look back on the baseline data you collect at the start of this unit and at the work students eventually produce and say, "Look at this progress!"

GETTING READY

Because in this unit children will be using a writer's notebook, you will want to create a certain fanfare around this very grown-up, professional writing tool. You will also want to make sure you have your own writer's notebook (or one borrowed from a colleague or downloaded from a famous writer on the Internet) filled with various entries that have been sparked by thinking about memorable moments with special people or events that happened in special places. If you plan to have your students decorate their notebooks with photos and pictures that might spark stories, then you should decorate yours also in a similar way. If you want your students to carry their notebooks with them always, then you should also, sharing stories of how you were able to jot down events right after they happened or how disappointed you were when there was a time you didn't have your notebook with you. You will probably be the first living, breathing author they know first hand, so everything you do as a writer will inspire them to do the same.

You will also want to gather examples of fifth-grade writing so your students have a vision of the kind of writing they will be doing. You can find some examples on the CD-ROM, but the best are examples that come from your own students or the students of colleagues because that way you know the inside story behind the stories, which children always find intriguing. In addition, throughout the sessions, we suggest returning to the same author, Sandra Cisneros, and the same texts, "Eleven" and "Papa," so that children can become used to reading closely like a writer. Of course, you can choose any author and book you love that has the qualities of good writing you hope to teach, but in either case, the important thing is to have an author who becomes like your coteacher in the room, sitting on your shoulder, whispering writing advice into your ear, and eventually into your students' ears.

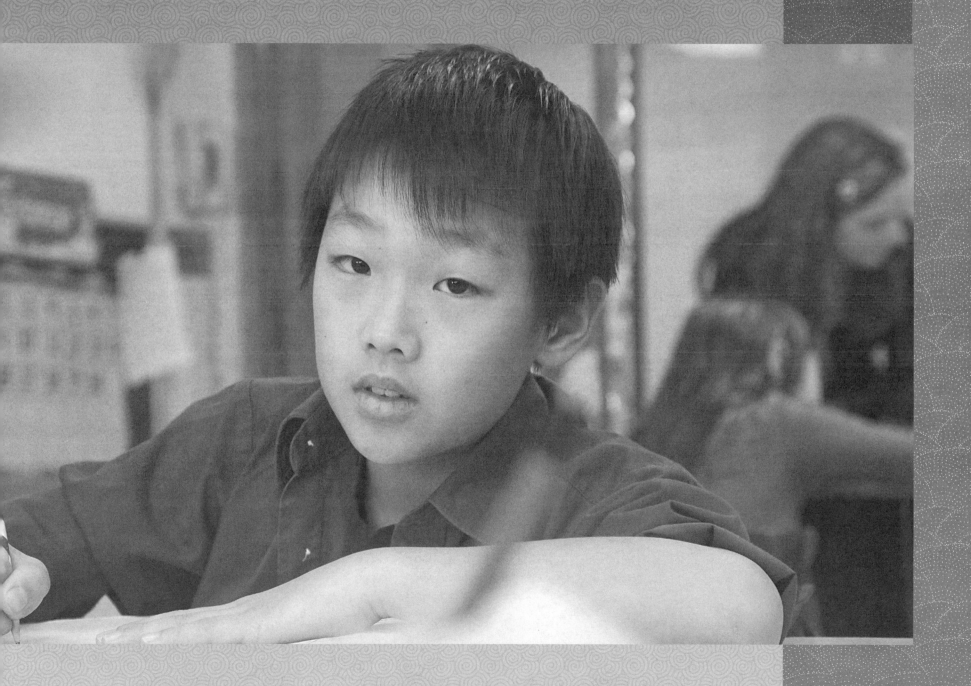

Starting with Turning Points

IN THIS SESSION, you'll teach students that to come up with ideas for personal narratives, it can help to think of turning-point moments.

GETTING READY

✔ The first minilesson assumes that just prior to it, you gave your children an on-demand, narrative writing assessment.

✔ Each child will need his or her own writer's notebook and a writing tool.

✔ On large chart paper, titled "Strategies for Generating Personal Narrative Writing," chart the first bullet ahead of time (see Connection). You'll have asked students (or their teachers) to report on collecting strategies they learned in the preceding year. If they do not seem to have a repertoire of strategies for generating narrative writing, alter the minilesson so that you do not refer to this background knowledge.

✔ Prepare your own example of a first time, last time, or time when you realized something important to include in your list of turning-point moments (see Teaching).

✔ Markers for writing on the chart

✔ Prepare your own example of a time when writing worked for you and a time when it was difficult (see Share).

COMMON CORE STATE STANDARDS: W.5.3, W.5.8, W.5.10, RL.5.2, SL.5.1, SL.5.4, L.5.1, L.5.2, L.5.3

WHEN I WAS YOUNG, every evening I rode my bike around Windover Drive, calling "Games in the circle at seven, games in the circle at seven" like a young Paul Revere. As day turned to dusk, whoever "it" was would kick the can and we'd scatter to hide. Some would be found, then the dusk would deepen, lights would go on in the houses, and mothers would appear in doorways to signal kids home. The final call would go out: "All-y, all-y in free, all-y, all-y in free. Come out, come out, wherever you are." Kids would drop from low-hanging branches and emerge from the back seat of the farm jalopy and from the bushes that lined the farmhouse.

That call—"All-y, all-y in free, come out, come out, wherever you are," happens whenever we teach writing. Young people come to us and they are hiding. Fifth-graders, especially, are hiding. They enter our classrooms on the brink of adolescence, writing in tiny scrawl, elbows covering their pages. Reading what they've written, I often find myself wanting to call, "Come out, come out, wherever you are."

Today, as you launch the fifth-grade writing workshop, you will call your students out of hiding. To do this, you will need to take the risk of reading your own writing aloud to your students, signaling to them that there is something powerful about putting oneself on the page. Throughout the workshop, you'll help youngsters write with honesty and voice. On the first day of his fifth-grade writing workshop, Roy wrote an entry that began, "One bright Saturday morning, my team played in the soccer finals and I almost made the winning goal."

In a conference, I told Roy about the writer James Merrill, who once said, "The words that come first are anybody's words. You have to make them your own." I told him that his soccer game story could have been anyone's story: one day I played soccer, I made (or did not make) the winning goal. "The end." I added, "Your job when writing is to put your story, your true, lived experience of that day, onto the page. Think about that day, and think about the story you haven't told."

"As you launch the fifth-grade writing workshop, you will call your students out of hiding."

We sat in silence for a moment, and I watched as he flipped through a mental rolodex of memories. Then he shook his head, ever so slightly, as if shaking away a memory, and said, "Nah." I knew better, and pressed him to tell me the story he'd just shaken off.

Roy told me this story.

> That Saturday, my dad said he wanted to drive me to my game and I thought, "Whoa. That's different" because other kids' dads drive them to the games all the time and sit in the bleachers cheering their heads off, but my dad was always working. So it was a big thing that he wanted to drive me. I could have carpooled but I knew he wanted to be nice, so I said great. When we got to the soccer field, he had work, so I got out of the car and started to walk towards the field.

> Then my dad called, "Son . . ." I turned back and as I walked to the car, I thought, "This is when he is gonna give me that little pep talk, those words to keep you going." And when I got to the car, Dad opened the window and leaned his head out and looked at me. Then he put his finger up, like to say, "One reminder." And he said, "Don't blow it." Then my dad rolled up the window and drove away, leaving me standing there, stunned. I walked back onto the field and all I could think was, "What was that?"

After telling this story, Roy reread his old draft—the perfectly okay draft about what happened at the soccer game.

And he realized that the real story wasn't the game, wasn't the score—the real story was about his dad. So Roy rewrote that first draft. He didn't just add a line or two to his draft, or fix his lead. Instead he folded up the first draft, and wrote a version of the story he'd just told me. And this time, he tried to make the story his own.

When Roy wrote this next draft, and read it to the class, you could hear a pin drop in the room. Something changed in that classroom, that moment. It was as if his story has issued the call, "Come out, come out, wherever you are." Children became present in a way they hadn't been, and the year's writing workshop was launched.

Today and tomorrow, you'll hope to accomplish something similar. The actual sessions may not be the most important parts of your teaching. Instead, it will matter tremendously that you wear a love for writing on your sleeve. And your absolute respect for your students as writers, and confidence in their willingness to invest themselves, heart and soul, in writing will matter.

The year ahead will be a fast-paced, demanding year for both you and your students. They are on the brink of middle school, and the expectations for their writing will accelerate quickly. During the upcoming weeks, you'll teach them to angle their writing to advance a theme, to work within the confines of story structure, to regard time in their texts as flexible, using backstory and foreshadowing to forward meaning.

It may be tempting to ready yourselves for the onslaught of new expectations, for the accelerating speed and scale of it all, by bypassing any effort to create a trusting community, hurrying past any effort to help students write the truth of their lives. Don't do that! Bypassing those essentials would be a big mistake. Your students are, in the end, no different than you and I. They are eager to work with heart and soul on projects that matter, but they need to know their contributions carry significance, their efforts and ideas and their lives are important. You'll convey that through the content of your teaching, and also through the values you embody.

Starting with Turning Points

CONNECTION

Support children's identities as writers by telling them that you've already begun to study their writing.

"Writers, yesterday during the on-demand assessment, when you wrote an entire story in just one writing workshop, I watched your pens rushing down the page and thought, 'This is a class of *writers*.' I took your stories home last night, curled up on my couch with a blanket, and began reading. Some of your pieces made me laugh; others made me want to cry. I jotted notes about each one of you, as a writer, listing the things you already know how to do. So now, looking out at you, I feel as if I know each of you already.

"An American writer named John Jakes once said: 'Be yourself. Above all, let who you are, what you are, what you believe, shine through every sentence you write, every piece you finish.' It seems to me that each of you is well on your way to becoming just that kind of writer—the kind of writer who lets your true self shine through every sentence you write."

Today the important thing will be that you show students how to use strategies to more powerful effect, keeping in mind that the goal is not just to produce text, but instead, the goal is to write well. This is not just a unit on writing personal narratives. It is a unit on raising the level of narrative writing. From the first day, you ask students to reach toward the goal of writing powerful stories—stories that will make readers gasp or laugh aloud or blink back tears.

Acknowledge that students already know strategies for generating narrative writing. Reference the year's new chart, encouraging them to make personal charts of strategies, sharing what they know.

"Today, as you begin to work on new pieces of writing, I want to remind you that *you already know* strategies for coming up with stories that make readers sigh and laugh and pull in to read more. I've hung a chart from last year, 'Strategies for Generating Personal Narrative Writing,' front and center in our classroom, because we'll draw on it all the time, and we'll add to it as we learn more. As writers, you each carry with you an invisible backpack full of all the strategies you've ever learned, and I know you are accustomed to pulling those strategies out as needed.

"I have *already* listed one strategy on our class chart. Many of you told me you already use this first strategy to come up with ideas for true stories. Right now, read this first bullet to the person sitting near you and signal to each other to show yes (thumbs-up) if you *have* used this strategy as a way to come up with ideas for true stories, and no (thumbs-down) if you *haven't* ever used this strategy to come up with ideas for true stories. Go!"

Sometimes I see teachers disguising the fact that children will recycle, in this unit, the same process they experienced in previous years. Don't downplay this! Instead, seize on the important opportunity you have to teach students to draw on earlier teaching as they continue their work. Until they learn to do this, they can't be independent writers. The image of an invisible backpack is one I use again and again.

> ### Strategies for Generating Personal Narrative Writing
> - Think of a **person** who matters to you, list Small Moment stories connected to him/her and write one.

"I saw a few of you going like this." I shrugged and lifted my hands up in an exaggerated 'whaaaaat?' way. "It is totally okay if you haven't already learned this strategy, because there are lots of kids all around you who can show you how to use the strategy if you are ever stuck on what to write about.

"How many of you have *other* strategies that work for you when you need a strategy for coming up with true stories?" Many children signaled that they did. Although some started to list these, I quelled that so I could continue. "I'm thinking, then, that you may each want to make your own private 'Strategies for Generating Personal Narrative Writing' chart, and you can tape it into your notebook or find a way to prop it up on your desk when you write. The important thing is that always, when writing, you use whatever is already in your invisible backpack of strategies to help you write as much as you can."

❖ **Name the teaching point.**

"Today I want to teach you another strategy—one that helps people write *powerful* stories. It usually works to jot moments that have been turning points in your life. These might be first times or last times, or they might be times when you realized something important. Then you take one of those moments and write the whole story, fast and furious."

TEACHING

Demonstrate the step-by-step sequence of using the strategy. In this case, generate ideas for personal narratives by listing first times, last times, or times when you realized something.

"Let me show you how I use these strategies—thinking of first times I did something, thinking of last times I did something, and thinking of times when I realized something important, because these are all ways for me to think of turning-point stories. Pay careful attention because then you'll get a chance to try this work in just a minute."

In order to come up with a first or last time, I take something—anything—that I do all the time. So, I'll pick ice-skating. Then I think, 'When is the *first time* I ice-skated?' And suddenly I remember a time (it might not have been the very first time, but it was an early time) when I skated out to an island, pushing a little red chair in front of me so I wouldn't fall. I write that time on my list, knowing I might come back and tell the story of it later. And writers, the exciting thing is that when I start to think of the first time I did one, usually a dozen other 'firsts' will just pop into my head and I can list of few of them, knowing that I can return to this list." I jotted quickly on the white board, scrawling a fast list.

Notice that I do not phrase the teaching point like this: "Today we will think of turning-point stories." That wording would have simply assigned children a task and that is not my goal! A minilesson is not a forum for telling children what you want them all to do in the upcoming workshop. Instead, it is a place for explicitly teaching children the skills and strategies of good writing—skills and strategies you want them to call upon as needed, not only today, but always. In today's minilesson, I am hoping to teach children one more technique that they can carry with them in their invisible backpacks of strategies.

For today, it will be especially important to convey to students that you hope they draw on strategies for generating narrative writing that they learned during previous writing workshops. Of course, as soon as children develop facility with these strategies, the strategies will become internalized, and the work of generating ideas will increasingly happen outside of the writing classroom, as people's lives become a giant form of rehearsal. As this unit unfurls, you should see that before long, your students enter your classroom already mulling over possible writing projects.

Turning Points

✓ **The first time** I went ice-skating and wobbled out on the ice, so scared I would fall.

✓ **The first time** I held my new puppy in my arms. I scanned the other puppies in the room and worried whether I would love mine.

✓ **The first time** we moved into our house. I walked around, so excited for what it would look like once all our furniture was in place.

As I worked, I said, "Doing this quickly is part of doing it well. The important work is not the listing, but choosing one of the times to write as a story. See how my hand is zooming down the page?"

So, see how I've got a bunch of first times here that could all make great stories? And I can go through the same process to think of story ideas if I push myself to think of last times, or times I realized something. In order to come up with a last time I did something, for example, I go through the same steps . . . and this time, I end up remembering the last time I saw my grandfather, on a visit to the hospital."

The last time I visited my grandfather at the hospital and said a sad, confused goodbye.

Debrief quickly, pointing out the replicable moves you have made and then continue demonstrating quickly coming up with an idea for a time you realized something.

"Writers, I can also think, 'What moment can I recall when suddenly I realized something important?' That's harder! But sometimes it helps to think about times when I've felt strong emotions and learned a lesson as a result. I do remember this one time. I was *so* angry, stomping around my house and yelling and crying. My mom didn't yell at me or punish me, though. Instead, she gave me a big hug and helped me calm down. In that moment, I realized that no matter what happens, no matter what I do, my family will always be there for me."

The time I was acting terrible and my mom gave me a big hug. I realized she would always be there for me.

Debrief. Remind children of the purpose for the strategy. In this case, remind them that thinking of turning points can help them generate ideas for personal narratives.

"When I want to pick a topic for a personal narrative that will make a really good story, one that will have the shape of a story—a beginning, a middle, and an end—and one that matters, it often helps to think about turning-point moments. And now you've seen that to do this, I sometimes brainstorm first times, last times, and times when I realized something important. My brainstorming leads to a list, and then I choose one moment from the list that I believe is the most significant to write about in detail."

Although I am not explaining this to students now, the truth is that I have found turning-point stories tend to turn out to be especially shapely. The writer tells what happened before, during, and after, and things are different from before to after.

Another way to generate turning-point stories is to list an interest that you care about—like teaching writing, for example—and then jot possible turning points.

Don't bypass this lesson! It works like a charm to ask children to think about first times, last times, and times when they realized something important. When children think about these turning points, they automatically generate story ideas that have a before and an after, or a beginning, middle, and end. In other words, finding topics in this way helps children build a story arc because the arc is inherent in the story. This is most obvious in the "times when I realized something" stories. For example, a child might tell about how he'd always taken his dad for granted. Then a turning point happened, and he appreciated him. Another child may have thought a particular teacher would be terrifying, but then a turning point happened and the child realized his fears were unfounded. Last- and first-time stories also often have a before and an after, or a beginning, middle, and end. This way of finding topics puts a tension into the personal narrative—an element so many good stories contain—even though the writer may not yet be completely conscious of crafting to create the tension.

ACTIVE ENGAGEMENT

Set children up to try the strategy.

"So now I want you to try it. Open to the first page of your notebook, and just like I did, make a quick list of the first and last times or times you realized something. Remember not to plan on telling the whole story but instead, try to really zoom in on an intense part of that time, just like I did."

After a moment, I asked for children's attention. "Notice this: for each time, I mentioned what I was doing specifically, the actions." I underlined that part on my three items. "And I mentioned what I was feeling some of the time, too." I circled that part on each item. "See if you can add what exactly you were doing and feeling to at least one of your items." Some children finished before others, so I signaled for them to do this work for their entire list.

As children worked, I voiced over, coaching into their work. "When you record an episode, it usually works to write more words. Not *getting my puppy* but *when I held Emma in my arms and I scanned the other puppies and worried whether I would love mine.* When you write more words, you figure out what exactly it is that you remember about that time."

Demonstrate and support thinking about moments in which you realized something, pointing out that realizations often occur during first and last times. Channel students to do this, first alone, quietly, and then by talking.

"It is harder to recall when you *realized something* important, but here is a trick. Lots of times, those realizations are right there in the first and last times. Like, the *last time* I saw my grandfather, I realized he was going to die, and only later, I realized that when people die, they are really truly with you still. (There's a whole story of me having to go up on stage, long after he died, and being afraid, and feeling my grandfather with me, but that is for another time.) My point now is that those first and last minutes are often times when you realize things. See if that's true for the moments on your list. If you realized something during those moments, or after them, jot that in the margins of your list. Or you might have other moments in your life where you realized things. If so, jot those. Do this jotting quietly for now, and then you can talk with each other."

Debrief. Remind children that whenever they want to write powerful true stories, they can use the strategy of listing turning-point moments and then select one to write.

"Writers, I hope you are seeing that when you want to pick a topic for a personal narrative that will make a really good story—and that will be a story that matters—it often helps to think about turning-point moments."

Keep your suggestions simple. Your goal is for children to be able to prompt themselves the way you are now prompting them. For a strategy to be useful, the writer has to be able to use it independently, without a teacher, later. Therefore make sure your prompts are the sort that kids can internalize and use for themselves.

Scanning students' work, I noticed most had generated first and last times and not times when they realized something, so I decided to insert another prompt and this time to provide a more concerted push to get them also considering times they realized something. You always want to enter this portion of a minilesson ready to adapt your plans based on what you notice when you do a quick assessment of your students' work.

Don't underestimate the importance of leaving little pools of silence after each injunction. Give children time to think and to jot. One way to do this is to have your notebook on hand, and to take a second after each injunction to do your own very quick thinking and jotting.

LINK

Remind children that writers draw from a repertoire of strategies to get themselves writing. Channel students to start writing, and meanwhile, add to the chart.

"So, writers, you carry with you an invisible backpack full of strategies for generating personal narratives, and that backpack includes this new strategy we have just learned and also all the strategies you have learned in your years in writing workshops. What has worked for you in the past might help you get started today. You may want to start writing by taking one of your turning-point moments and writing that story, fast and furious. That story will probably be at least a page, and I expect you will have time to start another story as well. If you end up writing a second story today, maybe that will be another turning-point story from today's list, and maybe that story will come from another strategy you know for generating ideas for true stories. For right now, while we sit here together, the important thing is that we write. So let's get started."

For a few moments, I ducked my head and gave full concentration to my own writing, not looking up to eye the group. Once I could feel that most children had begun writing, I silently signaled for those who were especially engrossed, one by one, to return to their seats and continue writing.

After three quarters of the class had dispersed, I convened the group of children who hadn't gotten themselves started and this time suggested a less open-ended version of the strategy. "You could write about first or last times you did anything," I said, "but lots of kids like to think about a first—or a last—time they had with a person, an animal, a place, a favorite activity. I'll help get you started. Right now, think about a person who has come into your life in the last few years—a friend, a sports coach, a relative. Jot that person down."

One child had no one, so I said, "Jot me down. You can write about meeting me on our first day."

Then to the group I said, "So turn and tell the person next to you the whole story of how you first met this person or first had contact with the person. Before you talk, think of where you were and what you were doing. If you can't remember it exactly, pretend, or choose a recent moment you spent with this person. Okay, after you thought of what you did or said first, think, what did you see or say or do next? Start by telling that and then keep going, bit-by-bit." As I heard one child and then another get started storytelling, doing so with momentum, I paused the talk and said to the storyteller, "Write that down." When possible, I dictated the first sentence from the account to the writer, who recorded it, and then gestured for the child to continue, whispering, "That's beautiful. Go off and write."

Once members of the group were launched, I added a few lines to the chart, displaying the second bullet point, so now the chart looked like this.

Today, and always, you will want to remind children that they carry a repertoire of strategies and that each day's learning is cumulative. Writers needn't go off and do exactly what you've taught in today's minilesson. Instead, teach children to be their own job captains, evaluating the strategies at their disposal and applying them to the work at hand.

It often pays to take a few extra minutes in the Link to make sure all your writers are launched and ready to go. You will not want to make this a habit, as you'll quickly want to teach children strategies they can use to launch themselves. For now, however, it ensures that all children will be a part of a productive, writing-filled workshop.

Strategies for Generating Personal Narrative Writing

- Think of a **person** who matters to you, list Small Moment stories connected to him/her and write one.
- Think of **first times, last times**, or **times you realized something**, list stories you could tell about each and write one.

Helping Writers Sustain Energy for Writing

BECAUSE YOU WILL WANT TO BE SURE the start of any new unit creates a burst of new energy for the upcoming writing, it helps to scan the day's plans in advance, asking, "What problems can I anticipate the children might encounter today?"

If most of the children in the class have participated in writing workshops during previous years, those children will probably not encounter much difficulty today because they'll be accustomed to generating ideas and writing narrative entries. If many children haven't had this prior experience, they'll be more uncertain and more in need of support. Either way, however, you are apt to find that despite all your efforts in the minilesson, some students will want to spend the entire workshop simply listing possible story ideas. This minilesson was designed to counter that tendency, but you may need to enforce the fact that lists should contain no more than three or four possible topics so that writers can get started writing.

Then too, you will probably find that some of your writers are not yet able to carry on without some cajoling. Although one-to-one conferences will be very important eventually, for now you probably can't afford the luxury of talking for five minutes with one individual and then another. To help all your students work productively,

---

MID-WORKSHOP TEACHING   Voiceovers to Keep Writers Writing

Today you will want to push your writers to keep writing without interrupting their flow. To do so, you might use voiceovers to encourage and validate your writers as well as to raise the level of their work. Think of yourself as a personal trainer encouraging someone next to you to keep doing push-ups without stopping what he or she is doing. One way to give voiceovers that are encouraging to all writers is to look for what one student has done well (or is starting to do well) and compliment that writer in front of the class. Guaranteed, all of your students will want to follow that writer's lead. Another time you will find yourself wanting to say the same thing to five or six writers. Turn that comment into a voiceover from which the whole class can benefit.

Some possibilities for voiceovers:

"Claudia already has five lines written! How fantastic! I'm betting she'll have half a page in no time at all!"

"I'm admiring how Henry just checked the chart to get another strategy for writing! How smart!"

"Writers, you should all be halfway down the page by now, writing furiously."

"Keep going, keep pushing yourself. Shake out your hand and keep going!"

"I love how when Amelia finished one story, she reached for another idea from on her list and started another story! I hope all of you will follow her lead!"

How many of you already have a page or more written? Give yourself a pat on the back and push yourself to try to get to a page and a half!"

you'll probably find yourself acting like the circus man who needs to get all his plates spinning in the air at once, racing around the room, catching one plate as it starts to wobble, sending it spinning, and then rushing to another that is wobbling. To move swiftly from one writer to another, you'll need to accept approximation—on your part and theirs. No one's work will be perfect right now. Don't worry just yet about whether the students' sentences are punctuated or the entries detailed. You can address those concerns in another day or two. For now, your goal is for kids to work hard, writing as much as they can. And you will want to teach writers how to be more resourceful problem solvers, finding ways to keep themselves going.

As soon as the small group of reluctant writers that stayed with you after the minilesson has been sent off to work independently, we recommend you move among all your students, using mostly nonverbal signals to celebrate and support their work. To one child, give a decisive thumbs-up sign, whispering "Love that you have five lines done already!" To another, admire the smart "revision" that is implied in three efforts to start an entry. Whisper, "I love that you are revising your lead!" although actually the child may not be doing anything quite so fancy. Look askance at the writer who hasn't gotten started, making a "What's going on?" gesture. Leave a folded note on another youngster's desk. After you move on, the child will unfold your note, and read, "Aim for a page and a half today." The important thing is that you realize that you can effect change with a decisive tap on one writer's page, a smile in the margin of another writer's page, a note—folded twice—that says, "You look like a professional writer!" or "Your hard work is amazing!"

Another method of keeping writers going and touching base with multiple writers is through table compliments. Look for what one writer is doing well at a table and compliment that writer, letting your voice carry to the others around her. "Yvette, I love how you are checking your list to grab another story idea to write about. It's so smart to realize that you should push yourself to start a new story once you finish the first. I hope all of the writers in this room will want to push themselves to always keep writing, just the way that you do! Writers," and this time eye the rest of the children at the table as you finish this compliment, "do you think you might be able to try something similar?" You'll find that they immediately jump to follow Yvette's lead.

Learning from Best and Worst Writing Times

Convene the writers in the meeting area, compliment them on their work today, and then give them a chance to discuss their work together and talk to them about the importance of building writerly lives.

"I've got to confess that I stopped teaching at one point today and just stood, watching you. It was actually a bit thrilling. I've said it before and I'll say it again: This is a class of *writers*. Because of that, I realized that we shouldn't just talk about the particular entry you have on hand. Instead, we should shop talk. You know—when you get a group of wrestlers together, or skiiers together, or teachers together—people talk shop. Wrestlers talk about the special chalk they use, skiiers, about the snow conditions. And writers talk about how that day's writing went. So right now, will you think about how writing time was for you today?" I left a few seconds for children to think about that question, then pressed on. "Now I want to ask you a really important question: 'How do you think writing time will go for you this year?' Again, I gave students a moment to think.

"I didn't ask you this because I want you to be fortune tellers, but because I want you to author writing lives that work for you. You've got to make writing work for you. You are the author not just of your writing, but also of your writing life. And it is up to you to make it work. Each one of you has a choice. You can make a writing life for yourself where writing is the pits, or you can make a life for yourself where writing is the best it can be."

Let writers know that one strategy to build a writerly life is to think back on best and worst writing times and learn from them.

"Right now, I'm going to ask you to think of a time when writing really *didn't* work for you." I left some silence. "What was it about that time that made it not work?" Again, I left some silence. "Will you tell the person beside you what you are thinking and talk about how you can avoid that problem this year?"

I let the children talk. Noticing that some needed a model, I said, "When I was in fifth grade, a lot of the girls in my class kept diaries. They wrote what they did each day, dutifully, so I thought I should do that too. Every night I sat there, cranking out the story of my day: 'I did this and then I did that and then I did this.' I knew it was terrible writing. That was a time when writing was the pits for me. So I know for sure that I can't use my notebook to just write reports of a day—I need to try to write well, about stories that matter to me, or I'm bored.

"But there have been other times that writing has been the best it can be. The important thing is to ask, 'What was it, *exactly*, that made writing so great?' And most importantly, 'How can I make it great again this year?'"

"Right now, think about what makes writing the pits for you and what makes it wonderful for you. Then push yourself to think about how you can make your writing life the best it can be. Jot what you are thinking."

As students leaned low over their notebook pages, scribbling away, I added, "We aren't going to share these right now, writers. Instead, keep working on this at home tonight so that you can make writing resolutions for yourself."

 # MAKING RESOLUTIONS

Tonight, continue to think about times when writing has been the pits and times when it has been the best it can be. Then, take a step back and ask, "What can I do, this year, to make writing the best it can be?" Begin an entry with the line: "To make writing the best it can be, I will . . ." and then write about your resolutions for the new year.

As part of this, think about the sources for your writing ideas, and think about whether you can imagine yourself coming to a stage where your life, itself, is rehearsal for writing. When Cynthia Rylant was asked about how she gets her ideas, she said, "We are talking about art, thinking about art, and creating art every single day of one's life. This is about going fishing as an artist, having relatives over for supper as an artist, and walking the aisles of Woolworth's as an artist" (1994). Rylant lives her life as a writer—opening her notebook and writing the story of shopping for slippers, spilling coffee on her wrist, or of other tiny events that make up her life.

For many writers, being a writer changes the way they see the world. Every second carries the potential for stories. Tonight, after thinking a bit about your past and your future as a writer, will you go ahead and live this one evening as a writer? See if you can come to school tomorrow bursting with ideas and ready to write.

The homework is meant to be distributed to students, not read aloud.

Dreaming the Dream of the Story

"G ET STARTED!" I want to tell students. I'm hoping many of them came to school with ideas for writing in hand, and that they are chomping on the bit to write, write, write. But writers the world over agree that the blank page is terrifying in its blankness. And fifth-graders, especially, are apt to worry what others will think of their topics. This makes it important for you to equip students with a repertoire of strategies for getting the ideas and memories—the words—flowing. You have already taught them that they can ponder turning points in their lives.

In today's session, you will teach them that writers sometimes think of a place that matters to them and list significant moments that have happened there. By prioritizing

---

"Every writer of stories needs to learn to write from inside the story."

---

setting, you'll be working within a grand tradition. Setting plays a vital role in the best literature, from Mark Twain on the Mississippi to E. B. White in a farmyard. You can bet that setting also plays a crucial role in your children's lives. Merely evoking the memory of a place will help them remember stories of "a time when . . . ."

But while learning new strategies for generating story ideas is important, it is not the most important work of today's session. Today, you will teach your students that narratives are written from inside the story.

IN THIS SESSION, you'll teach students that narrative writers sometimes generate story ideas by thinking of places that matter to them and the episodes that occurred in those places. You'll then teach students that in order to write effective narratives, writers re-experience the episode before writing it, reliving it so that readers will be able to experience it, too.

GETTING READY

✔ Have students bring last night's homework to the meeting area (see Connection).

✔ "Strategies for Generating Personal Narrative Writing," chart from Session 1 with today's strategy added on (see Connection)

✔ Begin a chart titled, "Techniques for Raising the Level of Narrative Writing" (see Teaching).

✔ Be ready to list a place of significance from your own life, as well as a couple moments you remember from that place. Prepare to re-experience the story of one moment or plan to adopt the Luka Story (on page 98) as your own (see Teaching).

✔ A chart you've created, listing a strong emotion and several instances when you experienced it (see Mid-Workshop Teaching)

✔ Each child's writing from the day, brought with them to the meeting area (see Share)

COMMON CORE STATE STANDARDS: W.5.3, W.5.4, W.5.5, W.5.8, W.5.10, RL.5.4, SL.5.1, SL.5.4, SL.5.6, L.5.1, L.5.2, L.5.3

These words seem simple when in fact they encapsulate some of the most complicated, challenging, and wondrous work in narrative writing. Every narrative writer wants to dream the dream of a story in ways that allow readers to become lost in their storyworld. Gerald Brice writes, "It's not enough for a writer to tell a reader about a person or a place, he must help readers be the person . . . the basic failure of most writing is a failure of the writer's imagination . . . he is not trying hard enough to live moment to moment in the very skin of his character." It's only when the writer writes with rapt absorption that readers can read with a similar absorption. As John Cheever says, "For me, a page of good prose is where one hears the rain [and] the noise of battle."

At the heart of strong narrative writing, then, is the ability to place readers directly inside the story. And to be able to place readers inside the story, you need to be able to write from inside the story. So, today, you will remind your writers that they need to step into the story and let it unfurl in front of them, conveying the events and experiences to others with precision.

Dreaming the Dream of the Story

CONNECTION

Channel students to share their resolutions for the upcoming year. Use that conversation to explain that your aim is to teach them how to write particularly powerful true stories.

"Writers, I've been hearing some of you talk about the resolutions you made last night. Let's take a minute to share those. How will you make your writing life be the best it can be? Turn and share what you came up with." The meeting area was filled with eager buzzing.

"Writers, I'm blown away by your resolutions. Becca said that she will try to get her partner to help her revise in ways that make her writing better. And Jake said that he will find a quiet place at home to write. We can all help him to make that resolution come true here in school, as well.

"So now I have a confession to make. I have been so impressed with how knowledgeable you are about narrative writing that I have decided to change my plans for this writing unit. Before I met you, I thought our first unit of study was going to be on writing personal narratives. But now I realize that you guys are ready for something more ambitious. You have the skills necessary to write not just any ol' personal narratives, but instead to write *powerful* personal narratives. What this will mean is that your job won't be to put any ol' true stories on the page, but instead, your job will be to write those stories *really well*.

"If you are game for doing this, it means that about halfway through our unit, you'll take the on-demand pieces you wrote a few days ago and put them in a display case with a sign that says, 'This is how I *used to* write,' and then beside those pieces, you'll put the text that you write later in this unit, with a sign that says, 'This is how I write *now*.' Have any of you seen those make-over TV shows where they make over a car or a house or someone's whole wardrobe? This will be like that, only you'll be making over your writing."

Teach and recruit children to join you in trying another strategy for generating narrative writing.

"I've got something important to teach you today, but before I do that, it would be good for you to have a topic in mind for the writing you will start soon. How many of you spent some time last night, thinking about possible stories and have come to class today with a story in hand?" Only a few students signaled they'd done that. "You already know some strategies for generating writing"—I gestured to the chart where we'd listed these strategies. Skimming the list,

It is helpful to remember that the first few mini-lessons in a unit must launch not only this particular day's writing workshop, but also the unit itself. This connection is aimed to recruit students to the big goals of this unit. It is really important that your instruction clarify and communicate goals to students. Notice the drumroll I give around the concept that in this unit, students' writing will get vastly stronger.

I said, "Writers can think of a person who matters and generate small moments spent with that person. Writers can zoom in on first or last moments, or can write about times when they realized something. Here's one more strategy to add to your list: Writers can think about a *place* that matters, list small moments that occurred in one of those places, then choose one and write it, long and strong.

"Even if you have a topic in mind, will you try this newest strategy, just to see what it yields for you? Do the work while I do it as well." Then I picked up a pen and said, "I'm going to jot a place that matters and list Small Moment stories that occurred in that place. I'll be jotting up here, while you work in your notebook. Let's take just a minute."

I waited until most children's heads tucked and they began writing, and then I picked up a marker and approached the blank chart paper, chin in hand, and muttering audibly to myself, "Places, places . . . what are some places that are important to my life? Places that I return to . . . places where some important parts of my life have been lived . . . ." I could write about my bedroom, when I was a child, or the field behind my childhood house, or the rocks beside the lake.

Then I muttered, "Let me pick one. Which holds memories, stories?" I wrote 'The field behind our house' and mused, "What are some things that happened there?" Then I began a new list.

> The field behind our house
>   1. Planting trees
>   2. Burying Luka

"By now you all should have a small moment whose story you'll be writing today—perhaps the one you've just come up with, perhaps one you had decided upon earlier."

❖ Name the teaching point.

"Today, I want to remind you that writers of stories—and this is writers of true stories as well as fictional ones—climb inside the story, walking in the shoes of the character, experiencing the story as it unfolds and putting that onto the page so readers can experience it too."

TEACHING

Explain that the secret to writing effective narratives requires you to experience the story so that readers can experience it too.

"I know you've heard that writers don't tell what happened, they show it. Instead of saying, 'I was sad,' writers say, 'I brushed a tear away with the back of my hand, and bit my lip to keep it from quivering.' You know that.

Teachers, the story that is begun here—"Burying Luka"—weaves through this entire book and is used repeatedly to make different points. You may decide to adopt this story, as if it is your own, or you may decide to write your own. If you make the latter decision, it will probably help you to read ahead to the other instances when this story reoccurs so that you anticipate the ways you'll use your writing later and set yourself up for these uses.

No doubt you are wondering to yourself, "What is going on here? This is still the connection and yet she has taught the children something new and asked them to try it." And you'd be right to wonder. I have chosen to take children through the process of listing small moments quickly, knowing it will not take them long to catch onto this new strategy—listing moments associated with places. Students are skilled at collecting strategies, so I didn't want to devote another full day's teaching to the process of listing, choosing, and then writing an entry. Instead, I quickly offer them yet another collecting strategy and reserve my most supportive teaching for the heady work of today—dreaming the dream of the story and imagining it as you write.

"But what you may not know is that many people think that the single most important thing a writer can do is to dream the dream of the story, as the writer writes the story. In his book about writing powerful stories, Gerald Brice has said, 'It's not enough for a writer to tell a reader about a person or a place, he must help readers be the person . . . he has to try hard to live moment to moment in the very skin of his character.'

"Another writer, John Gardner, advises writers to write 'as if you were a movie camera. The trick is to get it down. Getting it down precisely, what you really noticed . . . .'

"If you let your readers see and hear and feel all of the precise details, this means that when readers read a page of your story, they won't see *words*—they will instead see the field that you are tromping through. And when readers read your story, they won't hear pages turning—they will instead hear the rain falling on the trees overhead. To do this, you need to go back to the start of your story and step inside it, writing and imagining in such a way that you get lost in the story. You need to dream the dream of the story as it happens right around you."

Ask students to watch as you demonstrate, working with an entry you settled upon when thinking of stories that take place in an important place in your life. Ask, 'How did it start?' and then let the story unroll from there.

"Writers, watch me do this work and then you'll be able to try. So I'm going to tell the story I listed earlier, of burying Luka. First, you'll remember, I need to ask: How did it start?" I began talking in a lower voice, showing that I was musing to myself. "How did it start? Oh yes, I remember. I was taking Luka out for a walk. Wait. Let me see the precise details of that moment." I closed my eyes in front of the children, taking myself back to the field with Luka, letting them see my true process. "I was standing in the field. It was cold that day and the wind was whipping all around me and my hair was blowing everywhere. I see it. I'm there. Now let me dream the dream of what happened so I can tell it." I was quiet for a minute, then picked up my pen and started scribbling on my clipboard, voicing over as I did so.

> It was freezing out. Wind whipped around me so I pulled my coat closed. "Luka!" I yelled as she ran into my legs. "Silly dog!" I huffed. She looked up cheerfully, wagging her tail. Then she bounded down the field, happy to be outside. "Why do I have to take her for walks?" I grouched to myself, shivering in the cold.

Debrief, pointing out the replicable steps you have taken.

"Writers, do you see how I've put myself back into my story and made myself relive the details of that moment so I could story-tell it?"

In this instance, when you scrawl your draft onto paper on your clipboard, you don't actually need to write every word. You may in fact have slipped in a transcript of the text, and you may be reading it aloud as you "write" fast and furious. Later you can copy the story over onto chart paper.

ACTIVE ENGAGEMENT

Set writers up to choose one of their stories and put themselves back inside of it.

"So writers, now you'll get a chance to try this. Remember the story you've chosen to tell. Will you close your eyes and put yourself back in that moment?" I waited until the children had closed their eyes, then I spoke quietly. "Where are you, exactly? What are you doing, exactly? See what's before you in that moment." I gave the children time to think. "Okay, now let the story start to unfurl in your mind. Just let it all play out before you." I was quiet. After a bit I added, "Watch it happen."

Again, I gave them time to do this work. "In a minute, you'll story-tell to a partner, telling your story in a step-by-step way so that you put your partner right inside the moment. Rehease a bit in your mind before starting." I gave them one more long minute.

"Okay, in a minute will you turn to the partner beside you and story-tell? Decide which of you will be the storyteller and which will be the listener." I gave the children a minute to decide. "Listeners, you close your eyes, listen closely, and see if you can see all the details of what happened. Don't be afraid to give your partner feedback."

LINK

Send children off with the reminder to use all they know to write stories in a way that put readers inside of them.

"Writers, usually I send you off and tell you that you can use the strategy you just learned if it is helpful to you, and not use it if it isn't helpful. But today I want to tell you that each and every time you write a personal narrative, you should try to write it in a way that brings your reader right inside the experience. And to do that, *you* have to write from inside of it. So writers, today, make sure that when we read a page of your writing, we don't just see the words—make sure we see the world of the story." I revealed the following chart:

> ### Techniques for Raising the Level of Narrative Writing
>
> - Dream the dream of the story and then write in a way that allows readers to experience the moment along with you.

When I introduce a strategy, I make a big deal of the steps, turning it into a concrete—almost mechanical—process. This may feel unnatural at first, but I believe that when we teach any complex activity, it helps to demonstrate each step, giving exaggerated attention to the procedural details, keeping in mind that soon the learner will master the procedure so that it becomes one flowing, almost automatic activity. For example, the tennis coach will show the novice how to grasp the tennis racket and then how to swivel the racket so that the angle in the hand is perfect. But before long the learner will just grab for the racket, swiftly taking—but no longer fussing over—the same steps.

I use today's link as an opportunity to begin a second anchor chart—"Techniques for Raising the Level of Narrative Writing"—that will live in our classroom through much of this unit, reminding children of the cumulative nature of their learning and primary focus of our work.

Settling Down to Confer
An Overview of the Conference

TODAY'S MINILESSON COULD HAVE RAISED THE BAR for your students in ways that have paralyzed some of them. Instead of thinking only, "What story should I tell?" some of your students may be starting to think, "How will I tell my story in a way that brings my reader into it? Maybe I need a different story, a better story." The voice of the inner critic can overwhelm even experienced writers, and you want to rush to the rescue of any writer you see perched uncertainly before the page, crossing out one lead after another. Offer immediate reassurance: "If a moment sticks out in your memory, rest assured that you can tell it in a way that makes it stick in your reader's mind, too. Sometimes a writer just needs a *sense* that a story is important." The last thing you want is for your teaching to slow down your writers!

(continues)

MID-WORKSHOP TEACHING   More Strategies for Generating Personal Narrative Topics

"Writers, I love the feeling that your minds are bursting with stories, because this means that during writing time, you aren't just *thinking* up stories, you are *selecting* the stories that you feel will especially work.

"As I was meeting with some of you, I remembered one more collecting strategy that is often helpful when we want to write not just any story, but a story that really matters. I want to remind you that it is often helpful to write about times when you've had strong feelings. You can jot down a feeling—worry or hope or embarrassment—and then think, "What are a few *particular* times I felt that feeling? Then choose one and write the story of that time.

"Let me show you a quick example I made last night, when I was planning this lesson." I revealed the following:

Embarrassment

The time my whole class took a field trip to my house to see the monkey I pretended to have—only I didn't have one after all.

The time when the kids told me the dress I was wearing looked old-fashioned enough to be a costume for our Abe Lincoln play.

"I picked a feeling (in this case, embarrassment) and then quickly jotted a few times I felt that feeling. Once I've listed a few moments, I can pick one and write the story of that time. I'll add this strategy to our chart of ways to develop ideas for personal narratives. Next time you are stuck for an idea, remember you can try this strategy, too!"

Strategies for Generating Personal Narrative Writing

- Think of a **person** who matters to you. List Small Moment stories connected to him/her and write one.
- Think of **first times**, **last times**, or **times you realized something**, list stories you could tell about each and write one.
- Think about a **place** that matters, list small moments, that occurred in that place and write one.
- Think of a **strong feeling**. List stories of particular times you felt it and write one.

However, for the most part you probably feel that your students have settled into the rhythms of the writing workshop enough that you can begin to confer with them.

If you have ever worked with a trainer or coach or mentor of any kind, chances are good that person has conferred with you. You no doubt have memories of times when a coach interacted with you in ways that made a world of difference, and you probably also can recall times someone interacted with you in ways that disabled you and left scars that last to this day. Think about the characteristics of interactions that helped and of interactions that hurt. You'll probably come away from this aware that it helps if the coach:

- ◆ **Listens** to what the learner has done and to what trying to do

- ◆ **Conveys optimism** in the learner's ability to do much better

- ◆ **Teaches skills or strategies** that the learner will be able to use often

Usually teachers confer by drawing a chair alongside a writer and sitting at eye level, side by side. Teachers ask the writer to hold his or her writing in a way that conveys, "You are the owner, I'm merely an advisor." Usually the teacher begins by researching to understand where this piece of writing fits into the writer's trajectory as a student of writing, to understand what the writer has been trying to do, and to determine the writer's self-assessment. Then the teacher responds—sometimes to the piece, for a bit, and always to the writer's work and progress. Generally, the teacher notes things the writer has done well that seem to show progress, supporting this work in ways that are transferable to other days and other texts. Then the teacher teaches the writer something, often demonstrating or coaching to help the writer know how to do the new work. Either at the end of the conference or in a follow-up interaction, the teacher names what the writer has done in ways that are transferable to other days and other pieces.

That's a quick overview of conferences. Another time, we'll illuminate further parts of the conference, but for now, it is important to say that once you really understand a writer, the conference is infinitely easier to conduct well.

Today when you research what students have been doing, you'll probably find that some children are still summarizing the broad steps in their stories rather than telling the stories from within them. You can decide what will help. For some, you may decide that it will help if you show children how to tighten the focus of their writing, starting closer to the main action.

Celebrate the Powerful Writing Children Are Already Doing

Plan a way for every child to read a bit of his writing aloud to the group as a means to celebrate children's stronger and stronger writing.

"Your goal this month is to write in ways that make readers stop in their tracks. I thought we would spend the next few *weeks* trying to put some powerful writing on the page, but you've *already* written drafts that are powerful! Wouldn't it be a shame if we just tucked all this beautiful writing into our folders and forgot about it? Instead, I've thought up a way for you all to share a bit. I'm going to be the conductor of your orchestra. Only you won't be playing instruments, you'll be reading aloud snippets of your stories." I put my hand up, pretending to grasp a baton. "When I point my baton at you, read aloud a tiny excerpt from your writing. You may read your lead, or you may choose any portion of your entry to read aloud. I'll give you a minute to look through what you've written and choose what you'll read. Practice reading your words in your head to show their meaning, to help your listeners understand."

After we got my bike we asked
Camillo's dad if he can take
the training wheels off for us
We put it on the Side walk
I balanced on the bike with
my feet. I looked down on the
long hill, gulp! I swallowed hard
Camillo pushed me. The wind
was blowing hard. I keep going
into the dark night. Would
I crash! I held the steering
wheel! I turned around, "Yes, I
made it. The grownups came
out and clapped. Now I know how
to Ride a two-wheeler

FIG. 2–1   Khalid's writing excerpt

Soon I gestured with my "baton," and one child after another read aloud. Khalid read this excerpt (see Figure 2–1).

I balanced on the bike with my feet. I looked down the long hill. Gulp! I swallowed hard. Camillo pushed me. The wind was blowing hard. I kept going into the dark night. Would I crash? I was kind of scared.

Then I tipped my baton to Sabrina and she read:

I spent about three seconds in the air, partly tripping and partly jumping. As I was in the air, I thought, please let me land on my feet. I don't want to fall with Mya in my hands. Mya is just a baby, what if she gets hurt? It will be all my fault if Mya gets hurt. I really don't want Mya to get hurt!

You'll decide whether storytelling is an important way for your writers to rehearse, and whether your children benefit from props that may have been used in previous years, such as storytelling using fingers and booklet pages, and dots on a timeline to remind them of the march of time. If possible, I'd let those props fall away for most of your children, as they can limit as well as support.

After a few minutes, I put down my imaginary baton and gestured for the sharing to stop. "Wow—what a beautiful song all of your words make.

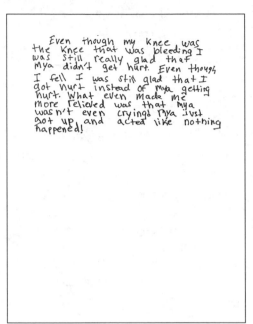

Sabrina
I took a mini jump off of the moving truck. And as I took that mini jump off of the moving truck I tripped over a string that was attached to the moving truck.
I spent about three seconds in the air partly tripping and partly jumping. As I was in the air I thought please let me land on my feet. I don't want to fall with mya in my hands. Mya is just a baby, what if she gets hurt? It will be all of my fault if Mya gets hurt. I really don't want mya to get hurt. "Your knee is' bleeding" shouted my uncle from the inside of the moving truck.
I thought I hope he's not talking about Mya's knee. On my gosh, please don't tell me that "Mya's knee is bleeding. "whos knee is bleeding." I questioned my uncle. "Your knee is bleeding Sabrina" replied my uncle.
I said "It's okay, all I need is some cream and a bandage." I'm just glad that Mya's knee isn't bleeding."

Even though my knee was the knee that was bleeding I was still really glad that Mya didn't get hurt. Even though I fell I was still glad that I got hurt instead of Mya getting hurt. What even made me more relieved was that Mya wasn't even cryings Mya just got up, and acted like nothing happened!

FIG. 2–2   Sabrina read from this entry

LIVING LIKE A WRITER

Robert McCloskey, the author of *Make Way for Ducklings*, was driving in Boston one time, and the traffic stopped completely. "What's going on?" he thought, wondering if there had been an accident or something. So he got out of his car to look and walked ahead a few cars—and saw a long line of ducks crossing the highway. The traffic on all sides had stopped while each little duckling waddled along. McCloskey said to himself, "I could write a story about this! I could tell about the day I was driving in traffic, then everything stopped. I could tell about how I got out of my car and watched." That story became *Make Way for Ducklings,* a book that has sold millions of copies.

Robert McCloskey, like so many other authors, lives differently because he is a writer. He lives every second waiting for stories to surface. He's not alone. In the *New York Times* there was a story about how a tourist, visiting New York City from Arizona, saw a homeless man, ragged, tired, sitting sprawled on the sidewalk. The man had bare feet, blistered, sticking out from too-short trousers. As the tourist looked at the homeless man, a policeman came by, crouched alongside the homeless man, and said, "Your feet looked cold so I got you these boots," and he produced boots with a soft fuzzy interior, which he slid on the homeless man's feet. But here is the thing: the tourist said to herself, "This moment matters. This is beautiful." And she used her phone to take a picture of that policeman doing that act of generosity. Later, she wrote about the small moment she'd experienced, and sent her writing and the photo to the police department, thinking the policeman deserved a note of appreciation. Before long, hundreds of thousands of people had heard the story.

Both Robert McCloskey and that tourist from Arizona lived like writers, seeing small moments that they experienced and then saying, "This matters. I could write about this."

Tonight, continue to collect entries in your notebook. As you try to imagine the stories you might write, remember that writers see the potential for stories *everywhere*. Give yourself the eyes to find them!

When there is an interaction between family members, watch it as a writer. Notice how people talk, move, and act. Think about the meaning and significance behind the small things, and see if you can let your life prompt your writing. Meanwhile, we'll add this to our chart as a strategy for generating narrative writing.

Strategies for Generating Personal Narrative Writing

- Think of a **person** who matters to you, list Small Moment stories connected to him/her and write one.
- Think of **first times**, **last times**, or **times you realized something**, list stories you could tell about each and write one.
- Think about a **place** that matters, list small moments that occurred in that place and write one.
- Think of a **strong feeling**. List stories of particular times you felt it and write one.
- **Live differently** because you are a writer. Notice small moments and capture them in entries.

Letting Other Authors' Words Awaken Our Own

IN THIS SESSION, you'll teach students that writers read great stories in order to write great stories. That is, writers allow another author's words to spark ideas of their own.

GETTING READY

✔ An excerpt from Eloise Greenfield's *Childtimes*, or any other memoir excerpt that can serve as a catalyst for your own students' story ideas (see Teaching)

✔ "Strategies for Generating Personal Narrative Writing" chart (see Teaching)

✔ Your own entry idea, ready to be written in the wake of the literature you choose to read aloud (see Teaching)

✔ "Techniques for Raising the Level of Narrative Writing" chart (see Mid-Workshop Teaching)

✔ Prepare writing partnerships and ask children to sit next to their new partners with their notebooks in hand (see Share).

✔ "Questions to Ask Yourself as You Edit" checklist (see Homework)

YOU'VE HAD IT HAPPEN. You are reading a book, and suddenly you are transported back to your own life—sometimes to a corner that you'd long since forgotten. From the nooks in your memories, a particular incident works its way out onto paper, clearing the way for other images to come spilling forth. Soon you are writing, writing, writing. And the amazing thing is that the writing you do has passed through the sieve of the original text, and invariably it contains some hint of that text—a phrase, a structure, a literary aura.

Take advantage of this in order to teach students that one of the most trustworthy ways to generate powerful writing is to find a beautiful text—one that resembles the sort of text you want to write—and then to read that text aloud, perhaps many times, and in the wake of the text, to start writing.

In this session, then, you'll teach children to look no further than the bookshelf. You'll teach them to turn to other writers for inspiration. This is an age-old writers' trick. Tell them that the sights and sounds of another author's memories will tug and tweak responsive memories. Allowing another author's words to wash over you will wake your own horde of words. It is a beautifully simple and effective strategy: read aloud to your students in ways that help them get their minds and their pencils moving. Ideas are borne of ideas.

Be sure that when you teach this new strategy for generating writing, you remind writers that you do not expect that during today's writing workshop, they will all draw upon this particular strategy for generating writing. Instead, they can call upon any strategy you have taught this year or that they learned in previous years, or they can do this work with automaticity, not needing a strategy at all.

COMMON CORE STATE STANDARDS: W.5.3, W.5.4, W.5.5, RL.5.2, RL.5.10, SL.5.1, SL.5.4, SL.5.6, L.5.1, L.5.2, L.5.3

Letting Other Authors' Words Awaken Our Own

CONNECTION

Provide an analogy that will help children understand how one writer's words can provide a spark of inspiration for another writer.

"Writers, do you know my favorite thing about a birthday cakes? I love watching as someone—perhaps someone's mother—lights one birthday candle and then uses that one candle to light another candle and another and another. Ever since I was your age, I've always loved seeing one tiny flame create many flames.

Teachers, at the risk of sounding like a pyromaniac, I am leading up to the idea that one piece of writing can "spark" another. By all means, if you have a different way to make this point, use it.

"When I read a well-written text, it acts like that first candle. It sparks more memories and ideas—the text acts like a spark of inspiration. Many writers cite specific books and authors as their 'muse.' For example, you might have heard of *Wuthering Heights* or *Pride and Prejudice*—those novels were written two centuries ago. They served as the first candles for lots of other great literature, so that many authors today, when interviewed, will say they got the idea for their hero from Heathcliff in *Wuthering Heights* or Mr. Darcy in *Pride and Prejudice*."

❖ **Name the teaching point.**

"Today I want to teach you that writers *read* great stories in order to *write* great stories. An author's stories and ideas will often spark the reader's stories and ideas."

TEACHING

Model reading a text and writing in the wake of it.

Will you watch how the work of another writer can spark us to have our own memories? Right now, listen as I read a story to you, and see if it sparks memories for you. I'll be doing this too." I began reading:

This lesson uses an excerpt from Eloise Greenfield's Childtimes, *but you may choose to read aloud a portion of any memoir that feels like it will have particular resonance for your class.*

> *I don't know why Mama ever sewed for me. She sewed for other people, made beautiful dresses and suits and blouses, and got paid for doing it. But I don't know why she sewed for me. I was so mean.*
>
> *It was all right in the days when she had to make my dresses a little longer in the front than in the back to make up for the way I stood, with my legs pushed back and my stomach out. I was little then, and I trusted Mama. But when I got older, I worried.*

Mama would turn the dress on the wrong side and slide it over my head, being careful not to let the pins stick me. She'd kneel on the floor with her pincushion, fitting the dress on me, and I'd look down at that dress, at that lop-sided, raw-edged, half-basted, half-pinned thing—and know that it was never going to look like anything. So I'd pout while Mama frowned and sighed and kept on pinning.

I paused for a moment, letting the effect of the words ring in the silence. "Writers, is this story in some weird way reminding you of anything that ever happened on your life?" When some writers signaled yes, I nodded. "The same with me! This story is reminding me of a time in my life, too. So watch what I do." Leaning over my clipboard, I began scrawling my own story, and voicing it as I wrote:

Those of you with parts in the play, stay after class to talk about your costumes," Miss Armstrong said ten minutes before the bell rang. My classmates and I continued working.

When the bell finally rang, I saw the children who, like me, were remaining in the room. I thought, "Eliza, Becky, Richard, and I have the main parts in the play!" I thought about how we'd probably need to stay late often. We'd probably go to each other's houses on Saturdays to study our lines.

I paused from writing to look up and read the parts I had just written. Aloud I added, "I knew Eliza's house because, many times, the school bus had drawn to a stop in front of it and she and a whole group of girls had thronged off the bus. Now I'd find out what they did there." I began writing again.

"Let's meet," Eliza said. I pulled my chair to the back corner of the room to where she and the others had already gathered. Eliza ripped a page from her spiral, and said, "It's from the 1860s, so we'll need antique costumes . . . Oh!" She giggled and pointed at me. "You won't need a costume. You can just wear the dress you have on!"

"But, but, but . . . ," I answered.

Debrief, explaining how the read-aloud spurred you to generate a corresponding entry.

Writers, did you see that I am not writing *about* the story I just read, I am writing my own story? It is not about a mother sewing. I can't say why this story came to mind for me, but it did. Eloise Greenfield's writing evoked a memory from my own life.

Teachers, I'm writing this on a clipboard so children hear rather than see the story because, frankly, I won't actually need to write all of it (if they can't read my writing). Instead, I essentially dictate this as I scrawl, and then after the minilesson, I will reveal that I have a copy of this written on chart paper for all to see. It is a powerful mentor text so one way or the other, I will want it enlarged.

You'll notice that this entry is much longer than those you'd normally write in the modeling portion of a minilesson. The reason for this is two-fold. First, it is important to have a strong entry that can serve as both a mentor and a teaching aide as the unit progresses. Second, it can be beneficial for students to watch you and I write and write and write, ushered on by the power of the memory and the desire to capture it in words. If you do this right, the children will be entranced by the story along with you. That said, there are certainly ways to shorten your modeling. You might choose to only write part of the entry, revealing the finished version at another time. Alternately, you can simply 'write the story in the air,' not even pretending to scrawl, and then to transfer it to chart paper at a later time.

I deliberately share stories in which I admit my vulnerabilities because I know that writing is a risky, revealing thing to do. I try to create a place of safety and compassion in the room by being willing to share hard, though appropriate, parts of my life.

ACTIVE ENGAGEMENT

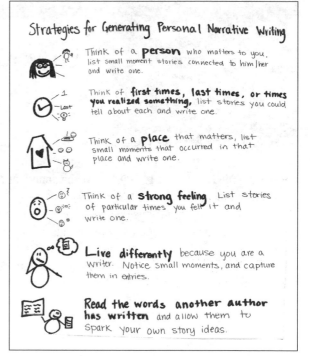

> Strategies for Generating Personal Narrative Writing
>
> - Think of a **person** who matters to you, list Small Moment stories connected to him/her and write one.
> - Think of **first times**, **last times**, or **times you realized something**, list stories you could tell about each and write one.
> - Think about a **place** that matters, list small moments that occurred in that place and write one.
> - Think of a **strong feeling**. List stories of particular times you felt it and write one.
> - **Live differently** because you are a writer. Notice small moments, and capture them in entries.
> - **Read the words another author has written** and allow them to spark your own story ideas.

Reread the excerpt again, this time giving children the opportunity to write from it.

"I know that as you listened to Eloise Greenfield's story, stories probably came to your mind as well. Right now, I'm going to read the story aloud again—let it spark memories in you of 'one time when . . . .' After I finsh reading, let's all write." I reread the story. Then, without saying I word, I gestured for children to write and I joined them, writing furiously myself, not looking up even as I did so.

After I heard the scratch of pens and knew almost everyone had begun writing, I crouched around the meeting area, whispering to the few children who seemed stuck.

If you find that more than half your class struggles to get started, consider voicing over tips rather than whispering in.

LINK

Send children off to continue writing, reminding them that writing in the wake of literature is yet another strategy they can add to their toolkit.

"Writers, I don't want to break the spell that Eloise Greenfield has cast on you. Once you are set and ready to write, you can head back to your spots and continue on from there. And remember, whenever you are looking for story ideas, you can turn to literature and let other writers' words spark memories of your own. For today, you can continue writing this story, or you can go back to a strategy from yesterday, or just write whatever true story you have in mind to write. Go!"

Uncovering Internal Details by Reenacting the Story

AS CHILDREN COLLECT ENTRIES, it will be important to make sure that they are carrying forward not just all they know about generating ideas, but all they know about good storytelling. Are they writing in the moment, using a storyteller's voice rather than the voice of a reporter? Are they incorporating action, dialogue, internal thinking, details, and all the other elements that make for powerful, lively stories? Inevitably, you'll find that some children are not doing these things and you will want to intervene as quickly as possible.

I pulled my chair up next to Becca. She'd already finished an entry on going beach combing, and a short, half-page piece of writing sat before her. "What are you working on as a writer?" I asked.

"Well, I wrote this entry and I'm writing about how I found a really nice piece of sea glass. And I wrote a little about it—details about it being lime green, and how I held it up to my eye. But it is still pretty short," she glanced down at her small entry. "So I

MID-WORKSHOP TEACHING   Revise Entries, Not Just Drafts

"Let me just stop you for a moment, writers. I was just talking with Ori, and I asked him what he was writing about. He told me that he was writing an entry about a time when he was very tired (and even a little grouchy!). I asked him what strategies he was using to make his writing particularly powerful and he realized that, in fact, his story was more of a summary. He had become so focused on collecting new entries that he forgot to carry forward all that he knows about good storytelling.

"Here's the really amazing part, though. After Ori realized that his entry was a summary, he took his pen and went like this." I made a giant, diagonal slashing motion with an imaginary pen. "He crossed the entire entry out, turned the page, and started to rewrite it." I glanced around with feigned shock, ensuring children grasped the magnitude of what Ori had done. "Now Ori is working on dreaming the dream of the story and writing in a way that allows his reader to experience the moment along with him.

"Sometimes, when we get focused on something new, we forget to carry forward the old stuff we already know how to do. Ori was brave enough to recognize that his

entry was just so-so and set out to revise it. Today, will you follow in Ori's footsteps? Ask yourself, 'Am I using everything I know about good writing to write this entry?' If not, revise it like Ori did! I'll add his strategy to our chart."

Techniques for Raising the Level of Narrative Writing

- Dream the dream of the story and then write in a way that allows readers to experience the moment along with you.
- Revise, using all you know about storytelling, not summarizing.

FIG. 3–1　Becca's entry

was gonna think, 'What else do I want to tell about?' and tell about the cool rides you can go on at the beach." I looked over her piece (see Figure 3–1).

"Becca," I said, "You have already done so much work. Even before I pulled up my chair, you had switched from being a writer to being a reader, and you reread your own draft and thought, 'Have I done the things I wanted to do?' I love that on your own, you boxed in a place that you thought was especially important, your focus. And I also love that you thought through the writing challenge that you face. Lots of kids just say, 'I don't know what to do next,' but you figured out that the hard part is writing extensively about a topic as small as a piece of sea glass. That sea glass is not doing anything much, so it isn't easy to describe it in detail, is it?"

Then I said, "You are right to think, 'My story is a bit short,' because it is, but the answer doesn't need to be to move on and tell about the rides. Because then you'd risk telling a story that is more like a watermelon and less like a seed. So instead, you can either make this sea glass story bigger or move on and find something else at the beach to highlight. I'll help you do either one of those. Which makes more sense to you?"

She answered, "The sea glass?" with intonation that suggested she wasn't too sure.

So I said to her, "Let's pretend it is right here on the floor. You see it. You reach down and pick it up."

Then I gestured, "Do that now." I picked up a similar piece of imaginary sea glass. "Hold it. Turn it over in your hand. What are you thinking? Feeling?"

Becca said, "I feel lucky. I can't believe I just found pretty sea glass for a change."

"Say more. What are you thinking as you hold that sea glass?" I said, and clasped imaginary glass in my hand. Soon Becca was writing. (see Figure 3–2).

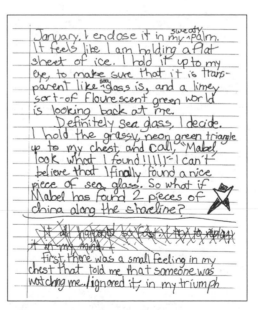

FIG. 3–2　Becca's revised entry, after reenacting the moment

"Becca," I said. "After this, when you want to stretch out a moment and write it in a way that lets your reader be right there with you, remember that it helps to reenact whatever it is you are describing, because sometimes when you act things out, you think up more to say."

Setting the Stage for Powerful Partnerships

Call students to the rug, setting them next to their new writing partner.

"Writers, you'll notice that I've set you next to a classmate for today's share. This classmate will be your new writing partner for the year, and believe me when I say that you are lucky to have each other! I studied each of your writing over the past few days and thought long and hard about a person with whom to pair each of you. I've made sure that each of you is matched with someone who can help you in big ways. So take a moment and get to know your new partner. One of you will need to be Partner 1 and the other will need to be Partner 2. I'll let you figure this out on your own. Once you've decided which partner you'll be, then take each other on a tour of your notebooks. Share the resolutions you've made so far this year. Let your partner know a bit about you as a writer. Go ahead."

Students turned to each other, tentatively at first, and after figuring out the logistics regarding Partner 1 and Partner 2, began to share their writing and resolutions. "Show your partner actual examples of what you are talking about," I told the class. "If you say, 'I'm the kind of writer who loves to use details,' then show your partner a place in your notebook where you have actually done this." Then, "Don't forget to tell your partner what you are working on as a writer. He or she may be able to help you!"

Call students back together and explain the importance of active, supportive partnerships. Ask them to re-do the conversation they had earlier, this time helping their partner to grow and change as a writer.

"Partner 1s, thumbs up. Partner 2s, thumbs up." After gathering the children's attention and ensuring that all partnerships had delegated a *1* and *2*, I continued on.

"I know that you have had writing partners before. But fifth grade is a new year and the expectations are higher. You are expected to do more as writers *and* you are expected to do more as writing partners. I read an article once that talked about people's abilities to change their bad, unhealthy habits. A group of doctors studied people who were obese and trying to lose weight, people who had high cholesterol and were trying to eat different kinds of food and exercise more, and other patients who were trying to stop smoking. The doctors found (and this is a little shocking) that no matter how much people wanted to change their bad habits, they usually failed. But here's the thing, they *didn't fail* if they had a support group, partners with the same goals, to help them. Now, you aren't trying to stop smoking or lower you cholesterol, but you *are* working hard to become stronger and stronger writers. Your new partner will be your support group." The children smiled and giggled, amused with the analogy.

In Writing a Life, *by Katherine Bomer, she cites Margaret Wheatley to remind us of the importance of not just writing our life stories, but of sharing them with others. "Many people are longing to be in conversation again. We are hungry for a chance to talk. People want to tell their story, and are willing to listen to yours. People want to talk about their concerns and struggles. Too many of us feel isolated, strange, or invisible. Conversation helps end that." (from* Turning to One Another)

"In order to be a supportive partner, though, you have to be an *active* partner. What I mean by this is that you can't just be polite listeners, nodding nicely as your partner reads his or her piece. Talking to a partner should not be the same as talking to a wall or a teddy bear. The wall and the teddy bear won't say, 'I don't really get how you think this meets your goal,' or 'What I think is most important about what you did is . . .' or 'Why don't you do that in more places?' So, will you rewind the conversation you just had, and this time, be an active partner! Partner 1, you be the listener and active partner for today. Partner 2, go ahead and share your work and resolutions again."

I listened in as Sabera shared her goals, referencing an entry she'd written about helping her mom.

Sabera began, "One goal I had was to add more of what I was thinking when my sister cried." She pointed to her entry, showing where she had added and said, "Why does she have to cry every day?" (See Figure 3–3).

Her partner Takuma added "That's good. I like that. It makes me feel like you are so tired of your sister crying. Is that what this is about?"

Sabera shrugged a bit and said, "Yah, she cries all the time."

"So what else will you do to make this better?" Takuma pressed.

When Sabera suggested she'd maybe show not tell to make the story more interesting, Takuma said, "I'm not trying to be mean. I like your writing. But maybe you could figure out what the heart of your story is. Then maybe you could show, not tell, there. You know, like if it's about how annoying your sister is you could say, "Her cry is like a siren on a fire truck."

After a couple of minutes, I called the partnerships back together. "Nicely done, partners. After this, remember—to be the best partner you can be, sometimes you need to speak up. Don't be afraid to ask questions, give tips, and help your partner make plans."

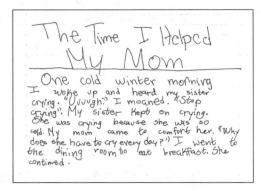

FIG. 3–3 Sabera shared this excerpt fom her notebook.

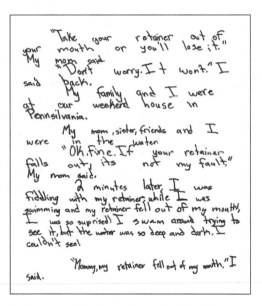

FIG. 3–4 Olivia shared an entry from her notebook with her partner.

SESSION 3 HOMEWORK

🔅 EDITING AS YOU WRITE

We often think that editing is something done just before publishing. We draft, we revise, we tinker with sentences and words, but it isn't until just before publishing that we set to making our writing readable. Strong writers, though, are in the habit of editing *as they write*. Throughout the process, the best of writers look back over their writing and ask, "Have I used everything I know about spelling, punctuation, and grammar to make my writing clear?"

Tonight, take some time to step back and ask this question. This doesn't mean this is all the writing you will do—I imagine you'll also have time to collect another entry or two—but spend a bit of time looking over your past entries and doing some editing. The list below will help you get started.

Questions to Ask Yourself as You Edit

1. Does this make sense? Are any words or parts missing?

2. Are all my sentences complete? Have I checked for run-ons and fragments?

3. Have I used correct capitalization (for names and the beginning of sentences)?

4. Have I used commas and quotation marks for dialogue?

5. Have I checked to see that all my verbs and subjects agree? Are my verbs in the right tense (past, present, future)?

6. Do the words all seem to be spelled right? Do they look right? Have I checked any I'm uncertain of?

7. Have I checked for frequently confused words (to, too, two; there, their)?

8. Have I paragraphed and indented?

Telling the Story from Inside It

I REMEMBER LEARNING TO PLAY TENNIS AS A CHILD. My mother would call from across the net, saying, "Keep your eye on the ball." And I would think, "What do you think I'm looking at—birds? Of course I'm watching the ball." But then one day, as I was playing tennis, I watched the ball as it came toward me, bounced on the surface of the court, then rose up. I saw the ball reach the top of its bounce, and hang there motionless for an instant, and I actually saw my racket meet the ball, and then I watched the ball sail toward my opponent. That day, I realized with a start, that I had never before actually kept my eye on the ball. "*This* is what my mother wanted me to do all those times when she'd call, 'Keep your eye on the ball,'" I thought, a bit chagrined.

Learning to write is not all that different than learning to play tennis. It is one thing to hear that the writer should experience the story so as to tell it in ways that allow the reader to experience it. One can learn the words enough to extoll the need to write from inside the story. But it is another thing altogether to actually pull off this feat.

You'll find, therefore, that although other teachers, in previous years, taught your students to story-tell, you'll end up teaching this all over again, and you will revisit this lesson again later this year as well. If there is a sense of déjà vu to some of these lessons, think about your own experience trying to change some aspect of your practice—say, of your practice as a teacher. Change is hard. I'm still working at keeping my eye on the ball.

Earlier, you urged children to step into the shoes of their character—who in this instance is themselves, in another place, at another time—and to reimagine the story in order to write it from the inside. This session builds on that one, helping students to become more clear about what it really means to tell a story from within the shoes, the skin, of a character (even if that character is themselves). You'll be teaching students to maintain a point of view as they write, and to be able to reread their rough draft entries and notice times when the point of view doesn't ring true.

I recall reading an entry that Ori wrote, in which he described looking into his parents' room and seeing his mom's "extremely large brownish bed." Later, he wrote that he walked down the "brownish stairs." When I reached for the words to capture why those descriptive

IN THIS SESSION, you'll build upon the earlier session, reminding students to experience the moment as they write about it so that readers, too, can experience that moment. In particular, the session teaches writers that to do this, it is important to write from inside the skin of the character—which in a personal narrative is oneself, at another time, in another place.

GETTING READY

✔ A "before" and "after" story, one in which you slip out of the narrator's point of view and then fix the problem in the second version (see Teaching)

✔ A story for children to practice the strategy off of (see Teaching)

✔ Each child's notebook, with them in the meeting area for the minilesson

✔ Two student samples illustrating poor and effective use of details (see Mid-Workshop Teaching and Share)

✔ "Techniques for Raising the Level of Narrative Writing" chart (see Share)

COMMON CORE STATE STANDARDS: W.5.3.a,b,d; W.5.4, W.5.5, RL.5.2, RL.5.6, SL.5.1, SL.5.4, SL.5.6, L.5.1, L.5.2, L.5.3

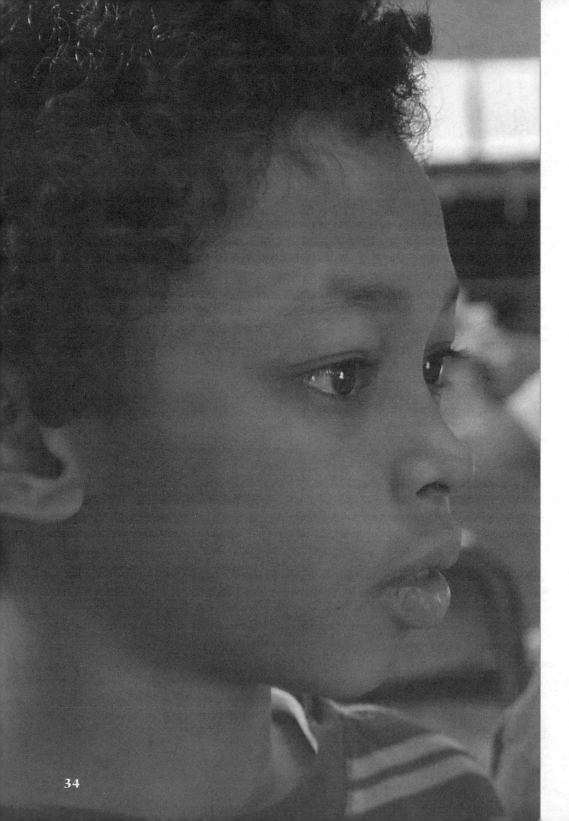

passages didn't work, I realized that the details reflected the fact that Ori found it difficult to maintain a point of view, to truly tell the story as if he had experienced it, as a nine-year-old boy. It was crystal clear to me that although Ori may well have stood in the doorway to his mother's room, it was very unlikely his focus would be on the brownish color of her bed. I suspected he inserted that detail later, presumably adding the color of the bed because he believed he was expected to add sensory details.

"You will teach students that telling a story through a narrator's eyes means keeping a consistent point of view throughout the piece."

Today you will teach students that telling a story through a narrator's eyes means keeping a consistent point of view throughout the piece. There are details a person in a particular situation would be apt to notice—and details a person in that position would be unlikely to note. If I've woken up in the middle of the night, and begun walking down the long hallway outside my bedroom, I might notice a patch of morning light on the hallway mirror, but I wouldn't attend to the details of the floral pattern on the rug at the end of the hall. And I wouldn't notice that the floor—the floor I'd grown up with and seen every day of my life—was brown.

Over the past few days you've been encouraging students to write with their full attention on their story, acting out the story in their heads, getting the whole true story down fast and furiously. This session focuses on point of view and extends the larger message.

Telling the Story from Inside It

CONNECTION

Celebrate the way children have learned to write from inside the stories, reimagining them as they write.

"I've been thinking about the ways your writing is getting better, and this morning, driving to work, I realized that the most important improvement I've seen in your writing so far is that you are bringing more imagination to your writing." I paused, and looked around. "Does that puzzle you? Are you thinking, 'Huh? I'm not writing imagined stories, I'm writing true stories.'

"Because I think deep down, you are coming to realize that even when you are writing true stories, to write those stories well, you have to imagine them. You have to recreate the movie of that event, and it needs to be so real to you that if it's night in your story, when you look up from the page and see the sun streaming into the classroom, you blink to get used to the light. You've been writing with that sort of imagination—with the kind of imagination that allows you to walk in the shoes of your character, to see what he, what she, saw. Today I want to ratchet up the level of that work even further so that the entries you write get better and better, each day."

✥ Name the teaching point.

"Today I want to teach you that when you write personal narratives, it is important to put yourself inside the skin of the main character (the character is the writer, of course, just you in a different time and place), and then tell the story through that person's eyes, exactly the way he or she experienced it."

TEACHING

Tell the story of one time when you wrote a story, staying inside the constraints of your particular perspective.

"The term that people use for telling a story through a narrator's eyes is called *point of view*. I first learned about writing inside a point of view when I was in the middle of washing dishes (in a story I was writing) and the phone rang. My arms were deep in the soapsuds, so I couldn't answer it. My sister picked up the receiver and I heard her say, 'Hello?' into the phone."

J. K. Rowling gave the commencement speech at Harvard a few years ago, and in it she spoke of the centrality of imagination. She added that she wasn't speaking of the kind of imagination that allowed a person to create creatures of all sorts. Instead, she was speaking of the sort of imagination that allows a person to walk a mile in the shoes of another person. That speech echoes in my mind as I teach these kids.

When I use the phrase narrator's point of view *throughout this session and this series, I don't mean it as a way to distinguish the first-person (meaning* I*) or third-person (meaning* he *or* she*) points of view. Instead, I mean the words more literally: what exactly is in the mind's eye of the narrator at any given time? I use the phrase* narrator's point of view *to help writers understand that if details of the scene aren't in that narrator's perception at that moment, perhaps they don't belong in the writing either!*

I held my arms down in front of me, acting out the scene. "I was still at the sink (arms down, in the suds) when my sister picked up the phone." At first, I wrote the story like this:

> My sister picked up the phone. It was my mom telling her that she had been to the doctor.

"But here's the problem! I was at the sink. My hands were all wet and sudsy. The phone was across the room. How would I know whose voice was inside that phone? The story has to unfold as I experienced it. I'm standing at the sink, my hands in the suds, looking at my sister as she talks on the phone. So the story, as I experienced it, must sound more like this:"

> My sister picked up the phone. I heard her say, "What'd he say?" and "Did he give you anything for it?" After she hung up she said, "That was Mom. She's been to the doctor."

Debrief.

"Writers, do you see why that second version worked? When writing, I have to stand in the character's shoes (my shoes) and to write from the character's point of view, capturing what happened from his or her perspective."

ACTIVE ENGAGEMENT

Set children up to practice telling a story from within the narrator's perspective. Ask them to reread a pretend draft where the point of view needs to be remedied.

"Once you get used to staying inside your own perspective, it's not that hard to watch for instances where, oops, you slip out of it. To practice noticing when a story suddenly loses its grounding, listen to my story and decide, 'Is the point of view working?' in which case make a thumbs-up gesture, or 'Did I just lose it?' (then, make a thumbs-down gesture)." I pretended to write on my spiral pad, zooming quickly along, and meanwhile voiced this story aloud.

> I stood alongside my bike at the top of the hill. My brother, Alex, waited as I made up my mind. In front of me the road lay like a ribbon. "I'm ready," I thought. I swung my leg up, climbed onto the seat, and pushed on the pedal.

I glanced out at the children. "Thumbs-up or thumbs-down so far?" They all put their thumbs up.

> Soon I was slipping down the road, faster and faster. The world zoomed past me: trees, boulders, woods . . . browns, grays, greens—a blur of color.

I like the visual effect of this minilesson. I know that when giving this part of the minilesson, I'll always act out how my arms are elbow-deep in sudsy water. I want students to grasp that as I stand there, arms immersed, my sister picks up the phone. I can imagine that just by my intonation the children will discern that something has been knocked asunder by the sentence, It was my mom telling her that she had been to the doctor. *My intonation and my gestures can make it easy for children to grasp why this story defies reality.*

Again, I paused, and the children put their thumbs-up.

> Then something darted in front of me. I swerved to avoid it, lost my balance, and headed into
> the wild brush on the side of the road. [Thumbs-up.] My bike flipped and suddenly I saw nothing.
> [Thumbs-up.] My brother went inside for help because he wondered if I was alive.

I paused after this last line, looking around the room to see if the children had caught the moment where I slipped out of the narrator's perspective. Slowly, then more confidently, they put their thumbs down. "Turn and tell the person beside you why that last part doesn't work." I listened in as children explained that because I was unconscious I could not know that my brother had run for help.

Ask children to continue saying the story aloud, maintaining the point of view.

"Partner 2, pretend you are the author. Continue the story from where I left off. Make it up, stay in the point of view of me, lying on the ground after the accident." To get children started, I went back and reread the last part of the story before I lost the point of view. "'My bike flipped and suddenly I saw nothing. I blinked my eyes open. . . .'" As one partner continued the story, I listened in. Silas continued the story with Ori,

> Above me I saw my brother's face. 'You . . . you alive?' he asked. I turned my head this way and
> that. It felt like thunder inside my brain. "I guess so," I answered, and wondered if anything was
> broken.

LINK

Rename your teaching point. Send children off to copy their leads and to climb into the skin of their narrator.

"So writers, right now, think of the entry you will be writing today and think, specifically, of how it will start." I gave them a few seconds to do this. "Remember that before you can write, you need to put yourself inside the skin of the person in the story, in that place. Think, 'Where, exactly, am I? What, exactly, am I saying and doing?' Be detailed. You are not 'going to the airport.' You are unbuckling your seatbelt and getting out of the car." I gave them a few more seconds. Then I said, "Open your notebooks to the page for your next entry and go! Get started!"

While sitting on the carpet in the meeting area, the children started writing. I moved among them, watching, whispering a tip or two. Then I voiced over, saying, "Don't say you talked—use the exact, actual words."

After another moment, I said, "Tell what thoughts occurred to you as you write the step-by-step story."

By this time, most children were writing, and one by one, I tapped those who were writing, sending them back to their seats. Then I convened the remaining children and got them storytelling to each other before sending them off, too.

It's always challenging to think, "How can I set things up so children can have a few minutes to practice and apply the concept I've taught?" Part of the challenge is that we want to act as training wheels, enabling children to have success with the concept. In my examples, I deliberately try to use words which make it clear when I'm writing within the first-person point of view, and when I slip out of it. But intonation helps as well.

The children won't all grasp this, but just the fact that they are aware that point of view is something to consider will help their writing. Watch for times when their writing reads like this: I stood on the balcony, looking down at my sister. She had a cardboard box in front of her and was doing something with the contents. It was a tiny kitten with blue, blue eyes. *That story works until suddenly the narrator, standing far away on the balcony, peers into the box and into the eyes of the little kitten. The character would have needed to leave the balcony, to rush beside his sister, and to peer into the box from close up in order to see the kitten's eyes.*

Using Details that are True to the Event

YOU'LL FIND THAT BY STUDYING YOUR STUDENTS' WORK and trying to understand their understandings of writing, you become much smarter as a teacher. I suggest you pay special attention to children's use of details and try to articulate what you ascertain. My observations tell me that when children are taught to add details or descriptions to their writing, especially to add sensory details, the resulting text often doesn't ring true. It is as if plums have been added to the plum pudding after the fact. The details that work are not those that are inserted after the text is completed, by the writer, who is now standing back from the story, objectively assessing it and correcting deficiencies. Instead, the details that work are those that rise to mind when the writer imagines the story, walking in the shoes of the character, seeing what he

---

MID-WORKSHOP TEACHING   **Noticing If the Details Ring True**

"Writers, when you are writing from inside the skin of a character, remember that the details you see and include in your draft will be the details that the character notices in the moment of the story. Do your details ring true? For example, last year, one of my students, a boy named Andy, wrote about sitting down at the lunch table. Think about the real, true details you focus on when you sit at the lunch table." I left a moment for the children to do that, and meanwhile I did the work as well. "Listen to Andy's piece and see if the details he has added are those that you think a kid would truly notice when he goes to sit at the lunch table."

> I carried my tray full of food from the lunch line. I went over and put my tray on the yellow metal table. I pulled the red metal chair in as I sat beside the table.

"Turn and talk, what do you think?"

The room was filled with hubbub, as children told each other that there was no way that kid really paid attention to the metal or to the color of tables and chairs in his cafeteria.

I spoke above the hubbub. "I agree with you all. He was probably thinking that it was good to add sensory details so he stuck those details in, but he'd forgotten that sensory details need to be true ones that the writer notices when reliving the story from the narrator's point of view. Right now, will each of you reread your story and

see if you can locate places where your story gets derailed, where you stop telling it bit-by-bit and stop writing from within a clear point of view?" After a moment of doing this work silently, I interjected. "And remember, whenever you are writing, make sure that all your details ring true."

I carried my tray full of food from the lunch line. I went over and put my tray on the yellow metal table. I pulled the red metal chair in as I set beside the table. Everyone was sharing snack. William had cupcakes and I wanted some. Thomas shared some popcorn with me. He put it on my tray. "Thanks, Thomas," I said.

FIG. 4–1   Andy's writing

---

felt, hearing what he heard. The best way to produce details that ring true is for the writers to dream the dream of the story, imagining and recalling all that happened in the sequence with which it happened.

You'll want to remind children of James Merrill's words: "The words that come first are anybody's words. You need to make them your own." If a child wrote, *'I walked up the walk and inside the front door. I had a snack. Then I went to my bedroom.'* you might say, "Your story could tell about walking inside *anybody's* front door. Listen to how Jean Fritz, in her memoir *Homesick*, describes walking inside *her* house:"

> *I flung open the iron gate and threw myself through the front door.*
>
> *"I'm home!" I yelled.*
>
> *Then I remembered that it was Tuesday, the day my mother taught English at the Y.M.C.A. where my father was the director.*
>
> *I stood in the hall, trying to catch my breath, and as always I began to feel small. It was a huge hall with ceilings so high it was as if they would have nothing to do with people. Certainly not with a mere child, not with me—the only child in the house. Once I asked my best friend, Andrea, if the hall made her feel little too. She said no. She was going to be a dancer and she loved space. She did a high kick to show how grand it was to have room. (13)*

I might show this excerpt to a child in a conference, saying, "Do you see how Jean Fritz describes that hallway in a way that reveals not only the hallway, but also reveals her as a person? If your first draft read, 'I walked up the walk and inside the front door. I had a snack. Then I went to my bedroom' and you wanted to revise this to show yourself—your point of view, your kitchen—what might you write? Would you write, 'I walked into our kitchen and opened the refrigerator to see if Mom had made the casserole for tonight's dinner'? Would you write, 'I sifted through a pile of mail but it was all bills for my mom. This time they had threatening, brightly colored labels that said things like 'Third bill,' and 'Urgent.' What might you say to show that this is not just anyone entering any kitchen?"

Then I'd look for a few places in the child's draft where he or she could apply this same concept and help the child continue writing like that. It was that sort of conferring that led Francesca to draft an entry about the day her cat died. Part of her entry read like this:

> It was a Sunday, a strange Sunday. I knew that something was going to happen. Sam was walking weakly, as usual, but worse than other days. I went to play with my friend Lucy. When I came home, Sam was barely walking but still alive.
>
> Camilla (my little sister) picked Sam up and put her on a soft white chair. Everyone was looking at her, even Lucy. I knew she was probably going to die so I cried. My dad started making tea to calm us down but it did not help. What would it be like without Sam? "It will be really quiet," I started thinking. I looked at Sam, with her little white paws and her cute tail. She was almost dead. She took three breaths of air. On the last one, I was looking at a dead cat. The room was silent. Too silent. I could feel Sam's spirit floating up to heaven. I don't know why but I had a big feeling that today was her 19th birthday. I looked at the candles. They were still burning like Sam's spirit was still alive and here. It was a good feeling.

As you support students with this important work, you might want to tell them about a strategy that poet Georgia Heard was once taught when she was learning to draw. Her instructor suggested that she fix her eyes on a subject—say, a tree—and draw fast and furiously, never once glancing away from the subject. The drawings that resulted often contained a life force that was remarkable. You can teach the students to apply this same kind of focus to the stories they are working on. You'll suggest that a life force, or power, can emerge in their writing when they keep their eyes (and minds) intently on the mental movie of their memories as they write them.

Using Details from the Moment

Share an example of a child's writing that includes details from inside the story.

"Writers, I want you to think about how you might describe a brand-new house that you just moved into. You *could* write something like this: 'There are three bedrooms along the hall. Each is about the same size. There is also a dining room.' But *anyone* could see those things. A stranger to the house or a real estate agent might describe it that way. In a really good story, characters (and you are the main character in your story) let the reader see the world as they saw the world in the moment of the story.

"I think Kim Yung does this really well. The way she writes about the new house—the one she's just moved into—lets me feel as if I am seeing that new house through her eyes. It's almost like she's got a video camera, and as she goes from room to room, we go from room to room with her. Remember what rooms look like when there is no furniture in them yet—when they contain just carpet and sun? Listen to how Kim Yung writes about her new house:

> After looking through this never-ending house, I went to my room that I chose and sat down on the furry carpet. The sun shined through all the windows until it reached the soft carpet. It was nice and warm when you stepped on it. It made you want to stay in that spot. I was going to like this house. It had everything. I would rise up every morning with a happy and bright smile. I would like that feeling. I would go downstairs and eat a healthy breakfast. Life would be the greatest in this house.

"Sensory details work in a story when they are the details that the character (that's you) really, truly notices in the moment of the story. Kim Yung's details about her new house ring true.

Channel students to share their own writing and to talk about places where their details ring true, and places where they don't.

"Will you read your writing to each other, and talk about whether you've been able to write with real true details?"

I listened as John discussed his piece about leaving for summer camp. "I'm not really sure if my details make sense," he admitted. "I really wanted my reader to picture everything I was seeing. I was trying to show not tell. When I wrote 'Hot tears spilled down my face like a river as I climbed on the bus,' I think that's good. That part's important. His partner,

FIG. 4–2   One page of a very long entry by Kim Yung.

Yvette, agreed, peeking over John's shoulder to see the rest of the entry. John continued: "But I think this part might be too many details." He began to read from his piece again. "I sat down next to Gail and looked out the window. She had floppy ponytails and the bus window was greasy and dark." Yvette shook her head, agreeing, and I moved on.

While children talked, I added our newest strategies to the class chart and then called for their attention. What each of you are realizing is the importance of living *inside* the moment you are writing about, and telling only the details that rang true at that particular time. Generally, the details we add later are less true than those that come to us as we re-experience and write the story. As you continue to write, keep this in mind."

SESSION 4 HOMEWORK

MAKING AND USING TOPIC LISTS

Writers, I love the feeling that your minds are bursting with stories, because this means that during writing time, you aren't just *thinking up* stories, you are *selecting* stories that you feel will especially work. Just to make sure you are brimming with possible stories, take some time tonight to gather a list of possible stories on a special page of your writer's notebook. That way, if you ever finish an entry, and for a moment can't think of something to write about, you can draw from your very own well of ideas.

One way to develop a topic list is by freewriting using a recurring phrase. It could be *I remember*, but be sure to remember very specific moments. 'I remember standing at the base of the lake, up to my ankles in freezing water,' or 'I remember throwing my first strike.'

Once you are done freewriting, you can spend a bit of time collecting an entry or two. I'm sending you home with a copy of our chart, "Techniques for Raising the Level of Narrative Writing," so that you can remind yourself of all you've learned while you write.

Techniques for Raising the Level of Narrative Writing

- Dream the dream of the story and then write in a way that allows readers to experience the moment along with you.
- Revise using all you know about storytelling, not summarizing.
- Use all you know about grammar, spelling, and punctuation to edit as you write.
- Tell the story from **inside** it.
- Use details that are true to the event and that ring true.

Taking Stock and Setting Goals

IN THIS SESSION, you'll teach children that writers sometimes pause to take stock, using a checklist to assess their own growth and set new goals.

GETTING READY

✓ Each child should be asked to bring his or her notebook, which hopefully contains all the entries the child has written since the start of the year, as well as perhaps the initial on-demand writing, to the meeting area for the minilesson.

✓ A copy of the Narrative Writing Checklist, Grades 5 and 6, for each child and a chart-sized version for class display with only a few categories unveiled (see Teaching) ✸

✓ A copy of "Goosebumps" for each child and a chart-sized version (see Teaching) ✸

✓ "Techniques for Raising the Level of Narrative Writing" chart (see Link)

WHEN TEACHING WRITING, you are teaching a skill—like playing the oboe or swimming. One of the important things about teaching a skill is that the learner needs to do the work. The words you say in a minilesson are important because they channel learners to do some work that will, in the end, accelerate their growth.

Studies of the factors that accelerate achievement have important implications for your teaching. John Hattie, author of *Visible Learning* (2008), has done a mega-study compiling thousands of studies from every walk of life that attempt to understand the factors that support achievement. When looking at data from 20 to 30 million students to see the factors that were especially influential, Hattie came away saying that it is incredibly important for learners to work toward crystal-clear, challenging but accessible goals, and it is important for them to receive feedback that includes compliments on what is working and instruction on the next steps they can take.

In any unit of study, then, it will be important for you to illuminate for students what it is that they are trying to accomplish. It is not enough for youngsters to work toward writing "a great story." What, exactly, constitutes a great story?

Of course, this is a complex question, and any one answer will be provisional. But that doesn't mean it isn't important for you to help the students in your care develop clear images of what they are working towards. Linda Darling Hammond has said that learning is accelerated when the learner, like a person training to be an Olympic diver, has studied examples of what he or she is aiming to do and then has opportunities to work towards that goal, repeatedly practicing, and receiving feedback. This session adds to work you have been doing since the start of this year to help youngsters crystallize their images of effective narratives, to self-assess, and to set goals. The ultimate aim is to accelerate achievement.

COMMON CORE STATE STANDARDS: W.5.3, W.5.5, W.5.10, RL.5.1, RL.5.2, SL.5.1, SL.5.4, L.5.1, L.5.2, L.5.3

Taking Stock and Setting Goals

CONNECTION

Introduce children to the work of the minilesson—assessing themselves as writers and setting goals.

After students had settled in the meeting area, notebooks in hand, I said, "Writers, would you look at your first entry, written earlier this year, and then look also at your most recent entry, and will you ask yourself one of the most important questions you can ask: 'Am I getting better as a writer?' Do that silently, right now."

After leaving some silence for this work, I said, "As you know, our goal this year is not just to write a lot. It is to get better as writers. That means that every day, you'll be taking all you know, and working to outgrow yourself. You know how runners are always timing themselves and trying to beat their average? Well, you'll be doing similar work as writers this year—only the measuring stick you'll be thinking about is not your time, but the quality and power of your writing.

"Researchers have studied what it takes for human beings to get better at something—whether that something is basketball or running or chemistry or painting or writing . . . and those researchers have found that one of the most important things you can do is to set ambitious, star-in-the-sky goals for yourself and then work like the dickens to reach those goals. You get better by deciding on big and important ways to outgrow yourself, fixing your mind on those goals, and then working to actually make those changes.

"Calvin Coolidge, who was president of the United States about one hundred years ago, was famous for saying, 'All growth depends upon activity.' I think you have seen that yourself already. You haven't gotten better as writers by putting your writers notebook in your desk or under your pillow and hoping you luck out and write better the next time you are asked to produce an on-demand narrative. Instead, you've worked at your writing. You have rolled up your sleeves and worked at writing from inside the story and writing long and strong."

❖ **Name the teaching point.**

"Today I want to remind you that it helps to pause sometimes and to look back on your progress as writers, asking, 'Am I getting better?' and also asking, 'What should I work on next? What will help me keep getting better in big and important ways?'"

This session is inspired by the song from South Pacific *that reminds us that you have to have a dream in order to have a dream come true. It turns out that practice does not make perfect, in life. The brain surgeon who has been doing this work for twenty years is not apt to be more proficient than the rookie surgeon who has been doing this work for five years. This is because most people reach a level of proficiency and then plateau. The one thing that allows people to continue their growth curve is for them to be deliberate learners, self-assessing themselves, working on concrete goals, and receiving feedback. This session is dedicated to that idea.*

Tell students that when working to get better, it helps to have tools for measuring progress and then tell them about the Narrative Writing Checklist for fifth and sixth grades and introduce a snippet of it.

"Writers, whenever you are trying to get better at something—say, running or lifting weights, playing Ping-Pong, or writing—it helps to use tools of one kind or another to measure the work you've done, asking, 'In what ways does my work measure up? In what ways do I need to improve?'

"Over the past few days, some of you have brought your writing to me and asked, 'How is this? Does this measure up?' Those are terrific questions, but here's the thing. You need to not only *ask* but also *answer* those questions. To do this, you need a clear sense of what makes for a powerful piece of writing so you can hold a piece of writing up and ask, 'In what ways does this measure up?'

"I have a checklist here that you can use to measure yourself. The checklist shows the expectations for the *end* of fifth grade, and though it is early in the year, I think that many of you are ready to meet and soon, even, to exceed these expectations. This checklist will live in our classroom through several units, and many of you will find yourselves reaching toward *sixth-grade goals* as you write.

"Now, writers, you're going to have a chance to score one of your entries. But before you score your own piece of writing, let's look at a personal narrative another fifth-grade student has written, 'Goosebumps.' Teachers all over the country have come together and decided that this piece of writing represents what most fifth-grade students should be able to write as an on-demand, written in forty-five minutes, by the end of fifth year. I bet if you really work at it, every single one of you can create writing as strong as "Goosebumps"— and can do that at the *beginning* of fifth grade!

"Since today is our first day using this checklist, let's start by focusing in on a few parts of it—*elaboration* and *craft*. You'll see these parts contain skills you've been working especially hard to improve during these past few days." (The entire Narrative Writing Checklist, Grades 5 and 6, can be found on the CD-ROM.)

Who is it that said, "You can't hit a target if you don't know what that target is"? I want to help children see, with crystal-clear clarity, what is is they are aiming for. Exemplar writing helps ensure the students have a vision for good writing. The checklist gives them the words to name what they see and the language to express what they are working toward.

Narrative Writing Checklist

	Grade 5	NOT YET	STARTING TO	YES!	Grade 6	NOT YET	STARTING TO	YES!
	Structure				**Structure**			
Overall	I wrote a story of an important moment. It read like a story, even though it might be a true account.	☐	☐	☐	I wrote a story that had tension, resolution, and realistic characters and conveyed an idea or lesson.	☐	☐	☐
Lead	I wrote a beginning in which I not only showed what was happening and where, but also gave some clues to what would later become a problem for the main character.	☐	☐	☐	I wrote a beginning in which I not only set the plot or story in motion, but also hinted at the larger meaning the story would convey.	☐	☐	☐
Transitions	I used transitional phrases to show passage of time in complicated ways, perhaps by showing things happening at the same time (*meanwhile, at the same time*) or flashback and flash-forward (*early that morning, three hours later*).	☐	☐	☐	I used transitional phrases to connect what happened to why it happened, such as *If I hadn't . . . , I might not have . . . , because of . . . , although . . . , and little did I know that . . . .*	☐	☐	☐
Ending	I wrote an ending that connected to the main part of the story. The character said, did, or realized something at the end that came from what happened in the story.	☐	☐	☐	I wrote an ending that connected to what the story was really about.	☐	☐	☐
	I gave readers a sense of closure.				I gave readers a sense of closure by showing a new realization or insight or a change in a character or narrator.			
Organization	I used paragraphs to separate different parts or time of the story and to show when a new character was speaking. Some parts of the story were longer and more developed than others.	☐	☐	☐	I used paragraphs purposefully, perhaps to show time or setting changes, new parts of the story, or to create suspense for readers. I created a sequence of events that was clear.	☐	☐	☐

"Let's look just at the points listed under *elaboration* and one under *craft*." I revealed a chart-sized version of the categories as I spoke. "Take a moment to read and discuss them with your partner."

Ask students to join you in assessing a benchmark narrative for fifth grade against a portion of the checklist and do this in a way that allows you to demonstrate how to use the checklist with accountability.

After children had a minute to read and discuss the small section of the checklist I'd uncovered, I continued. "I'll read 'Goosebumps,' and I want you to listen for examples of these items on our fifth-grade checklist. Use the copy of 'Goosebumps' I have given each of you to mark and annotate the places where the writer *does* things called for on the checklist."

Goosebumps

I held up my knee-length nightgown. My mom held up my fleece ankle-length PJs.

"Why should I wear those?" I said. I wondered why she wanted me to wear fleece on a warm summer night in Montana.

"It gets very cold in the night," my mom said with a serious look on. I gave her a look, she looked right back at me. For a moment there was silence. Then she let out a long sigh. I could tell that I had won because she was putting away the PJs.

As I slid on my nightgown I could feel my mom herding me to my bed. I stopped and climbed in. I pulled up my light sheets. My mom opened her mouth and said "Put your wool cover over you. I'm serious!" I gave her a look. She let out a sigh. She hugged me and whispered in my ear, "Good night."

I woke up with a tingle, I sat up in my bed. I looked at the clock, only ten minutes went by. I looked at my arms they were covered in goosebumps. So were my legs. It felt like it had dropped thirty degrees. I bent down and grabbed the wool blanket and pulled it over me with a sigh of relief.

As I got comfy my mind soared. I thought about all the times my mom had been right. Like the time I didn't wear rainboots when my mom told me and got cold. Then the time my mom told me to put on sunblock. I didn't and got a really bad sunburn. But out of all my thoughts I wondered why I acted like that? Was I cranky or mad? But before I could think my eyes got heavy and started to close, before I knew it everything was black and then gone.

"Let's look at those points and think about how the 'Goosebumps' writer measures up." I read the first few paragraphs of "Goosebumps" aloud and then let my eyes travel between "Goosebumps" and the checklist. "What do you think? Touching one portion of the checklist, I then touched portions of the story that matched the checklist and said, "Each part of the story is told bit by bit, often including thoughts, action, and dialogue. I can definitely see that." I underlined two of those parts, and briefly annotated them in the margins.

The students will soon assess themselves against the whole narrative checklist. For now, however, you are asking them to focus their attention on just two significant categories. First off, this gives children the opportunity to take in the checklist in a more accessible, bite-sized fashion. Then too, this is the focus of students' most recent work and by championing these sections of the checklist, you steer children to work toward goals within these categories. Don't fret if you see things on the checklist that you have not taught children yet. Because these are end-of-fifth-grade standards, that is just as it should be. Know that throughout the unit you will touch on everything that is addressed in the checklist.

Notice that you are not whipping through this, just sort of going check, check, check. Model close analytical reading, and show that you hold yourself accountable to providing evidence for each conclusion you draw. It would be just as effective to do this work with a text that is not entirely up to par—but we wanted to introduce "Goosebumps" to the class for other reasons. It will resurface in later minilessons.

I touched another portion of the checklist, and then looked at the draft. "Hmm. Would you say the writer writer develops the main character—the narrator? Hmm. What do you think?"

I gestured to Sandy, who pointed out places where readers got to know the narrator, and I underlined them as well, saying as I did this, "You are right. I can tell exactly how she feels not only about wearing those heavy winter PJs, but also how she feels about her mom telling her what to do. The dialogue between the writer and her mother shows that the writer is . . . what would be the words . . . a bit stubborn, do you think? Pigheaded? What do you think?" I looked up at the children, and they settled on *stubborn*.

"Wait, wait," I said, and pointed to the relevant portion of the checklist. "It says that the writer develops characters, with an *s*—more than one. Let's reread and see what we think about that." The room was quiet, and then, as students looked up, I channeled them to talk quickly to their partner. As they did, I listened in, and soon convened the class. "I hear you saying that this piece develops the mother as well as the daughter. The mother's actions show what kind of person she is. I underlined portions of the text that showed that she gave a serious look, a long sigh. "It's like the mother is aware of her daughter's obstinate ways." Then looking at the snippet of the checklist as a whole, I said, "If I were going to score 'Goosebumps' based on the categories here, I would definitely say that it does match most of the fifth-grade descriptors."

Debrief in ways that help students extract transferable lessons from what you have just taught.

"Do you see the way I did that? Using a checklist is not an exact science and I didn't spend hours trying to figure out *exactly* what the writer has and hasn't done. Instead, I quickly looked at what a strong writer does, and then checked to see how the writer of 'Goosebumps' measures up. I looked for evidence before deciding 'yes' or 'no,' and I annotated the text, marking up places where I found that evidence."

ACTIVE ENGAGEMENT

"Now it's your turn. Take a few minutes and talk with your partner about what you noticed about 'Goosebumps,' and then reread either your fast draft or your partner's, and talk about ways you have—and haven't yet—done the work of elaborating and describing. Partners, your goal is to help each other get better, okay? Turn and talk."

LINK

Restate your teaching point, reminding children that to grow and develop as a writer, it is important to stop and take measure of what they've done so far and make plans for how to improve.

"Writers, can I stop you? I know many of you haven't finished assessing your writing in light of our checklist and our exemplar text ('Goosebumps'), but that is okay because although it is helpful to do this with a partner, the truth is that this is the work each one of you needs to do all the time as a writer. So today, as you look back at your entries, you'll be looking at your work and trying to come up with some 'starting to' or 'not yets' that can give you goals. I've put a

Notice that there are tiny, brief ways in which you include children in the teaching portion of your minilesson. If doing so means that you can no longer just teach, uninterrupted, for a couple of minutes without them on their knees, trying to pitch in, then you may need to back down and tell them that during minilessons, there are times for them to be active (active engagement) and times for them to listen (the connection and the teaching components).

Be sure to hold children accountable to identifying specific places where they have done things on the checklist. You want to avoid a "Yup, I did that! Yup, I did that! Yup! I did everything" kind of mentality. Instead, teach children to look at their work critically, noting the good work they have done as well as the work they've yet to accomplish.

Read Chapter 5 of Writing Pathways: Performance Assessments and Learning Progressions, K–5 *as this gives a much more detailed overview of how you can recruit children to self-assess.*

copy of the full Narrative Writing Checklist on each of your desks so you can do this. After you assess and set goals for yourself, plan for your writing work. Some of you will decide to revisit old entries and revise them based on the goals you are setting now. Others of you will make a new entry, but this time keeping your new goals in mind as you write.

You just have today's writing time, and tonight's, before you'll be looking back on your entries and choosing one as a seed idea that you will work on for the next few weeks. So you definitely want to be sure you have written an entry that has the potential to become an important piece of writing. Whatever you do today, be sure that you hold yourself to the highest of standards. The Narrative Writing Checklist can help you do that." I added our newest strategy to the class anchor chart.

Techniques for Raising the Level of Narrative Writing

- Dream the dream of the story and then write in a way that allows readers to experience the moment along with you.
- Revise using all you know about storytelling, not summarizing.
- Use all you know about grammar, spelling, and punctuation to edit as you write.
- Tell the story from **inside** it.
- Use details that are true to the event and that ring true.
- Use tools like the Narrative Writing Checklist to ask, 'In what ways does my writing measure up? In what ways do I need to improve?' Then, revise your work to make it stronger.

Setting Goals for Your Writers

TODAY YOU ASKED WRITERS TO SELF-ASSESS AND TO SET GOALS. You taught them the important work of self-reflection and instilled in them a sense that writers don't just write, they also aim to improve. This does not mean, however, that all your children will have picked "just right" goals for themselves. It will also be important for you to have goals in mind for each of them, and much of today's small-group and conferring work might focus on directing students toward several goals that you think are especially key.

For now, look over your students' writing with an eye toward the essentials of effective narratives, letting the checklist be your guide. Look first for patterns across the whole class—areas for development that many children need, and that might influence the direction of your whole-class teaching. Next, look for smaller groupings of children with similar issues, planning for the strategy groups you'll hold across the next few days. For instance, let's read over Olivia's writing and then list the positive work she has done as well as ways in which she can improve. (see Figure 5–1).

> I took a sip of my hot choclate and turned the page lof my book. It was snowing outside and I was nice and cozy inside, reading.
>
> "Perfect," I said. My mom walked in and wiped her hands on her jeans.
>
> "Well, laundry's done," she said looking out the window. She didn't look at the blue jay or the dog running across the field. She looked at my brother and sister playing in the snow.
>
> "Olivia, why don't you go play with them?" she said.
>
> I looked down at my book and back at my brother and sister struggling to get the head on the snowman.

FIG. 5–1   Olivia's writing

1. The beginning sets the reader up to understand the events of the story, but not the deeper meaning or the problem.

2. The writer is beginning to show the internal lives of the characters but could do more to develop both the internal story and the character's relationships.

MID-WORKSHOP TEACHING   Keeping Track of Goals

"Writers, let me stop you for a moment. I just walked past Aalia's desk and saw something that she had created." I put Aalia's chart on the overhead. "Aalia decided to make a personal goal chart for herself, which she'll keep taped to her desk to remind her what she's working toward as a writer.

> My Personal Goal Chart
>
> I need to work on show, not tell.
>
> I also need to work on stretching out the heart of my story.

FIG. 5–2   Aalia's personal goal chart

"As you set goals for yourself as a writer, you'd be smart to follow Aalia's lead and find a way to capture those goals in writing. You might make a 'personal goal chart' like Aalia did, you might use Post-It notes, or even highlight or circle your goals right on the checklist. You could even save a small section of your writer's notebook and label it 'Goals and Resolutions.' Use whatever system work best for you. But remember, it is important to not only set but *remember* your goals each day.

3. The writer uses details, actions, and dialogue to build up this part of the story, but without a clear sense of what it is really about.

4. The ending provides closure, but like the beginning, does not help the reader understand the larger significance of the story.

Don't feel as if this assessment process needs to be long and arduous. Instead, try quick assessments, glancing over children's shoulders to see where they are in their development. One trick for doing this is to focus on one part of the assessment rubric at a time. For instance, you might circle the room once, looking only for children who have summarized rather than told a story, jotting their names on a list as you go. Then take a second spin around the room, this time jotting down children who need work with paragraphing, then those who have an over-abundance of dialogue, and so on. If a child is on more than one of your lists, you will have to make some decisions about which focus will help him most as a writer. These kinds of quick assessments are not meant to replace lengthier, more thoughtful and comprehensive assessments, but assessment is so important it can't always wait until you have a long stretch of time. Don't delay assessing children's progress and setting goals—even if you don't have hours to devote to it at this point in the year!

As you develop your own hunches about the children, be sure to fold in the self-assessment work they did on their own. In instances where your goals diverge from the student's own, validate what the writer has chosen, and then, when possible, help him or her to see how that goal goes hand in hand with other goals (your goal!). For example, for the child who struggles to focus his story, you might say, "John, I love that you've set a worthy goal for yourself to elaborate in more ways. I can imagine all that you might add in. Dialogue, descriptive details, internal thinking. I think this will really help to spice up your writing! Can I give you a tip about elaboration? When writers elaborate, they don't just do it everywhere." Draw a big, invisible circle around his story to illustrate your point. "Instead, they focus in on the most important part of their story, the part where they want to slow down the action for their readers, and they stretch that out. Let's take a look at your piece and see if we can do some of this work together." In this way, you have married your goal (getting John to elaborate without compromising focus) with his goal (varying the methods by which he tells his story).

Mentoring Yourself to a Classmate's Work

Guide students to mentor themselves to a classmate's work.

"Writers, when I have a goal, I do things differently. If I want to get a part in the play, I don't just say, 'That's my goal.' Instead, I practice the part. I watch videos of the play. Today, I saw many of you work differently, because you've selected goals for yourself and that is great." I put Will's writing up so all the children could see it. I ushered Will to the front of the meeting area and asked him to tell us about his work.

"Well," Will began "I looked at my old entry about going to the Packers' game with my grandparents and I didn't think it was really that great. It said on the checklist that it's important to show why characters say and do things. I didn't really tell anything about how excited I was to go to the Packers game. I was also nervous. So I decided to rewrite the beginning of my story. In the better one, I show how nervous and excited I am."

I readied Will to read his first and then his revised entry aloud. "Writers, as you listen to Will's revised draft, will you ask yourself, 'How, exactly, did he show more of his feelings? What did Will do as a writer to help us understand what he is experiencing at that moment?'" Will read his two versions aloud.

FIG. 5–3   Will's first lead

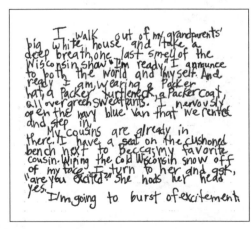

FIG. 5–4   Will's revised lead

Will's Revised Lead

I walk out of my grandparents' big white house and take a deep breath, one last smell of the Wisconsin snow. "I'm ready," I announce to both the world and myself. And ready I am, wearing a Packer hat, a Packer turtleneck, a Packer coat, all over green sweatpants. I nervously open the navy blue van that we rented and step in.

My cousins are already in there. I have a seat on the cushioned bench next to Becca; my favorite cousin. Wiping the cold Wisconsin snow off of my face, I turn to her and ask, "are you excited?" She nods her head yes.

I'm going to burst of excitement.

Ask the students to share what they notice about the student's revisions.

"Go ahead and share what you noticed with your partner. Be specific. What did Will do as a writer to make this second version stronger?" I listened in as children spoke.

Khalid began, "I think in the first one you don't even know that he is talking about going to a Packers game. He doesn't even mention it!" His partner Henry agrees. "I know, it seems like it is all about the snow."

I intervened, "So what exactly did Will do to bring out his nervous excitement? Try to be precise."

"He used dialogue when he said, 'I'm ready,'" Khalid said.

"Yah," Henry added, "and he used details like when he said he nervously opened the navy blue van."

I called the children back together. "You are noticing many things that Will did as a writer to raise the level of his lead to this story. You are right that he worked to bring out his excitement about the game by zooming in on the details that matter, using dialogue to let us in on his internal thinking, describing how he nervously opened the car and stepped in, and so much else."

Ask the students to share their self-assessments with their writing partners and set goals for moving forward with their drafts.

"Today ends Bend I of our unit and tomorrow you'll have the chance to pick a seed idea to take through the writing process. When you rehearse for and draft and revise your new piece of writing, it will be important to keep your goals in mind.

"Take a few minutes now and show your writing partner your checklist. Talk to them about a few of the goals that you have set for yourself after really taking a hard look at your writing. Be specific about where you tried new things. Then, tell your partner what you'll do next. How will you continue to work to make your writing as strong and powerful as it can be?"

YOUR LAST CHANCE TO WRITE A DROP-DEAD POWERFUL ENTRY

Writers, every day you come to school and I try to do a bit of drumroll to help you write well. Tonight, I'm going to ask you to give yourself that drumroll, to design your own minilesson or work your own magic so that you set yourself up to write the most powerful entry you've written yet—giving you more entries to choose from next week, when you will choose one entry to work on for a very long time.

To do this for yourself, you'll want to decide whether you want to rely on our chart of "Strategies for Generating Personal Narrative Writing," or whether you can just sit, pen in hand, waiting for an idea to nibble. "It's like fishing," as William Stafford says.

The other thing you will need to decide upon are the conditions in which you can do your best writing. Will you be writing alone, doors shut, away from everyone? Will you write at the kitchen table, in the midst of the hubbub? Will you be listening to music? Many writers have almost a fetish about the conditions they need in order to do their best writing. One famous writer writes standing up at a counter. Another needs the smell of sliced roasted apples to do his best work. Some go to busy coffee shops and write admist the hubbub. Annie Dillard built herself a writing shed so she could be all alone, and even though the shed has a picture window looking out over the ocean, she puts her desk to the wall, looking away from the ocean, because she's desparate to focus.

So do what you need to do to write a smashing entry.

Moving Through the Writing Process: Rehearsing, Drafting, Revising, and Editing

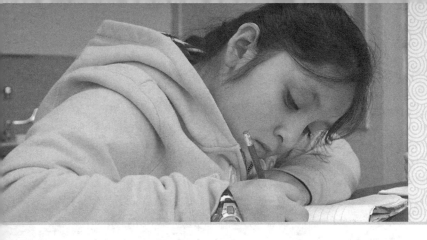

Flash-Drafting
Putting Our Stories on the Page

IN THIS SESSION, you'll remind students that writers draft by writing fast and furious, working to capture the experience on the page.

GETTING READY

✔ A paper clip for each child to mark the seed ideas they select to turn into a story (see Connection)

✔ Each child's writer's notebook, in the meeting area for the lesson

✔ Loose-leaf, lined paper or a drafting pad for each child

✔ Corners of the room where prechosen children can share their flash-drafts with a small group of peers

COMMON CORE STATE STANDARDS: W.5.3, W.5.5, W.5.10, RL.5.1, SL.5.1, SL.5.4, SL.5.6, L.5.1, L.5.2, L.5.3

T ODAY BEGINS THE SECOND BEND in the road of this unit. The bend will start with students rereading their entries and thinking, "Which, of all of these, will I choose to develop further?" This bend will end, almost a week and a half from now, with students having taken the entry they select today through the entire process of writing so that it is publishable (and published in a mini-celebration). During the third bend, your students will generate more entries, selecting one to develop further, and they will then take that entry, that seed idea, through the entire process of writing, this time working with more independence and with more attention to a mentor text. As the unit draws to a close, writers will publish a final piece in a grander fashion.

You will not necessarily lay out this entire trajectory now for your students, but you will want them to understand that they are in a new section of the unit. They should expect that their work will fundamentally change. Before today, they were generating entries, which essentially meant that many students were writing a new narrative, on a new topic, every day. They were working to try to make each day's writing better than the writing they had done on the previous day, and meanwhile they were developing their knowledge of effective narratives, but they had not yet committed to one entry, to one story. Today that changes.

Today you will ask students to pick a seed idea, and then flash-draft a first draft of their story, writing in ways that you have taught them to do during the first portion of this unit. It took me several decades before I realized the importance of writing a draft in a splurge of writing, scrawling fast and furious. Over many decades of teaching writing, I have come to realize that if students crank out their drafts perfectly, producing a paragraph or two a day, working over a sequence of days, the resulting drafts are apt to be wooden and disjointed. In contrast, something magical happens when writers fix their eyes on a story they can imagine with vividness, and then write with their attention fixed on that drama. In these instances, writing becomes an act of empathy, of imagination, of dramatic play. As we have emphasized extensively in the first portion of this unit, when writing stories, a writer becomes himself or herself, living in another time and place. The writer writes "fast and furious," outrunning censors. Donald Murray likened the writer to a bike rider, peddling fast. Because the writer loses himself or herself in the story, readers can do the same.

"Something magical happens when writers fix their eyes on a story they can recall or imagine and write with their attention intently fixed on that drama."

We discovered the power of flash-drafting after we had developed learning progressions for assessing writing and began asking students to write on-demand pieces (which were sometimes narratives). Students were expected to begin and finish those pieces within an hour, while also aiming to write in ways that illustrated their best work. Lo and behold, in those pressure pots, students produced writing that was often significantly better than drafts they produced when they worked more slowly, in class, cranking out rough drafts by working dutifully on them across four or five days of cautious, deliberate work. The pieces that were written in a day had a cohesiveness and a voice, a life force, that hadn't emerged when writers belabored their early drafts, eeking out a few paragraphs a day. Soon we'd asked all students to always flash-draft a first discovery draft, and to do this quickly, expecting that they'd try more than one flash-draft so the one was not a commitment, but a try. In this unit, we expect students to write not just one draft of their final piece, but several, allowing them to later make choices between those drafts. The result is that when students write this way, their work has a new kind of power, and their subsequent revisions are more large-scale, dramatic, and helpful.

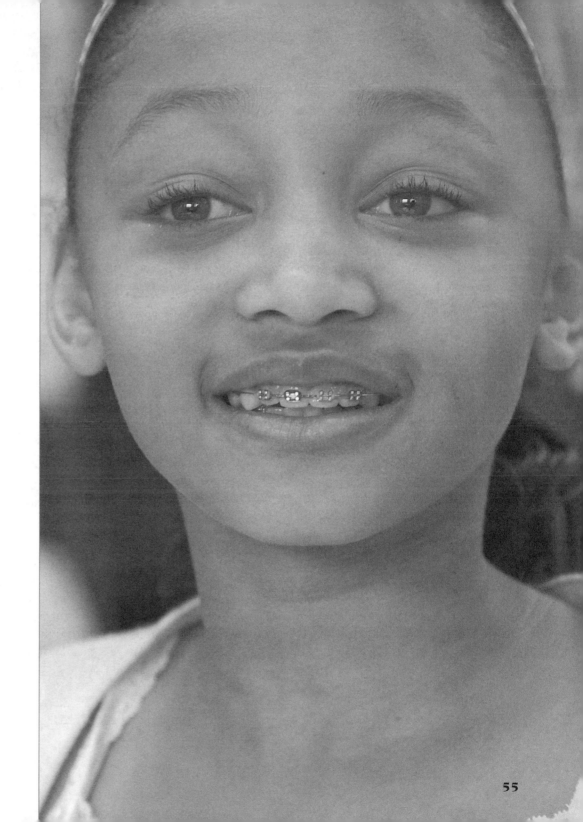

Flash-Drafting
Putting Our Stories on the Page

CONNECTION

Tell children that today begins a new bend in the unit, and overview the work ahead. Then locate students who know how to choose a seed idea, and ask them to teach others nearby.

"Writers, today is a big day. Starting today, the writing workshop changes, so that instead of generating new stories almost every day, you will, today, choose one of those stories to be what writers sometimes call a seed idea, and then you will grow that seed idea across a bunch of days into a piece of publishable writing. How many of you are experienced at rereading your notebook and choosing one entry to function as your seed idea? Thumbs up if you have done that work before."

Half the class signaled a thumbs-up, so I said, "Those of you who are experienced at doing this work, will you quickly teach the kids around you what to do, since we're going to spend just three minutes right now, sitting right here, doing this really important work? Think about how to explain what writers do at this stage. Talk quickly so you leave your friends time to do the work."

Highlight your hopes for the story ideas they settle on. Highlight the value of focused narratives that carry large significance, without overdoing focus.

As children who'd done this work the previous year talked to others near them, many of them gestured toward their notebooks, pointing out that this process involves rereading. I stopped them after a little bit of time. "Whoa! The insights I am hearing. Some of you are suggesting that choosing a seed idea doesn't mean looking for an entry that is *already* great—the seed idea could be a teeny tiny passage, really. Instead, what you are looking for is something that you think might *become* a good story, with a week or so of work. Wise. And you are wise to remember what you know about good stories. That will make you lean toward choosing a focused 'seed' story rather than a big 'watermelon' topic like 'My summer at camp.' And I heard some of you say—wisely—that it is great to choose a seed idea that is important to you, that has a big meaning, even if that meaning isn't yet on the page. So right now, do that work. Reread and choose one entry to become your seed idea. Go."

As students worked, I voiced over. "I love that you aren't just rereading your entries like this." I flipped mindlessly through my pages. "You aren't just flip, flip, flipping through your notebooks. You are taking the time to reread

The fact that the writing process is cyclical means that you are freed from always needing to teach children what their next step as writers should be. You need only to reference that next step, and meanwhile you can teach your students how to do that step especially well, or you can address the predictable problems they'll encounter. On some occasions, you will want to let children assume the role of teacher, imparting the knowledge they already have mastered, doing this in ways that free you up to spotlight something new.

Notice that I reinforce the work I hope children will do with simple accolades. It may be that only a few students are rereading entries, but by bringing this strategy to the class's attention, I ensure that more students will jump on the bandwagon and do the same.

thoughtfully, like real writers do." After a bit more time, I said, "I'm going to come around and give each of you a paper clip so you can mark your seed idea once you've found it."

As the students put their paperclips in place, I called for their attention. "Congratulations, writers. You have just found your first seed idea of the year, and we are going to grow that seed into something wonderful!"

Convey that good writing will come from rapt absorption in the subject.

"Today, writers, you'll be writing outside your notebook, working on clean sheets of draft paper. You'll be flash-drafting your story, writing the story as *literature*. You'll be writing a story that's not all that different than this book." I held up a book. "Or this one." I held up another class favorite. "But it will be a true story of you and of one episode in your life."

"So what advice can I give you as you start? I want to tell you that writing a flash-draft has a lot in common with drawing a portrait. A friend of mine is studying to be an artist, and in her class on drawing portraits, her professor taught her that one way to get unbelievable power into her drawing is to look at her subject, to gaze deeply at the person she is portraying, and to sketch what she sees *without even looking down at her paper*. My friend keeps her eyes on the person and sketches with the goal of putting down the truth of what she sees—all of it—onto the page. Writers do something similar."

❖ **Name the teaching point.**

"What I want to remind you of is that writers fill themselves up with the true thing that happened, recall how they've decided to start the story (the where and the how), and then, keeping their minds fixed on the mental movie of what happened, let their pens fly down the page. Writers write fast and furious, pages and pages, finishing (or almost finishing) a whole draft in a day."

TEACHING

Name ways that writers can get deeply absorbed by their stories—listening to, or reliving, their subject.

"In a few minutes, I'm going to send you back to your writing spot. The room is going to be absolutely quiet. I won't even confer with any of you because I don't want any talking to break the spell. Instead, I'm going to write as well—a story of my own. Each one of us will write pages and pages. We will each write almost as if we are reliving that time, putting the truth of our experience all down on the page. The writing might be amazing, and it might not be, and that is okay. That is why it is called a draft.

"But there are things you can do to make it likely that this is a magical day for your writing. And this is what you do." I listed across my fingers as I spoke.

✓ You are silent.
✓ You listen. You listen for the part of your story that makes a sound in your heart.

I tell the story of my friend because I find it particularly inspiring. This friend is Georgia Heard, an author of poetry books who also takes painting seriously. I encourage you to make these lessons your own so of course you needn't tell stories about Georgia. Think about the stories that will resonate with you and with your students. If you have a class full of avid sports players, you might tell the story of the basketball player who envisions his three-pointers before ever trying to take the shot. He imagines the heaviness of the ball in his palm as he aims, the curve of his wrist as he sends the ball flying toward the net, the swish of the net as the ball falls perfectly through the round, metal hoop.

You should notice that really, the point of this lesson is no different than points you have taught earlier in the unit.

If I leave students with one message today, I hope it is this: The writer who is scared to fail, who fears imperfection, is the writer who sits frozen with nothing but a blank page before him. I want children to understand that our goal today is not perfection. Instead, we aim to capture the truth of a moment in all its intensity—a moment that we will then carve into a more perfect, nuanced piece of writing.

- ✓ You replay that part again, like a movie in your mind.
- ✓ You listen, you watch, you try to remember what you can't quite recall.
- ✓ You re-create something that feels right.

"Say I'm writing about a hike to the sea. As I write, I see the path. Ahead, there's a hedge of brambly bushes crowding the path. I duck under some of the branches, push past others—writing all that down—and suddenly I'm there, with the glimmer of the blue, blue sea stretching before me. I take off my sneakers and run barefoot over the hot sand to the edge of the water. My sister, behind me, doesn't stop at the edge of the sea but keeps running and plunges in. She is bobbing in the waves. I'm writing, but I'm also standing by the sea, sneakers still in my hand.

"You'll be wherever your story takes you. Remember those words from Gerald Brace, who says, 'It's not enough for a person to *tell a reader* about a person, or a place. The writer must help readers *be* the person . . . the basic failure of most writing is a failure of the imagination. . . . The writer is not trying hard enough to live moment to moment in the very skin of his character' (1969)."

ACTIVE ENGAGEMENT

Set students up by encouraging them to reread their entry, recall their storytelling efforts, revise their lead, and signal when they are ready to be released to write.

"So get yourself ready. Reread your original entry, your seed idea, and begin to imagine how it will unfold on your draft paper. For some of you, it might help to hold a blank sheet of notebook paper in your hands and to pretend your finger is a pen, saying in your mind the words that you might write. For others of you, block out the rest of the world, and relive the episode. No matter what, you'll partly make things up because you'll need to supply details that you can't actually recall. I'll be doing my own work to get ready, too, and once any one of us leaves this meeting area, that person will be writing, writing, writing. This is the remembering place, the planning place, so stay here until you've got the beginning thread of your story and can write, write, write."

I, meanwhile, tried to recall the details of my own story. Sitting at the front of the meeting area. I worked mightily to resist supervising and instead tried to model a rapt attention to my own storyline. I didn't want to be available, as I wanted to signal that writers can dig deep and find resources within.

LINK

Get out of their way and let them write.

"When you are ready, signal to me, and you can get started writing—absolutely quietly."

This is not a usual teaching section of a minilesson, because you are not demonstrating, you are not detailing a strategy. It is probably more accurate to say that you are giving a keynote address, aiming to inspire. Although this is not an everyday minilesson format, it is one that can make a big difference when used at the exact right time.

I have tried to keep today's teaching short, allowing plenty of time and energy for the actual work of flash-drafting. By asking students to think and plan in the meeting area, I let them know that once they leave for their writing spots, it is expected that they will write with speed and purpose.

Launch Kids Who Need Help
Then Take Time to Assess

YOU HAVE SENT YOUR STUDENTS OFF WITH A CLEAR MESSAGE—today, you write—and you will not want to confuse that message by asking children to stop and talk with you. Once you've gotten all your students off the carpet and writing at their desks, then, you can use today mostly as an opportunity to watch children and gather data that can inform the rest of your teaching. It is rare that we have an opportunity like this, one in which you can truly step back, watch, and take note.

But before you get to the stage of assessing, you'll no doubt have a few children who don't signal to you that they've got a story in mind. They're stuck. Later in the school year, you'll know these children better and will know which of them are chronically stuck and really need to be told that they can solve their own problems, and if they can't, that's okay because they can stay in and write some more during recess and also during gym, if they need the extra time. For now, though, you won't know the dynamics behind why some children seem unable to choose a topic and get themselves started, so you'll probably want to pull out your "get kids started on their writing" tricks.

Try this. "So did you reread your notebook and think which of the entries—or which part of one entry—kind of, sort of, interests you? Did you think which *might* be a reasonable seed idea for a story?" Then, after the child rolls his eyes, and says, "Well, *maybe* I could write about this one when I played hide and go seek and no one found me ever" (speaking as if the topic were probably duller than dishwater), you say, with utter fascination in the story, "Really?! They just left you hiding? Did they end the game when you were still there?" If the child perks up a bit, amplifying the story by saying, "Yeah, they forgot me," then you listen with more rapt attention and with empathy. "Oh my gosh. What a thing to live through. No wonder you are thinking of writing about that. Whew. What a story." And then you turn toward actually supporting the writing. "So how did it all start? Who said what at the very start? Was it your brother who said, 'Let's play . . . ' or who?"

Once the child has dictated a few lines at the start of the episode and you have dictated them back to the child as the youngster gets them onto the page—lines that actually start off the story, progressing in a bit-by-bit fashion—then you can leave, saying to the child, "This is going to be an amazing story. I can feel it in my bones. Write fast and furious today. It'll probably be this long," and you can gesture that the story will be well over a page.

If you need to do so, you can use that tactic to help the few remaining children get themselves started. Then, you need to do as you suggested you would be doing, and sit yourself in a very prominent spot and write publicly in front of kids, doing this with total absorption in your writing. You can be sure that students will peek up at you and wonder what you are doing, so resist the temptation to be giving them eagle eyes. You'll convey the same "get working" message if you instead are intent on your writing.

Once you have gotten some payoff for demonstrating that you love the chance to write, you'll probably want to put your writing aside and to use this valuable window of time to do some assessing. If you decide to circle the room as children write, watching their

(continues)

MID-WORKSHOP TEACHING   **Supporting Velocity**

As students wrote, I did voiceovers to the whole class. "You should be on your second page by now. Write fast and furious." Then again, "Remember, see the place. See the sun dappling the wall behind you and feel its warmth. Feel the bushes scraping against your legs. And write fast to get that onto the page." Then again, "One of the greatest writing teachers in the history of this country—a man named Donald Murray—said, 'You have to write fast to say what you did not know you needed to say.' Do that."

behaviors and perhaps reading over their shoulders (still not talking to them), it is a good idea to first decide on a particular lens with which to watch the students. You'll want to think about engagement and about their writing habits, for example. Notice children who seem distracted or who struggle to get started. These students may be struggling to conjure the image of a moment in their mind. They may encounter anxiety when putting pen to paper. Then, too, they may be so intent on getting their writing "perfect" that they are frozen over how to proceed. Jot a note about each of these children and remind yourself to check in later, inquiring into the source of their hesitation or lack of engagement. In the meantime, rely on small gestures and whispered prompts to spur them on. A simple, "Don't be afraid to get started. Go ahead and get something down. . . . Tomorrow we'll worry about making it better!" or "Take one more moment to choose a seed idea and rehearse it across your fingers. Then, get started!" can be enough to get a writer going.

For the children who are writing up a storm, you'll want to try to see what writing entails for them. How often do those children seem to reread? To look up at classroom charts? Do they sit in a way that suggests they are absorbed by their writing, intent on capturing a moment, or does their body language suggest they are somewhat detached, merely completing an assignment and waiting for the bell to ring?

You can also look at the children's written products so as to get a sense for where their writing development is in the learning progression that underlies the Narrative Writing Checklist. As mentioned in earlier sessions, the checklist can give you a list of items to look for. Begin with one item on the checklist or one category and survey the room. "Who seems to need help storytelling rather than summarizing?" you might ask, and then jot the names of students who would benefit from a small group in that area. Then, move to leads and endings. Do students' leads orient the reader to the characters and setting, all the while setting the stage for the problem or tension that will unfold? Circle the room asking this question, and again, jot the names of students who would benefit from support with leads. In the end, you will leave the workshop with a list of potential small groups around particular subsets of writing skills and habits. Be prepared to change and adapt this list (after all, your whole-class teaching may quickly alleviate some of the issues you see today), but you have at least collected some baseline data that can help inform the trajectory of your work across this bend.

Reading Our Drafts Aloud to Imagine Ourselves in the Story

Ask children to convene in four groups, one in each corner of the room, and in each corner, a different child will read aloud his or her draft.

"Writers, your goal today was to write a first draft, and to write as you have learned to do, writing from *inside* your story—reliving the moment and putting it onto the page, fast and furious. Many of you have done just that. I've asked a few children to share their writing." I divided the class into four groups, and explained how each quadrant of the meeting area was going to work in a different section of the classroom. As the children dispersed to their areas, I collected the youngsters who had already been asked to read aloud and I said to them, "Those of you who will be reading to a group, wait until everyone's eyes are with you, until the group is totally attentive."

Once the children had settled into their new spots, I said to the whole class, "Writers. Really listen, *really listen*. Try to put yourself in the story and to imagine the moment as the writer tells it."

Seated in one corner of the classroom, Zora began (see Figure 6–1).

> "Nice to see you back here again Julie." He looked down at me, "Chin up Zora." Then he turns and walks off to the "Employees Only" room. As soon as he left my mom took a deep breath and said, "Zora, why are you in such a dull mood?" I jump up and stare at my mom like she is a three-headed donkey that talks. I never noticed but my mom just doesn't understand. I have a lot of things on my mind. There's a lot to do when you're 9 and 3-and-a-half-quarters.
>
> "I've been very busy lately mother" I finally respond in a highly sophisticated voice.
>
> "Busy, huh?" my mom rolls her eyes and stares out at the watery gray sky. She squints her eyes and looks at the bright lipstick red off in the distance, the sun.
>
> "No really," I say trying to regain her attention. "Tours for middle school, after school, homework and school, mother, there are simply not enough hours in the day. . . ." My mom looks at me like she is not quite believing what she is hearing. Her big brown eyes getting wider and wider with every word that comes hopping out my mouth. She looks completely amazed by the time I'm finishing my lecture!! "That's why I'm feeling moody today. . . ."

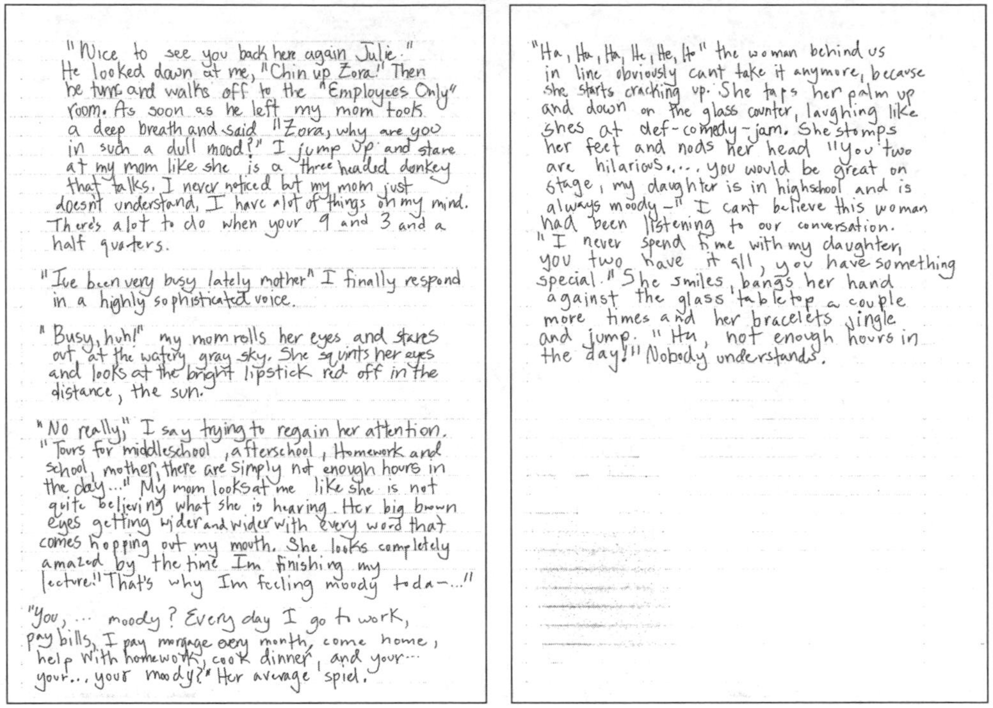

FIG. 6–1   Zora's flash-draft

"You, . . . moody? Every day I go to work, pay bills, I pay mortgage every month, come home, help with homework, cook dinner, and you're . . . you're . . . you're moody?" Her average spiel.

"Ha, Ha, Ha, He, He, Ho" the woman behind us in line obviously can't take any more, because she starts cracking up. She taps her palm up and down on the glass counter, laughing like she's at def-comedy-jam. She stomps her feet and nods her head. "You two are hilarious. . . . You would be great on stage, my daughter is in high school and is always moody—." I can't believe this woman had been listening to our conversation. "I never spend time with my daughter, you two have it all, you have something special." She smiles, bangs her hand against the glass tabletop a couple more times and her bracelets jingle and jump. "Ha, not enough hours in the day!" Nobody understands.

Meanwhile, in three other corners of the room, other students read, and students responded. When all groups were finished, I said, "Listeners, will you tell someone near you what you noticed that your reader did that you are going to try as well?" After children talked, I said, "I can't wait to hear more of your stories tomorrow."

Session 7

What's this Story Really About?

Redrafting to Bring Out Meaning

I RECENTLY OBSERVED A TEACHER LEAD A MINILESSON. She said to her class, "Yesterday you learned that you can improve your stories by making your characters speak," and she reminded the students that during the previous minilesson, they had added a line of dialogue into a little class story about a bike ride. "Today," she said, "I want to teach you that you can also improve your story by adding *details*." And she showed the class how she could use a caret to insert a description of the wind rushing through her hair as she pedaled fast. The teacher then dispersed children, telling them that they, too, could reread to identify passages that were general, and then insert details into a few of those places in their drafts.

Watching that teaching, I was unsettled because I knew the teacher was teaching what she had learned from studying writing process instruction, and I knew that what she had taught her children to do is what many children believe constitutes revision. In many writing workshop classrooms, children write first drafts and then, over a sequence of subsequent days, they tinker with those drafts by inserting a few details or inner thoughts or dialogue. Revisions are inserted into drafts with carets, and with arrows leading to marginal notes. Sometimes students write their first drafts, skipping lines, and then wedge revisions into the alternate lines. My uneasiness, watching this lesson, came because that sort of doctoring up of a draft is nowhere close to what writers do in the name of revision.

That teacher had been right, of course, to teach children that writers use descriptive details to help the reader picture the world of the story. But sometimes, in order to coax children into doing some work that we regard as important, we try to make the work seem like it's easy, like it's no big deal. And the problem is that the work of revision is a very big deal indeed. In the teaching of writing, most lessons can be taught either as little tricks that writers can do easily or as gigantic truths that underpin our entire understanding of writing. In this session and across this unit, you aim to show students that it is not a small thing to revise. Rewriting is as integral a part of the writing process as rehearsing or editing, and becomes all the more important when writers seek to bring out more complicated messages and themes in a narrative.

IN THIS SESSION, you'll teach children that the most important question they can ask as a writer is, "What's my story really about?" You'll channel writers to expect to engage in large-scale, whole-new-draft revisions.

GETTING READY

- ✔ A class story that you will tell so that it conveys one meaning and then another (see Connection)

- ✔ Two pieces of blank paper, which you'll use to model making and using planning booklets (see Active Engagement)

- ✔ Your own story, ready to be planned in two distinct ways (see Teaching)

- ✔ A chart, on paper, titled "Thinking Up a Whole New Way to Tell a Story" (see Teaching)

- ✔ Paper for each child to turn into a storytelling booklet (see Active Engagement)

- ✔ A child's work to highlight during the share

- ✔ "Techniques for Raising the Level of Narrative Writing" chart (see Link)

- ✔ A prepreared chart titled "Ways to Be an Effective Partner" (see Share)

COMMON CORE STATE STANDARDS: W.5.3, W.5.5, W.5.10, RL.5.2, RL.5.5, SL.5.1, SL.5.4, SL.5.6, L.5.1, L.5.2, L.5.3

In this session, you will loosen your students' hold on their first drafts. You'll act as if your writers, like writers the world over, expect that revision involves writing a sequence of entirely new drafts. Today, you'll lure your students into the job of writing whole new drafts of the stories they wrote the preceding day.

Of course, if you are going to make it nonnegotiable that your students all write another draft of the story they've decided to develop, it is incumbent on you to make this work rewarding. The new draft can't seem like the chorus-line of the song that says, "a little bit longer and a little bit worse." For today's drafts to be significantly better than those students have already written, go for the gold. That is, teach students that the one most important question writers of stories ask is, "What is my story really about?"

Your goal will be to teach youngsters that a story about going to the zoo could actually be a story of how nothing the narrator does is right in his father's eyes, or it could be the story

---

"It is not a small thing to revise. Rewriting is as integral a part of the writing process as rehearsing or editing."

of that child's realization that he wants to work with birds as a profession. And the story will be told differently depending on what it is ultimately about. It will begin differently, end differently, and include different details and quotations and descriptions and internal thoughts—depending on the message the writer wants to convey.

This work will call for significant revisions. When children reread their existing drafts, asking, "What is this story really about?" and then realize that they have a theme that has not yet been forwarded, they usually need to write an entirely new draft in order to forward that theme. Certainly they need to ask, "How do I start this story so as to bring forward the theme? What do I elaborate on in the middle of the story in order to bring forward the theme? How do I end the story so as to bring forward the theme?"

There is a risk that this emphasis on "meaning" will cause many students to forget earlier instruction, when they learned to envision the story as they wrote it. To help students do the complicated work of combining these two skills—making movies in their mind and also advancing a bigger meaning—you'll ask them to engage in multiple versions of storytelling, remembering that each time they tell a story, they are working to spin while also working to convey deeper meanings. Later in the session, you'll remind children to be the kind of partners who don't just listen but who also help strengthen each other as writers. You'll teach children that partners stop each other when a story is going off track or when meaning breaks down.

What's this Story Really About?

Redrafting to Bring Out Meaning

CONNECTION

Help children understand that revision is not about adding a word here and and word there. Instead, revision often means setting one draft aside, taking on a new lens, and then redrafting.

"When you were younger, and it came time for revision, many of you probably took out a special colored pen and added in a few words or sentences to spice up your piece. For instance, you might have looked at your opening line—*It was Monday morning*, and thought, 'Hey, I can do better than that!' Then, you might have changed that line to something like—*It was a warm, sunny Monday morning.* As you get older, you learn that revision is often about much more than adding in a few words with a caret.

"Writers and storytellers the world over know that the single most effective way to make a piece better is to write it once, then to think hard about the draft, and to try it dfferently, then to set to work, improving the best of those efforts. In my own writing, after completing a first draft, I usually set it aside and write a whole new draft. I might then talk to someone or get a new idea for my piece, and end up writing most of it yet again. Usually I find that what I write first is kind of the throat clearing that a person does at the start of a conversation before she settles down to a real, deep, true talk. Today I am going to teach you how to redraft by thinking about the true, big meaning behind your story. And you can expect that during writing time today, you will write a whole new draft of your piece."

Point out that you could look back on a story you wrote previously, and think, "Wait. What do I really want my story to say?" and based on the answer, tell the story very differently.

"Writers, in order to show you something huge, I'm going to ask you to pretend with me. Pretend the draft that I wrote yesterday was about the very important story (okay, not really, but pretend) of that time yesterday when I couldn't open the window in our classroom. I'm going to read my draft to you and will you think, 'What's the main thing the story is saying?' 'What is it really showing?'"

> Yesterday, I was reading aloud and for a moment, everything was okay. But it was so hot that with our air conditioner broken, the sweat was rolling down my cheeks. I stopped and went over to open the window. I pushed but it was stuck. I pushed again, and it was still stuck. I thought,

◆ COACHING

Ours has become a first-draft-only society. People use razor blades, cameras, cleaning rags once, then throw them away. They're always racing to new, new, new.

You are trying, from the start, to set your students up to expect that they'll be writing their draft differently. Instead of letting the cat out of the bag at the end of the minilesson, you might as well set them up from the start to expect this.

Things never work in this school." I pushed again and little paint chips flew down from the window frame, all over my hair.

I stopped, and asked children to tell each other what the draft was really, really, mostly saying. They agreed the story showed that the school is always falling apart.

"Pretend that I stopped now, and I thought, 'What do I really want my story to show?' and I remembered all of you helping me with that window and us heaving it open, so I decided what I really want to show is how this class is like a team, helping each other with things. How would I change that draft to bring out the way we work as a team?" I gave the students a little bit of time to think, and then pressed on. "I might write a version that sounds like this." I revealed a second version of the story, which now hung alongside the first version.

Yesterday, as I read aloud, I could see sweat rolling down the cheeks of all my students so I walked to the window, while still reading, and with one hand, tried to open it. The window didn't budge. Even after I put the book down and heaved, the window remained stuck. Then Gary jumped up, joined me at the window, saying, "I'll help." Soon four others were beside him, and together we heaved at the heavy window. . . . The class cheered as the window rose, and we felt like a victorious team.

"Do you see how I told the same event really differently so as to make sure the story revealed different messages? The important thing is that writers can tell the same story differently based on their answer to the question, 'What are you really trying to show?'"

❖ **Name the teaching point.**

"Today I want to teach you that when professional writers revise, they don't just insert doodads into their drafts. After drafting, the pros pause and think, 'How else could I have written that whole story?' Then they rewrite—often from top to bottom. Usually as writers rewrite, they are working with the question, 'What's this story *really* about?'"

TEACHING

Demonstrate that when you ask the question, "What's this story really about?" this leads you to want to tell your story differently, leading to another draft. Show children how you plan for this new draft by thinking and talking across the pages of a planning booklet.

"I'm not sure you all realized that the Luka entry is the one I chose for my draft. The draft I have already tells what happened first, then next, then next, but I think I can strengthen it by popping out what I really want to show. Last night, I asked myself 'What's this story really about?' and I decided that it is about guilt. I had been cranky with Luka before his walk because I didn't feel like taking him out. But after the accident I wished that I had been kinder."

I know that the message of today's lesson is a difficult one to grasp and so I've chosen to begin the minilesson with a clear, concrete example of how the same story can be told in ways that highlight two different meanings. I will break down the process of finding and forwarding meaning further when I model in the teaching. For now, I simply hope to give children a vision for the work they'll do.

Although I am not mentioning "Goosebumps" just now, that draft is written in a way that advanced a meaning. It is worth studying. I recommend carrying a copy with you today as you confer and pull small groups.

This is no small point, and I hope to convey its importance with the tone of my voice.

I quickly folded a sheet of unlined paper in half and then in half again, producing a tiny rehearsal booklet. "Let me think. In order to get this meaning across, I first need to show my reader how grouchy I was in the beginning of the story. Then, at the end, I need to show how guilty I felt. Let me try rehearsing the story across the pages of this booklet."

I touched the first page of my booklet and said, "I took Luka out for his morning walk."

"Wait a minute." I stopped myself dramatically. "I want to show that I was angry and grouchy. Hmm . . . oh, I know!" I resumed storytelling. "I took Luka out for his morning walk. I dragged my feet behind me, sulking because it was so early and cold. 'Luka, stop it!' I yelled as she ran into my legs. 'Silly dog!' I huffed. She bounded down the field, all her muscles rippling. I grouched silently, shivering in the cold wind and thinking of my warm bed.

"Do you see how I brought out my anger there?" Let me keep going. I touched the second page of my booklet. "It was then that I heard the sounds. There was a screech, a thud, and a whine so full of pain that my heart stopped beating."

I paused and turned to the third page of my planning booklet. "This last part of the story should show my guilt, my regret at having been mad. I'll need to make that pop out for my reader.

"'What . . . Where . . . Where's Luka?' I didn't know my older sister was running through the field behind me until I heard her panic-filled voice. I turned to look at her but found I couldn't talk. Together we ran until we were beside the furry body that had curled into itself, now heaving gently.

"'Luka?' I heard my voice break as I knelt beside him. 'Luka, it'll be okay boy.'

"'You deserved so much better than this' I thought to myself. I replayed that morning's events—Luka leaping and bounding and playing, me sulking. Why couldn't I have acted differently? I took off my warm jacket and wrapped his stiffening body in it. 'I'm sorry, boy.' I whispered."

Debrief in ways that highlight the transferable lessons you hope children will carry with them.

"Do you notice what I just did? I retold the story of Luka, but this time I told it in a way that would bring out a specific meaning. I wrote to show first that I was grouchy and angry at Luka, and later to show that I felt regret for having acted that way.

"In a moment you are going to have a chance to write the story that you wrote yesterday really differently, and you might find yourself saying, at first, "But, but, but . . . that's how it happened!" You'll want some techniques up your sleeve to draw on in order to push yourself to write a whole new draft. Here are some of the tips that have helped me:

What I've done here assumes some familiarity with planning booklets. If this is not something you or your children are familiar with, you might choose to say a bit more about how they work, explaining that writers can plan for the parts of their story across the pages of a booklet, touching each page as they say aloud what will go in that part of the story.

You'll want to pour your heart and soul into this part of the minilesson, hamming it up for students. When reading a book aloud to the class, it is likely you do everything in your power to pull children into the story. You emphasize some words and sentences, speed up others, and even pause at parts to impart the power of the text. Show children that the words they write, the stories they are composing, can be just as powerful.

> ### Thinking Up a Whole New Way to Tell a Story
>
> - Tell the story differently to bring out a different important meaning or message.
> - Start the story earlier or later.
> - Tell the story out of order.

"Just looking at this chart, I realize that I could tell the Luka story in a completely different way if I want to emphasize the role my sister played in the story. She helped me through this tough time, and I'm not sure I would have been able to do it by myself."

ACTIVE ENGAGEMENT

Set children up to ask themselves, "What's my story really about?" and to imagine that there is more than one way their story could be told.

"Writers, right now, sitting right here, will you look back at the story you wrote yesterday? You are going to do a completely new rewrite today—from start to finish. And today, as you write, you'll be absolutely clear that yours is not just an 'I did this and then I did that' story. Instead, your story is one that shows something important—a relationship that's important, a part of you that's important, a life lesson that's important. So . . . what will that be? Think." I let there be a bubble of silence.

"Take out a sheet of notebook paper, and fold it like this." I folded a page into halves, then quarters, making a little booklet. Keep in mind what your story will be about. If you want, you can jot few words onto each page to place-hold the part of the story that will go on that page.

"Now Partner 1, will you tell your story across the booklet, as I did, to Partner 2? Think, 'How can I *show* my readers what this story is really about?' Partner 2, listen like writing teachers do, intently, in ways that help storytellers tell their stories well. When you're ready, tap your first page and start storytelling."

As children told their stories, I added tips, including one at the very start. "Remember to use a storyteller's voice. Listen to how the start of Aalia's story sweeps her listener up into that world." I repeated Aalia's opening line, giving it grandeur and flair: "It was a cold, November morning. Leaves crunched beneath my shoes." I added to the rest of the class, "You might start over and try to sweep your readers up, or draw them in, with storytelling language." After a bit, I coached, "Be aware of what you want your reader to feel and build up the parts that will give the reader that feeling!"

Don't underestimate the importance of this silence. I have asked children to do something difficult and don't want to underestimate the challenge by asking children to do this sort of thinking in a flash-second. Instead, I hope to impart the importance of the work by giving students a moment to think.

LINK

Restate your teaching point. Send children off to rehearse their stories by storytelling them first.

"Writers, what you have just done is to rehearse for another draft of your story. Whenever you want to do something well, rehearsal matters. Whether we are hoping to hit a home run or give a great speech or write a great story, all of us—teachers, children, moms and dads, world leaders—rehearse the things we plan to do. We go over them in our mind, and our ideas change in the process. It takes courage to change your ideas.

"Usually at the end of a minilesson, I remind you that you are the boss of your writing and suggest you choose the work you want to do. Today, though, I think it will be really helpful if each one of you thinks, 'What is my story really about?' and then rehearses—perhaps by storytelling on booklets, like you just did, or another way. And above all, it will be important for each of you to put away your first draft, and to write a whole new draft that conveys what you really want to show.

On most days, you work hard to help children understand that each day's learning is cumulative—a tip they tuck into their pockets and pull out as needed. You encourage the students to make choices as writers about what they will do and how they will do it, which in turn supports problem solving, independence, and high levels of cognitive demand. Today is a bit different in that you will ask all children to go off and do the same thing—rehearse and then draft.

Techniques for Raising the Level of Narrative Writing

- Dream the dream of the story and then write in a way that allows readers to experience the moment along with you.
- Revise using all you know about storytelling, not summarizing.
- Use all you know about grammar, spelling, and punctuation to edit as you write.
- Tell the story from **inside** it.
- Use details that are true to the event and that ring true.
- Use tools like the Narrative Writing Checklist to ask, "In what ways does my writing measure up? In what ways do I need to improve?" Then, revise your work to make it stronger.
- Ask: "What is my story really about?" and then write to bring forth that meaning.

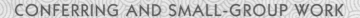

Rally Writers' Energy for Multiple Rehearsals by Teaching Partners to Listen

IF I HAD A WRITING TEACHER'S MAGIC WAND, I'd use it to make sure that every single writer had a personal teacher on a day like today, when each child is trying to rally herself to write a whole new draft, aiming to to write like literature. I'd tell all those one-to-one teachers to listen to the stories that kids say aloud, and to say to them "Wow. This story is going to be huge." Or, "Whew. You've chosen an important story, haven't you?" I'd help the teachers get students started telling their stories again, this time telling them in more detail. If one student began her story, "I went to the airport," I'd hope that her personal teacher would coach her to instead start more like, "I stepped on the doormat and the doors of LaGuardia airport slid open. I walked in, and stood looking for the Departures sign." I'd do all this because I know that when someone listens to a writer, then the writer listens, and all of a sudden the writer begins to tell her story with far more conviction. The writer begins to listen to her own story. Donald Murray, the Father of Writing Process, described the writing process by saying, "I must somehow, as a teacher, husband, son, father, citizen, busy, busy person, so proud of my busyness, find a way to listen so I will hear what I have to say."

On this day, try to make time for listening. Talk to youngsters about their writing outside of writing time, when you are bringing kids into your room in the morning, and in transitional moments when other kids are cleaning up or getting out their work. Use every chance you have to listen, and to show by the attentiveness of your listening that you have faith in this story.

But there will be more children than you can reach today, and because you and I do not have the magic wands that will allow us to produce a personal teacher for each writer, the wisest thing we can do is to teach children to become listeners for each other. You might tell your children that Donald Murray once said that in a good writing conference, the writer leaves wanting to write. The writer's energy for writing should go up. That's true whether the conference is with a teacher, or with a peer. If we could only all learn to be the sorts of partners for whom others want to write, then writing would flourish.

MID-WORKSHOP TEACHING
Helping Partners Work More Effectively

"Writers, something magical is happening. Your stories are coming to life! You all sound like *real* authors. And your stories sound like literature. I am impressed with the listeners, the active partners, too. For example, John was just telling his story, and I heard Joey call, 'Wait!' I stopped, wondering what was going on, and Joey said, 'I lost my picture of the story.' Then Joey said something so smart. He said, 'Can you rewind back to the part where . . . ?' And soon John was storytelling again, but this time really working to tell the story in such a way that Joey could experience it.

"I hope all of you are being partners like that—partners that will call out, 'Stop,' when you can no longer picture a story, who will say, 'Can you rewind and this time try it again?' And if you have trouble storytelling again in a way that is a bit different, remember you can draw on our chart. Great work writers *and* partners."

Thinking Up a Whole New Way to Tell a Story

- Tell the story differently to bring out a different important meaning or message.
- Start the story earlier or later.
- Tell the story out of order.

As students story-tell their stories, help them angle their pieces so that they bring out the big idea they want to convey. If some kids are telling their stories in perfunctory ways, help their partners act as therapists, listening deeply and then saying back what they've heard. "It sounds like you are really mad at your mother," the therapist says, using the technique of active listening. Active listening elicits far more from writers than does a battery of small questions. The important thing is not that a person says back what the writer has said. What matters is the listening. Model for children how to listen with rapt attention to just a chunk of the story, and then respond by reiterating, or responding to or exclaiming over what you've heard and then by *not talking*.

Of course, you will want to register that you heard the writer's message. "You were really worried as you stood there, ready to jump into that pond, weren't you? I can just picture it—with your friend John saying over and over, 'You can do it.' Whoa. What a story."

Then be quiet, and help children in the class to be quiet. Wait. Let the writer talk.

Of course, over time there are techniques you and students will learn for priming a writer's storytelling. Prompts like "I'm not sure I can picture it. Exactly how did it go? What, exactly, did he say? What did he do? Oh! So he said . . . . Then what?" can do

wonders. Once a child has told just the start of a story with voice, passion, and detail, scrawl those sentences down to help him hold on to that lead. Then say the start of the story back to the writer while he records it, and say, "You're off to an amazing start. Keep going." In this way, you'll help students not only story-tell, but also begin writing leads.

For experienced storytellers, or for those who are telling a story for the second or third time, your prompts can elicit a more angled piece. "At the start of the story, what do you want me to know you were feeling and thinking? And then later, toward the end?" Imagine a child responds, "I want you to know that I really wanted to win this award"; you can prompt, "So think what, exactly, you were doing that might show how badly you wanted to win it. Right now, stand up. Now act out what you were doing, and tell me what you were thinking, too." Then you could say to the child, "So try telling the story again, adding those actions and thoughts."

Sometimes I make an even more pointed effort to rally a child's energy for the work ahead. "Sabrina," I might say, "I have a feeling this is going to be the most important story you've ever written. Do you feel that too? You're onto something here." Or I might say, "Miles, I'm not sure you realize that the detail with which you're discussing your writing plans is incredibly special. I hope you take this talent of yours seriously."

Sharing Our Process and Progress as Writers

Share one student's process for choosing a great lead.

"Writers, Sophie has been thinking about her supper at Chuck E. Cheese's and that question, 'What's your story really about?' She wants it to be about how, at Chuck E. Cheese's, she and Claudia made the leap of committing themselves to be best friends. Sophie has put aside her first draft because it was more of an 'all about what we did' draft. She's wisely been thinking about how her next draft will go. Just now, she said to me, 'I can't decide whether to start before I pop the question to Claudia ('will you be my best friend?') or right when I ask it."

Sophie piped in, "No, I figured it out. I'm going to have a beginning part *before* I ask—to show how nervous I was about asking Claudia to be my best friend." Sophie dictated how she thought her draft would begin:

> We walked into Chuck E. Cheese's. I held Claudia's hand tight. My palm was sweating. I was really happy to be with Claudia. "Hey Claudia, what game do you want to play?"

"Do you see the way Sophie chose her lead carefully, making sure it connected to what her big meaning was and making sure it is not too far away from the main story?"

Ask students to share their own process and progress, and encourage partners to be not only listeners but coaches, as well. Then show the revised "Ways to be an Effective Partner" chart.

"Writers, right now, will you show your partner what you wrote yesterday and today, and will you talk about whether you are getting better at writing narratives, and about the things you still need to work on? It would be helpful to show them the choices you made about meaning, about what your story is really about, and how today's new draft highlights that meaning.

"Partners, be good listeners, but also be coaches. You might say things like, 'Can you show me where you did that?' or 'I'm not sure I understand. Can you say more about that?' to help your partner clarify his or her ideas. Then, just like the way I give you feedback in conferences, you might consider giving your partner a bit of feedback. Try saying something like, 'One thing I love that you've done as a writer is . . . ' and then 'One thing you might work on is . . . .'"

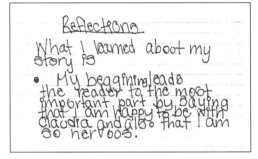

FIG. 7–1   Sophie's reflection on her lead

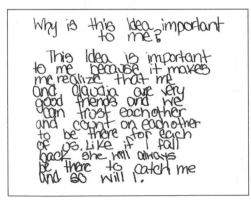

FIG. 7–2   Sophie asks, "What is my story really about?"

After giving children a bit of time to hold effective partner conferences, I revealed the "Ways to Be an Effective Partner" chart.

ANGLING YOUR WRITING AS YOU DRAFT

In her memoir, *Little by Little*, Jean Little (1991) wrote one scene about her first day in a new school. It happened in April, when all the other children already knew each other. Jean was struggling because of her poor vision, which made her different from other children. Read the first part of this scene, and mark up ways Jean angled her writing to show what it is really about. Label what she's done.

> "This is Jean Little," my new teacher told the class. She led me to a desk.
>
> "This is Pamela, Jean," she said, smiling at the girl in the desk next to mine. I smiled at her, too.
>
> Pamela's cheeks got pink. She looked away. I thought I knew what was wrong. She was shy. I sat down and waited for lessons to start. I was glad that reading was first.
>
> When it was my turn to read out loud, I held the book up to my nose as usual. The other children giggled. The teacher hushed them. Then she turned to me.
>
> "Are those your reading glasses?" she asked.
>
> I was not sure. I snatched the glasses off and switched. But I still had to hold my book so close that my nose brushed against the page. Everybody stared. Nobody noticed my good reading.
>
> That afternoon when the teacher left the room, Monica pointed at me.
>
> "Look!" she crowed. "She's got black all over her nose!"
>
> I clapped my hand to my face. The class bursts into peels of laughter. They only broke off when the child nearest the door hissed, "Shh! She's coming."

After you have learned from Jean Little's craftsmanship, take time to think again about what it is that you most want to show in your story. Jot a few notes to yourself about what you might change or add to strengthen your writing. Then work on your draft, making revisions that make a giant difference.

Ways to Be an Effective Partner

When Listening You Might
- Ask to see specific examples of what your partner has done.
  - "Can you show me where you did that?"
- Ask for clarification.
  - "I'm not sure I understand. Can you say more about that?"

When Giving Feedback You Might
- Start with a compliment.
  - "One thing I love that you've done as a writer is . . . ."
- Give some constructive (helpful) feedback.
  - "One thing you might work on is . . . ."

Bringing Forth the Story Arc

IN THIS SESSION, you'll teach students that one powerful way to revise their narratives is to bring out the story structure.

GETTING READY

✔ Each child's writer's notebook, with them in the meeting area for the lesson

✔ *Peter's Chair*, by Ezra Jack Keats (1998), or another book that children have already heard read aloud (see Teaching)

✔ A chart titled "How Stories Tend to Go," already drawn on chart paper (see Teaching)

✔ Story mountain for *Peter's Chair*, sketched on chart paper

✔ A marker pen and chart paper, to make a story arc of *Peter's Chair* (see Teaching)

✔ A copy of "Goosebumps," projected on the overhead (see Active Engagement)

✔ Student writing to share for both the active engagement and the share

COMMON CORE STATE STANDARDS: W.5.3, W.5.4, W.5.5, RL.5.1, RL.5.3, RL.5.5, RL.5.10, SL.5.1, L.5.1, L.5.2, L.5.3

TEACHING ALWAYS SEEMS TO INVOLVE RUNNING from one side of the boat to another. For a time, you emphasize one thing. Then you assess, and realize the work is lacking in another dimension, and so you "run to the other side of the boat" and emphasize whatever that missing element might be. Your teaching will have emphasized two things. First, you will have emphasized that writing narratives involves living inside a story, imagining the story, and writing in such a way that readers, too, can experience the story. And secondly, your teaching will have emphasized the importance of deciding what the story is really about, and angling the narrative to build that meaning, that theme.

Today, your teaching "runs to the other side of the boat" yet again. Your students may be surprised—the content of today's minilesson may be something of a shock. Today, you remind students that all this time they have been writing *narratives*, stories. And this means that they need to remember to draw upon all that they know about how stories go.

You can count on the fact that many of your students will not have thought to transfer the lessons they learned during last year's fiction unit into their work with personal narratives. They will not have been thinking about the character traits of their main character (themselves) and of their secondary characters. They probably will not have been thinking about plot and setting, or problem and solution. That's not surprising—they will have been doing a lot of other work. But the good news is that in this one session, you can remind them that yes, indeed, they do need to be mindful that they are writing stories. And this one bit of instruction can then help them tap into a huge amount of cumulated knowledge.

Today, the knowledge you forefront will be that of story structure. You'll remind students of the story arc. This emphasis on structure should not surprise you as it threads through these units of study. In the minilesson, you point out to students that there is an architecture that undergirds minilessons, "a way minilessons tend to go." Just as it hopefully is helpful to know that architecture when you go to develop minilessons, so, too, we suspect it is helpful to your students to bring their knowledge of story architecture to their personal narratives.

Today, then, you'll revive the anchor chart from last year's realistic fiction unit and you'll remind students that personal narratives follow the same predictable—and familiar—structure of short fiction. Both are stories. You'll remind children that stories are patterned into a story arc. They include a description of the situation, then something happens, and then there are results. Another way of describing "the way stories tend to go" is to say that stories revolve around a character who yearns for or reaches toward something, who encounters trouble, and who, as a result, finds new resources within himself or herself or the world . . . and changes in the process.

In this minilesson, your students will join you in analyzing Ezra Jack Keats's *Peter's Chair*, a picture book that is found in many first-grade classrooms. We chose to teach story architecture by studying a young child's picture book because this way students can get their mental arms around the whole text quickly. If you look at *Peter's Chair* closely, you will notice that Keats has no wasted words; every word forwards Peter's emotional journey through the story. We also chose this text because even though it is written for first graders to read, there is nothing elementary about this as an example of writing. If your fifth graders could *write* stories like this, you would be very pleased indeed!

This session, then, invites substantive revisions yet again, and gives students a substantial and important rallying cry to inform those revisions. Don't apologize or worry about the amount of work you are putting onto your kids' shoulders. It is through substantive revisions that young people come to understand how to make good work great. Just as the sculptor finds a lion emerging out of his block of marble and works the material to bring forth his vision, so, too, your young writers can see story arcs hidden within their rough drafts, and work to bring forth true stories. It's a wonderfully complex, rich way to revise—one which has everything to do with vision as well as revision.

Bringing Forth the Story Arc

CONNECTION

Let your students know that revision begins with seeing possibilities in drafts that at first we think are finished.

"Some of you have been coming to me saying, 'I've finished two drafts already!' That's a great feeling, isn't it? To write a draft, and then rewrite it, trying once again to put your story onto the page! When I get to the end of a draft, I sit back and enjoy being done. I take time to clean up my writing folder. I get a drink of water. Then, writers, I get back to work.

"Our motto in this bend of our unit has been that saying that I know you heard in previous years: 'When you're done, you've just begun.' Once you've written a couple of drafts of a piece, you're in a very special place. Now you can make your best work even better. I know you are thinking that this last draft is *already* pretty good—and you are right. But today, I'm going to teach you a secret that can make this 'already good draft' better. The word *revision* means, literally, 're-vision.' It means 'to look again.' Today I want to teach you one way to look again at your writing, so that you can then dig in, making your good draft, much better."

❖ **Name the teaching point.**

"Today I want to remind you that when you write personal narratives, you are writing . . . *stories.* And you already know that stories have a 'way they usually go.' One of the most powerful ways to improve your personal narrative, then, is to look at it as a story, and to think about whether you have brought everything you know about how stories usually go to bear on your draft."

TEACHING

Remind students of the essential elements in a story.

"Writers, by now you have come to realize that our writing workshops usually begin with a minilesson, then there is work time, then we meet to share. You can count on that. Stories, like writing workshops, have a pattern, a way that they usually go.

I want children to embrace the concept of revision and to anticipate major, significant changes. The message is that revision is not a time to tweak and polish. It instead offers a chance to reinvent, to reimagine. I want children to approach their revision work with zeal and resourcefulness.

Pause for just a second to realize how many words related to the teaching of writing are linked to sight: point of view, focus, zooming in, vision, lenses, perspective . . . but the greatest of these is revision.

When planning this unit, I went back and forth over whether to teach this lesson on story structure as part of planning, just before children begin their drafts, or as part of revision. For me, a sense of structure is one of several magnetic poles exerting a force on my content from the very start. But, on the other hand, I worried that children might let their sense of story and their attentiveness to form overpower everything else so that writing a narrative became filling in a format rather than dreaming the dream of an event. So this session is here, when students are revising content they will have written about twice—content I hope many of them will consider writing within an entirely new draft.

"So I'm going to remind you of how stories usually go, and as I do this, will you think about how you could write a whole new version of your piece, this time writing it more as a story? Doing that will mean changing some things around a bit, taking poetic license. We'll talk about that later.

"Okay, you ready to listen up? Most stories begin by introducing the main character, who has hopes, wants, or motivations. Then there is a problem. Maybe those hopes or motivations lead the main character to get into some sort of trouble or face some sort of tension. Anyhow, the problem gets worse, and finally, the story ends in a resolution. People talk about that whole flow of a story as a story arc. You learned all about story arcs in last year's realistic fiction unit, remember?

How Stories Tend to Go

- Main character
  - Motivations, hopes, wants
- Problem
  - Trouble or tension, often with some sort of emotional response from the character
- Things happen related to the problem
  - The problem gets bigger or another problem emerges
  - The tension increases for the character
  - Sometimes the character tries to solve the problem
- Resolution

Recruit children to join you in thinking how a familiar narrative is undergirded by story architecture.

"So let's think about the story arc in a simple story like Ezra Jack Keats's *Peter's Chair*." I held up the book for the class to see. "I know you all are reading much more complicated texts, but your personal narratives are actually a bit like this story in length—*and*, if you are really really talented, in design. So listen with me and see if you can find the character's motivations, the trouble, and so forth." I also pointed to the chart, "How Stories Tend to Go."

I read the story as if to myself, skipping nonessential parts to keep the rendition quick, and facing the book outward so that children could follow.

Peter stretched as high as he could . . .

The big difference between a timeline and a story mountain is that in the latter, one section of the story is given prominence. We can refer to that one section as "the heart of a story" or as the rising action and climax or peak of the story.

"Yup, there is the character and he's physically reaching for something. Page one and he already wants something—to make a tall tower. He may have deeper wants, too."

Crash! Down it came.
"Shhh. Remember we have a new baby."

"Yup, there is the problem! His tower falls down and all his mother worries about is waking the baby." Then I added, in an aside, "Do you notice that the author never comes right out and says that Peter has a problem? He just shows it: Peter has to tiptoe around because of his sister. His parents aren't paying attention to him; they are paying attention to his sister's needs."

"That's my cradle. They painted it pink!"

"More stuff is happening with the problem—and again, the author doesn't come right out and say it is a problem for Peter that his parents are taking his stuff and painting it pink for his little sister, but we can infer. As I keep reading, see if the ending of this story follows the plan for most stories."

Peter picked up the chair and ran to his room . . . "Let's run away, Willie," he said.

"The trouble is getting worse and worse, isn't it? Peter is responding to the hard stuff—he is upset enough that he picked his chair and ran away with it because he didn't want it painted pink too! I think this is the heart of the story. The problem Peter is facing has gotten so bad that Peter wants to run away with Willie. Let's read on and see if there is a resolution at the end, because that's how stories usually go, right?"

Skipping past other details, I read from the ending:

Then Peter says, "Daddy, let's paint the little chair pink for Susie."

"That definitely shows resolution. Peter has returned from running away, and he not only rejoins the family, but this time he wants to help paint his little chair pink for his sister! Ezra Jack Keats doesn't come out and say that the problem is resolved, but he shows it, doesn't he?

Diagram the story arc in the text you study.

"Writers," I said, taking hold of a marker pen and drawing a mountain-like arc across chart paper, "remember, we call this a story mountain because of its shape. The main character, Peter, wants his family to be the way it was: just him and his mom and dad." I located this in a dot at the base of the story mountain, and continued making dots, as on a timeline. "But then there's a new baby, Susie, in the house. Things happen to Peter that make the problem get worse." As I spoke, I moved up the incline of the story mountain, marking key moments and labeling each with just a word or phrase, skipping some altogether. "And so finally, he and Willie run away: Peter can't take it anymore." I pointed to the top of the story mountain. "Then comes the resolution, starting with Peter finding he no longer fits in his old chair

Structure is foundational to any human endeavor. Music has its minuets, waltzes, and sonatas; law has its hearings, plea bargains, and trials. Mastery requires an awareness and application of forms.

Pace is really important in a minilesson. Your point is to use their story to give children a quick glimpse at the way this story is structured. Don't get lost in the details.

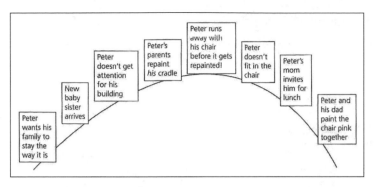

FIG. 8–1   Later you can produce a completed, detailed story mountain for *Peter's Chair*

and ending (and I pointed to the last portion of the story mountain), with Peter helping his dad paint his blue chair pink for Susie." (The in-class version will be far sketchier than the version, Figure 8–1, you produce later.)

ACTIVE ENGAGEMENT

Retell shortcut, using voice intonation to help children perceive the story's structure.

"Are you ready to have a go at this in another story? Here's a story all of you know well." I displayed a large copy of "Goosebumps." "I'm going to quickly remind you how this story goes and then you'll have a chance to figure out its story arc."

"So in 'Goosebumps,' you'll recall that the girl goes to bed, not wanting to use the wool blanket her mom recommends. They are in Montana, and her Mom cautions that it will get cold at night, but the girl resists. Then she wakes up with goosebumps! She reaches for the wool cover, thinks about all the times her mother has been right, wonders why she's questioned her, and drifts off to sleep.

"Okay, writers. It's your turn to give this a go. With your partner, try to plot 'Goosebumps' in the same way that I plotted *Peter's Chair*. Use a page in your notebook to make the story mountain—and use the chart to think about how stories usually go. Get started, and help each other."

As students talked, I listened in.

"The story starts with a character who wants something," Rie said to Caleb. "She wants to wear a nightgown."

"And not the fleece pajamas," Caleb added.

If you feel that students need another example, you could add: "Writers, do you see that all these stories have a structure that is the same as the one in The Little Engine That Could? *Remember from when you were little, that story of a train that makes it over the mountain, carrying toys and treats to all the good little girls and boys? It starts up the mountain, but the load is heavy, the train is small, so it chugs along, going, 'I think I can, I think I can, I think I can,' until finally—Hurray! Toot toot! It's on its way to all the good little boys and girls."*

"But maybe that's the problem," Rie said. I gestured for her to explain, and she added, "Her mom wants her to wear warmer things but she doesn't think she needs to—so it's like they have an argument."

"Yeah, but then another problem is that she's cold when she wakes up," Caleb said. "And that's when she realizes that her mom was right." I gave them a thumbs-up for explaining their thinking, and moved on to another duo.

Jack was saying to Rena, "I don't know if there's really a resolution," Jack said. "I mean, she puts on the wool sweater but then she thinks about how her mom is right all the time . . . only she never tells her mom. Like she doesn't say thanks or sorry or anything. So that doesn't seem like the problem is better."

After a few minutes, I reconvened the group. "Writers, listening to you just now, I realized that this is really just review for you. You know story structure! Most of you agreed that there's a clear want in this story: the narrator wants to wear a knee-length nightgown. Some of you even thought that there might be a deeper want: the narrator wants to decide things for herself. You threw out a few options for the problem—that the narrator and her mom can't agree, or that the girl gets cold in the middle of the night because she's not wearing the fleece pajamas. And you wondered about the resolution. Is it that the girl covers herself with a wool blanket? Or is it that she realizes her mother is often right and then is able to sleep?

"The fact that you have questions may be a sign that this writer needs to clarify her story arc a little more, or to spend more time making the problem get worse and worse. Some of you thought that the author could have a fuller resolution too. Jack came up with an interesting suggestion—he thought that a real resolution might come in the form of an apology or a thank you to the mother."

LINK

Remind children that stories, like the writing workshop, follow a form. Help them realize that a knowledge of story structure can help them revise their work and decide upon their next steps.

Will you return to your own writing, *reseeing* it as you've just *reseen* 'Goosebumps.' You may find that you can't draw a story arc for your draft yet because it doesn't yet fit into a story structure, which will give you ideas for revision. As you think about revising the draft you wrote yesterday and about all the narratives you will ever write, remember that stories, like the writing workshop itself, have a way they usually go. Knowing the way that a kind of text usually goes helps a writer to rethink earlier drafts.

"Because you know how stories usually go, you can look over what you've written so far and plan what you will do next, keeping in mind that your personal narrative will be stronger if you bring out the story arc that is buried in it. You can ask yourselves, 'Do I have a character with a want or a hope? Have I given my character a clear problem and then written some things that happen that are related to that problem?' and finally, 'Does my story have a clear resolution?' I'm expecting many of you will write a whole new draft to bring out the story structure in your writing—but at the very least, make sure you write a whole new beginning or a whole new middle. That is—you'll be writing and revising in big ways, not with just a little caret or some teeny tiny inserts."

At this point, I am setting children up to think not just about story structure, but about meaning. I highlight Jack's words in an attempt to highlight what will be a next step for us as writers—creating a text that not only has a strong story arc, but that is intricately tied to the meaning the author hopes to put forth.

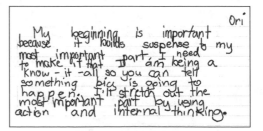

FIG. 8–2 Ori reflects on his writing and makes a plan.

Developing Elements of Story

I PULLED MY CHAIR ALONGSIDE SIRAH. I knew, even before I began the conference, that Sirah's last draft of her story was a fairly effective piece of writing. I looked forward to helping her make some substantial revisions that could help her make a good story into a great one. "Sirah," I said, "You've written two drafts by now. I'm wondering whether you are going to write draft three, or are you going to work to improve one of your drafts, or what?"

Sirah answered, "Well, I think my last draft is pretty good. I told the story the way it happened, and it was sort of like a story. I went to the hotel to go swimming and I was playing in the pool when a hurricane hit. Then we thought the hurricane was gone, so we all went in the pool, but then it came back so we all went home."

"So you remembered the way the story happened from the beginning to the end, and that's the way you wrote it?"

Sirah nodded. "Yep. The whole story was not even one hour, so it's focused."

"That's smart of you, Sirah. I'm glad you are thinking about keeping it focused, and you are right that one way writers focus is by limiting the amount of time that passes."

Then I said, "And Sirah, you said that this is a story—can you walk me through the draft and show me how each part fits with story structures?" We looked at the draft together and noted that Sirah had started the last draft when she arrived at the hotel for the swimming lesson.

"What's the work you are trying to do in the lead of your story?" I asked. Sirah explained that getting to the hotel was the first thing that happened so that was why the story started as it did. "Sirah, remember in the Narrative Writing Checklist, that your lead should orient the reader to the problem, it should hint at the problem that's coming in the story? That means the lead has to connect with the heart of the story, with the climax—which is what?"

(continues)

MID-WORKSHOP TEACHING **Taking Poetic License to Bring Out the Story**

"Writers, many of you are struggling a bit to think of the true thing that happened to you as a story. I think it will help if you realize that you some of you will need to include more than one small moment, more than one twenty-minute scene, in order to show the character wanting something and encountering trouble. You may need to jump ahead to show what happens in the end, as well. So your problem might be that you are trying to get the whole story arc into one small moment and that may be hard to do.

"The other thing is that you need to remember that you don't need to start the story at the start of the action. If you are writing about a ski trip, you needn't start it with the drive! You could start it with the moment when you slide off the ski lift at the crest of the mountain. Usually, it helps to start the story close to the trouble, to the rising action, when you can see the story's mountain peak rising ahead of you.

(continues)

"But here is the even harder thing. You can't just worry about writing this as a good story—you also have to think about that question, 'What's my story really about?' and be sure that your answer to that question links to your story (and your story mountain).

"If Rie's story is really about how she was very scared to surf and her father made her feel safe, she's not going to want to start her story with a description of eating lunch at the beach sitting under a colorful umbrella, even if that is what she did. She needs to start when she had scared feelings. So she can only have herself eating lunch at the start of the story if she's having a hard time swallowing because she is so nervous. (See Figure 8–3.)

"The thing is—Rie won't remember whether she could swallow during lunch that day or not. She's going to have to invent the small actions that make her story work. She might make her father put down his peanut butter sandwich and plead with her to go out in the waves. She might make him grab her hand and say, 'Come on, scaredy-cat.' Every single bit of the story need not be exactly true."

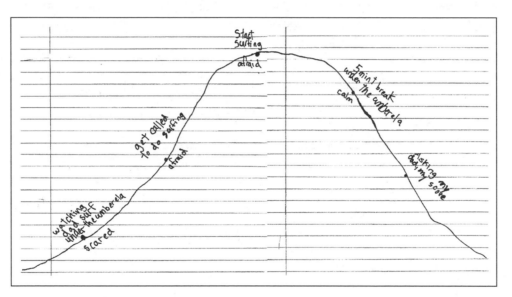

FIG. 8–3   Rie's story mountain

Sirah didn't answer. She was too busy studying her draft. "I guess I know how to revise this," she said. "Because I could start closer to the main problem—I could tell that my cousin and I were on the beach collecting shells. We had a whole bucket. That's where I first had a feeling that the hurricane was coming."

"Okay, so you might start it when you were on the beach and you had a feeling that a hurricane was coming?" As I spoke, I graphed what Sirah said on a story mountain.

Then I said, "Sirah, do you see that one way, then, to be sure your story is focused is to check that your beginning and your ending relate to the main part (the peak) of your story? You've done that for your lead; try it now with your ending. You have everybody leaving and going home at the end. But, just like your beginning, you want your ending to be related to the most important part of your story. Don't leave and go home! Think of other possible endings that stay close to the heart of the story." Then I added, "You have some big revision work to do today."

Mapping Internal and External Story Arcs

Show children a story arc drawn in "mountain" form. Show another story arc for the same story, this time for the character's internal changes.

"Writers, I've got to stop all of you because the work I am seeing right now is drop-dead gorgeous! I go from desk to desk, from writer to writer, and it's as if I'm on some sort of magic carpet. One moment I'm walking with Takeshi into a delicatessen, seeing the very same man behind the counter who was there five years ago, and the next minute I'm with Sirah, living through a hurricane. You are building up the important parts of your stories in such powerful ways that I feel as if I need to hold my hat or I'll be swept away by your words!

"Listen to Sirah as she reads to you just the part of her story where trouble grows. (See Figure 8–4.) Remember her story starts with her gathering shells when she was on the beach near her home in Senegal. She'd been taking swimming lessons at the hotel when she saw a dark cloud coming. She worried it was a hurricane but no one believed her. Then—listen. See if you think she has what writers call 'rising action!'"

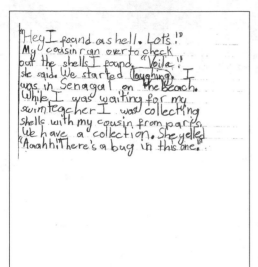
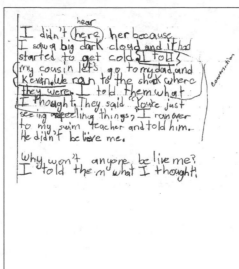
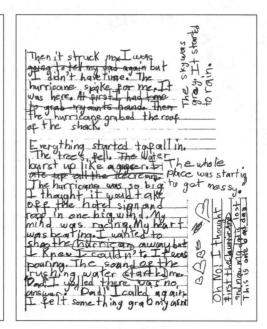

FIG. 8–4 Sirah writes with rising action

PLANNING REVISION WITH STORY ARCS

Tonight you'll be revising—writing at least a page and a half of writing in total, but this may be new endings, new beginnings, drafts of parts you are tinkering with . . . anything that makes your writing better. You may want to start your work by deciding which of your many drafts feels to you to be the best, then start to work on it. Then, look at your goals for narrative writing and make sure you are working towards them. By that, I don't mean make sure you write one good lead, or ending, or version of the heart of your story. Write one, draw a line, try it again.

Look specifically at the heart of your story. Have you built up that part? In *Peter's Chair*, the trouble seems to get worse and worse before it is resolved. Peter's feelings of jealousy, exclusion, and anger get stronger and stronger for a bit. You might think about the story arc for each of the characters in the draft you like the best, revising to bring out the rising tension.

You've got a lot of work to do—get started!

Elaborating on Important Parts

TWO DAYS AGO, you taught writers to ask, "What's my story really about?"—and to write and revise to bring forward that meaning. Since then, however, there have been more lessons—and now your children's minds are apt to be preoccupied with thinking about their accounts of true episodes as stories, complete with problems and solutions, character traits, and story arcs. Asking students to keep all the different priorities in mind at one time is like asking them to pat their heads and rub their stomachs at the same time. It's a feat!

Nevertheless, writers do need to balance seemingly conflicting priorities, and certainly narrative writers need to advance a theme while also bringing a story to life. One of the reasons that the question, "What is this story really about?" is so important is that the answer guides the other decisions writers make.

For example, writers know that it is important to bring forward the internal story. It is important to show what a character is thinking, feeling, wondering. But in order to decide which thoughts to bring forward, a writer needs to have decided what he or she wants the character to represent and do in the story. Then, too, writers can only decide how to pace a story when they have decided what to forward . . . and again, that relates entirely to the question of significance.

Today, then, you will return to the emphasis on significance but this time you will show students that asking, "What's my story really about?" allows you to make decisions about pacing and elaboration that reflect your decisions about meaning.

As you recall, earlier in this unit, when you asked children to assess their writing, you gave them the Narrative Writing Checklist, asking them to identify what they did well and what they still needed to aim toward. As your narrative units progress across the year, you will need to reflect not only all of the expectations for fifth-grade narrative writers, but those for sixth-graders, as well. Before you do this, you will want to teach your students the qualities of good writing that will eventually surface on those lists of expectations. Students have already learned that effective narrative writers elaborate using dialogue, actions, thoughts, and descriptions. In this session, you teach youngsters that the goal is for

IN THIS SESSION, you'll teach students that after writers have determined what their stories are really about, they use writing techniques to elaborate on the parts that show that meaning.

GETTING READY

✔ Each child's draft, with them in the meeting area for the lesson

✔ Your own story or the Luka story written on chart paper, and a preselected important part on which you will elaborate in ways that bring out a new meaning (see Teaching)

✔ A chart, titled "Strategies for Elaborating on Important Parts" (see Active Engagement)

✔ A selection of a few noteworthy pieces of writing from today's workshop that you'll hang around the room, and a plan for how to divide kids into observation groups during this "Museum Share"

✔ "Techniques for Raising the Level of Narrative Writing" chart (see Link)

✔ A chart, titled "Make a New Paragraph to Signal" (see Mid-Workshop Teaching)

✔ Questions to Ask Yourself as You Edit checklist from Session 3 (see Mid-Workshop Teaching)

COMMON CORE STATE STANDARDS: W.5.3.b,d; W.5.5, RL.5.2, SL.5.1, L.5.1, L.5.2, L.5.3

writers to control their elaboration. That often translates into controlling the pace at which a story unfolds so as to highlight whatever the writer wants to say and show. That is, as writers think about which parts of their stories deserve to be zoomed past and which need to be drawn out and played in super-slow motion, they are in fact thinking about their message.

"Once writers become mindful of a story's deeper meaning, they'll elaborate in ways that allow the deeper meaning of a story to pop out."

Elaboration, like other skills, will look different at different levels of development. A second-grader will elaborate by adding more details. A third-grader might elaborate by adding dialogue or actions. A fourth-grader might elaborate by including a character's internal thinking. Your fifth-graders, however, will elaborate by doing all of the above, and in a way that creates *cohesion with the story's deeper meaning or theme.* That is, once your writers become mindful of a story's deeper meaning, they won't elaborate randomly at just any point in the story. They will elaborate in ways that allow the deeper meaning of a story to pop out.

Elaborating on Important Parts

CONNECTION

Create an analogy that explains to children how different circumstances can require us to vary our pace and attention.

"Writers, over the past few days, we've been thinking about two important elements of narrative writing: meaning and structure. You've now drafted through the lens of meaning and redrafted through the lens of structure—and most of you have three solid drafts! I hope you feel proud. Quickly turn and tell your neighbor what you tried to do in each draft."

I gave them just a minute to do this, then said, "Given all you've already accomplished, I know you're ready to do something sophisticated—starting today, as you revise, you will be thinking about structure and meaning *at the same time*. Specifically, you'll ask yourself, 'How might the structure of my writing bring out its meaning?' (Don't worry, I'll help you think about how your three drafts will come together as one at the end of the lesson!)

"Let me explain this in another way. Imagine being driven through a new city. Imagine that the driver literally zooms through some neighborhoods that are kind of ordinary or typical but goes super slow through others that are beautiful and unique so you can roll down the windows and lean out, taking in the details of the scenery around you.

"When you're writing a story, it's like you are the driver and you're taking the reader for a ride through an area that you know better than anyone else. You *would*; you're its author. You can decide the parts of the story that need to be zoomed past and the parts where you want the reader to be wide awake and not miss a single detail because it is an important part. You literally have to drive the readers through the story so that their attention sweeps across and past the less important parts but lingers and stays with the significant moments. That's one way that writers use structure to bring out meaning.

"The question is, 'How does a writer decide which is a more important part and which is a less important part? How does a writer tell one from the other?'"

Don't skip over the accolades. Your children have drafted two to three versions of their story (depending on whether or not they did a full redrafting yesterday) and this is something to celebrate! Acknowledge how proud you are of them, and how they should be of themselves, before moving onto more revisions.

As you say this, you can bring out the meaning if you role-play. Writers have the option of being speedy, eyes-on-the road drivers, or of slowing down, opening the window, studying the scene around you. Those choices need to be enacted!

Let children know that to identify the most important parts, they have to know what the story is about, at its heart.

"The answer is simple, but very important, so I need open ears and full attention: the writer can only decide what the most important parts of a story are once the writer has decided what the story is *really* about! For example, if my story about Luka is about regret, then the important parts would be earlier where I was taking Luka for granted (calling him a silly dog and being grouchy about having to walk him) and also the part where I realized that he was gone (that there'd be no one running across the field beside me now). *But* if my story is about my relationship with my *sister*, then the important parts would be those where she and I interact, the parts where she helps me carry Luka's body, the parts where I cry on her shoulder."

❖ **Name the teaching point.**

"Today I want to teach you that writers vary the pace of a story for a reason. Writers elaborate on particular parts of a story to make readers slow down and pay attention to those specific scenes."

TEACHING

Set up a piece of your own writing so you can demonstrate the work of the teaching point.

"Writers, I want you to note how I do this with my story. I've decided I am going to write my Luka story so that it is about my relationship with my older sister." I uncovered an overhead display of a prewritten draft of a section of the story. Instead of writing out the entire story, I'd selected a portion where the work of elaboration could be supported. "Writers, watch. When I reach a part about my sister—a part where the reader could get a peek into what my relationship with my sister was like—I'm going to circle that part, and later, I will return to that part to *elaborate* on it, to make a bigger deal of it."

> "Luka!" I yelled as he ran into my legs. "Silly dog!" I huffed. He had too much energy for his own good. He looked up cheerfully, tongue hanging recklessly out of the side of his mouth. Then he bounded down the field, all his muscles rippling. "Why do I have to take him for his walks?" I grouched silently, shivering in the cold wind, and thinking of my warm bed.
>
> It was then that I heard the sounds. There was a screech, a thud and a whine so full of pain that my heart stopped beating.
>
> "What . . . Where . . . Where's Luka?" I didn't know my older sister was running through the field behind me until I heard her panic-filled voice.

This is as much a lesson on determining importance as it is on elaboration. In previous years, students likely learned to elaborate by adding dialogue, thoughts, feelings, and action to their writing. They will continue to use all these strategies in this unit. However, I expect they will do this in a more sophisticated way. I do not want them adding details just for the sake of adding details. In this lesson, I aim to teach them that they must be strategic in not only which details to add, but where to add those details to bring out their intended meanings.

I plan for my modeling carefully, considering what parts of my story I will choose and how I will clearly and efficiently demonstrate the use of a strategy. It helps to keep your entries small, so that students can focus on the work at hand and aren't bogged down in endless text. I often find that I need to create purposefully deficient writing (in this instance, writing that does not elaborate on the important part of my story), so that I can fix that problem in front of the children.

You'll recall that often in minilessons, you highlight what you want writers to do by juxtaposing that alternative with its opposite. Here, too, juxtaposing is used to make a point. Luka is energetic, his muscles rippling . . . then his furry body will curl into itself, heaving.

I turned to look at her but found I couldn't answer, only shake my head. Together we ran 'til we were beside the furry body that had curled into itself, now heaving gently.

"Luka?" I heard my voice break as I knelt beside him. His eyes had never looked like this, glazed with shock, as if he couldn't see me at all. My sister, too, was talking—softly.

I circled the sentence that introduces my sister into the story: "Together we ran . . ." I glanced meaningfully at the children and then also circled the last sentence.

Think aloud as you demonstrate the process of elaborating on an important part.

"Writers, when we elaborate on a part of the story, we stretch it out and fill it with details, to help the reader's imagination see it clearly. Watch how I take one of these parts that I've circled," I pointed to the second circle I'd made, "and elaborate on it."

I made a star near my final sentence and then made a star on a blank sheet, connecting the two parts. I began drafting aloud and writing large enough for children to read as I thought aloud. "Let me replay that moment in my mind. What was my sister doing? What was she saying? What did I do, think?"

My sister, too, was talking—softly. Her face as she bent close to Luka was white. "It's ok . . . It's ok . . . It's going to be ok," she murmured. Her hand came up to hold my shoulder and I realized it was me, not Luka, that she was trying to comfort.

Debrief. Repeat that writers elaborate on parts that reveal what their story is really about.

"Writers, I elaborated on this little part of the story. First, I showed some *small actions* that my sister made: bending her face toward Luka, murmuring, reaching up to hold my shoulder. Second, I put in some *dialogue*, with my sister saying, 'It's ok . . . It's going to be ok.' Third, I gave a *visual detail* about her face, that it was white, suggesting she was upset. Fourth, I told some of what I was thinking—my internal story.

"The *most* important thing about elaborating is that I didn't just pick any old place in the story to do it. I picked a specific part, a part connected to what this story is really, really about—in this case, my sister's support during a tough time."

You'll note that if my answer to the question, 'What's my story really about?' is that it's about my relationship with my sister, I have some work to do! She's almost entirely absent from my draft. This, of course, is deliberate. I removed her from the original draft so I could make my point. In minilessons, I find it's important to not be too subtle or my intended meaning flies right over the heads of children.

ACTIVE ENGAGEMENT

Ask students to circle an important part of their story so they can center on that for elaboration and then to elaborate, in various ways, as you've demonstrated.

"Right now, turn to your own writing. Ask, 'What is my story really about?' and then, once you know, find parts in your story that relate to that and could be elaborated upon, and circle those parts." I gave children a moment to do this and then reclaimed their attention.

"Now, you'll want to take a part you've selected and make time go slower, so that the reader can't help noticing details. Add what you saw—the visual details—maybe what you heard and smelled too, if that goes. Add dialogue and small actions if you can. Remember, your reader's attention will linger here. Keep reminding yourself that this part will truly show your reader what your bigger story is about. You can use this chart to help you think about techniques you can use to really slow your readers down, to help them understand that this is a really important part of your writing." I revealed a chart I had made earlier.

Strategies for Elaborating on Important Parts

- Slow down the action, telling it bit-by-bit
- Add dialogue
- Give details
- Show small actions
- Add internal thinking

LINK

Send children off to elaborate on strategic spots in their stories.

"Writers, you'll want to pick up your pens and start at once. Remember, you're the author. That means that you decide on the work you need to do to make this the best story it can be. You may do any of the things on our chart of strategies for elaborating, or you may decide to write a whole new flash-draft of this story, perhaps bringing out an entirely different meaning. Here's another thing you might do—you might pick a part (or two) of one of your three drafts that you think works especially well, and add it into your favorite draft—probably the strongest one. I put scissors and tape in the writing center, so if you want to do this kind of patching together work, you can.

"Right now, take just a minute to think about a plan, and then turn and tell your partner what you will do today. I've hung our anchor chart in the meeting area for you to reference. "

Notice that this is an extended link. Normally, you send children off to do their work with fairly little ceremony. Today, however, we feel it is important to honor all the drafting and redrafting students have done, which is no small feat, and to give them a chance to think about next steps. Therefore, we suggest keeping children on the rug a little longer to help them reconcile their three drafts.

Techniques for Raising the Level of Narrative Writing

- Dream the dream of the story and then write in a way that allows readers to experience the moment along with you.
- Revise using all you know about storytelling, not summarizing.
- Use all you know about grammar, spelling, and punctuation to edit as you write.
- Tell the story from **inside** it.
- Use details that are true to the event and that ring true.
- Use tools like the Narrative Writing Checklist to ask, "In what ways does my writing measure up? In what ways do I need to improve?" Then, revise your work to make it stronger.
- Ask: "What is my story really about?" and then write to bring forth that meaning.
- Bring out the story structure.
- Elaborate on important parts—parts that relate to what your story is really about.

After a minute I said, "Writers, you are in charge of the work you'll do—you decide. But hold yourself to producing at least a page and a half of writing today. Off you go!"

Supporting Elaboration

IN NEARLY EVERY PERSONAL NARRATIVE, there will be an example of the author stretching out a moment that is laden with importance. While students may try to emulate that stretching of a moment, it is not easy, and you may find it useful to use some of your conferring and small-group teaching today to help them do this more effectively. To do this, you might share examples of students who have stretched out a moment successfully.

For example, you might convene a small group of students and introduce them to the work Cameron did while trying to elaborate. "Cameron selected his seed idea and jotted notes about it across the pages of his booklet. His notes are simple," you might begin.

> page 1: At tennis match
> page 2: Saw ball coming
> page 3: Catch it

"That's all he started with! But pay attention to the way Cameron helps us appreciate that this moment is monumental to him. Watch the way he stretches out the important

---

MID-WORKSHOP TEACHING **Using Paragraphs to Clarify Meaning and Emphasize Important Parts**

"Writers, many of you have been elaborating to highlight your story's theme. Sometimes when people get going on an important project, they forget to stop and dot the *i*'s. I want to caution you that you will want other people to be able to read your writing. I don't expect your drafts to be perfect, but you *do* want to write in ways that allow others to be able to read your writing. You might want to take out the Questions to Ask Yourself As You Edit checklist I gave you in the first bend. If it takes just an extra thirty seconds to remember to paragraph as you write, you need to take those thirty seconds. And the same goes for remembering that every syllable contains vowels, or that there are certain words on our word wall that you should 'just know,' and so forth.

"Paragraphs are especially important. They give readers a second to make the movie in their minds. The white space gives readers a little nudge to stop and envision. In general, writers use new paragraphs when . . . ." I pointed to a new chart I had prepared, and read from it.

Make a New Paragraph to Signal

- A very important part that needs space around it
- A new event
- A new time
- A new place
- A new character speaking

"In a little bit, I'm going to organize a small group for those of you who still need help paragraphing. Before that time, go back and use the paragraph sign to add any paragraphs you've missed. Back to work."

---

parts, telling not just the external story but also telling the internal story of what he is remembering and wondering and noticing." (See Figure 9–1.)

Channel the students to study Cameron's example and name replicable, transferrable moves he made as a writer. The key will be for them to understand not just that he elaborated, but *how.* "Cameron, like all good writers, stretches out the most important parts of his story, telling not just the external story but the internal story, as well. Let's look at Cameron's work closely and see if we can name the exact ways he did this."

Be sure that students have a copy of Cameron's writing to annotate, so they can not only name what they notice but point to specific examples. Don't be afraid to "rename" some of what they say in words that are clearer and more accurate. For instance, a student might say, "In this one part he keeps saying 'Will I catch it?' over and over again. You 'll want to help that student name the craft move Cameron made, perhaps noting that he includes internal thinking that reveals his emotional state, or that he uses repetition to emphasize an important feeling. You'll also want to help students see that Cameron creates mood through his choice of details. For instance, the line "Seconds turn to minutes, minutes turn to hours" creates a sense of suspense and rising tension for the reader. Then too, Cameron's word choice is powerful—there is a *rage* of excitement at the beginning. Later, suspense *melts* and is replaced by *elation.*

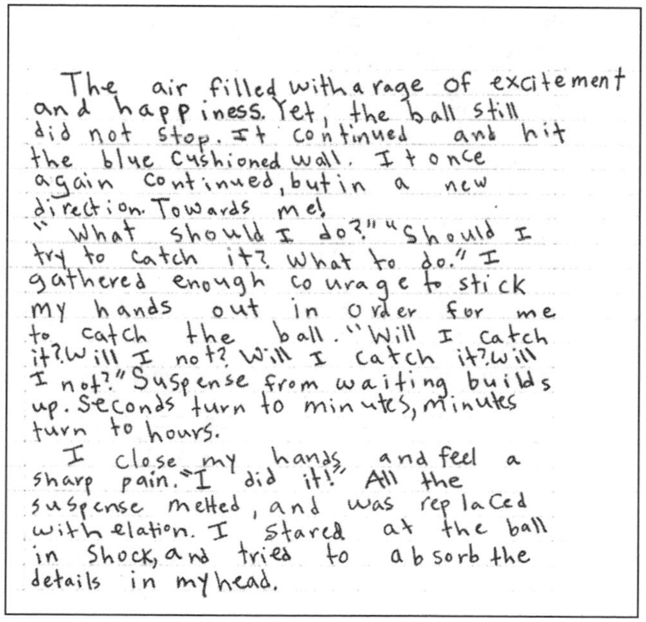
The air filled with a rage of excitement and happiness. Yet, the ball still did not stop. It continued and hit the blue cushioned wall. It once again continued, but in a new direction. Towards me!
"What should I do?" "Should I try to catch it? What to do." I gathered enough courage to stick my hands out in order for me to catch the ball. "Will I catch it? Will I not? Will I catch it? Will I not?" Suspense from waiting builds up. Seconds turn to minutes, minutes turn to hours.
I close my hands and feel a sharp pain. "I did it!" All the suspense melted, and was replaced with elation. I stared at the ball in shock, and tried to absorb the details in my head.

FIG. 9–1 Cameron's writing can be analyzed to show the weave between actions and thoughts.

After annotating Cameron's writing, ask children to decide on one or two moves they will try when elaborating. You'll want to stay with them a bit while they get started, making sure that they are able to transfer the work you just did together to their own writing.

Using Our Classmates as Writing Teachers

Highlight the fact that some children have chosen to elaborate on portions of their writing to bring out a specific meaning, while others have brought out story elements.

"Writers, many of you have decided to elaborate today, and most of you found places where there was an opportunity to convey a big message to your reader. (See Figure 9–2.) Others of you have been working on story elements—developing the story arc for your characters, bringing out their traits. I've posted a few samples of writing you all have been doing around the room and we're going to end today by pretending our classroom is a museum. I'll split you into four groups and everyone will have a chance to spend a couple minutes in front of another student's work. While you are there, see if you can spot cool techniques that that writer has used. Admire their work, and then try to quickly bring that technique into your own draft. You won't have long before I say 'Switch to the next museum station,' so be ready to read, think, and revise your writing with a lot of intensity."

Divide children into groups and set each group in front of a piece of writing. Coach children to carefully study what each student has done.

I then herded the class into four groups, one sitting on the floor alongside each of the four pieces of student work. As the first groups worked, I circulated the room, coaching children to be careful apprentices. "What *exactly* did Miles do when he elaborated? Try to name it so you can do the same." Then later, "Don't be afraid to talk with the person next to you. Sometimes two minds are better than one!" And, "Use our 'Strategies for Elaborating on Important Parts' chart to help you name what the writer has done. Then, quick as a wink, try it yourself."

After writers visited at least a few of the stations, I recapped. "Writers, today you saw that each of your classmates can be a writing teacher to you. You won't need me much longer!"

Then I got to thinking. I dont spend time with my mom. She works 5 days a week. She gets home really late and sometimes, Im already in bed. But I push myself to stay up late just to kiss her goodnight. I have never seen that lady in starbucks before, never. But still out of nowhere she copliments me and my mom. She calls us 'Special' and for a quick second I dont believe her. How can a relationship be special if you barely see her.

I wrap my arm around my mom's waist and squeeze, and she squeezes me back. Im sure my mom doesnt know why Im squeezing her, but the feeling is so warm, She doesnt care. What I have is special. She squeezes me tighter. Special.

FIG. 9–2   Zora revises her ending to show what her story is really about.

MAKE A MUSUEM IN YOUR HOME

Writers, tonight I'm going to ask you to set up a museum in your own home—like the one we set up in school. Will *you* select a few mentor texts and hang those texts up in a few places in your house, and then move from one station to another, studying what the authors have done and then borrowing a strategy you admire, using it in part of your draft?

You don't really need to hang the pieces as if they were in a museum—though it might be fun—but study and write off from one piece for ten minutes, then another piece for ten minutes. I've given you copies of a few texts, including the pieces you studied today from your classmates. But really, you can take any narrative that you love and put it in your museum as well.

Note: sample texts are available on the CD.

Adding Scenes from the Past and Future

IN THIS SESSION, you'll teach students that writers use scenes from the past or future to bring out the internal story and add power to their narratives.

GETTING READY

✔ Your own story, on chart paper, to which you'll add a flashback or flash-forward (see Teaching)

✔ Passage from "Papa Who Wakes Up Tired in the Dark," by Sandra Cisneros, written on chart paper and read aloud before today's minilesson (see Active Engagement)

✔ Timeline of "Papa Who Wakes Up Tired in the Dark," written on chart paper (see Active Engagement)

✔ The stories (and accompanying pieces, if possible) from two children who successfully implemented a flash-forward and/or a flashback

✔ "Make a New Paragraph to Signal" chart (see Mid-Workshop Teaching)

W HEN WE WRITE, we take the booming, rich, nuanced chaos of life itself and we simplify and channel and shoehorn all that into a single line of print that unrolls across the page. When we write curriculum, we work in similar ways. We take the vastness, richness, and complexity of all our dreams and worries, all our disciplinary knowledge and practical know-how, and somehow cut and craft, select and simplify, until our plans and hopes are set onto the page in what is temporarily, at least, a best-going-draft.

To write a line or to create a curriculum, we make choices along the way that temporarily compromise the multilayered, multifaceted nature of what we want to say as a teacher and writer. And so, early in the year, when we sense that many children are accustomed to writing in such an unrestrained, unstructured manner that they record anything tangentially related to the last word they've written on their pages, this series of books suggested teaching children that stories proceed chronologically, with a character doing one thing and then the next in a step-by-step fashion. But, of course, that was oversimplifying. Today you will teach children that in the midst of their tightly controlled sequential narratives, they—the main characters—can blast through barriers of time and space by the simple miraculous act of remembering or of fantasizing.

COMMON CORE STATE STANDARDS: W.5.3, W.5.4, W.5.5, RL.5.2, RL.5.5, RL.5.6, SL.5.1, L.5.1, L.5.2, L.5.3

Adding Scenes from the Past and Future

CONNECTION

Invite children to recall a fantasy story in which the character suddenly steps into another world. Explain that time travel can happen similarly in personal narratives when the narrator remembers the past or envisions tomorrow.

"Most of you have read or seen the film version of *The Lion, the Witch and the Wardrobe*. You'll remember that in the midst of a hide-and-seek game, Lucy hears her brother's footsteps coming and slips into a wardrobe, a closet. It's full of coats. She pushes toward the back of the closet, rustling in through the soft coats, and suddenly something cold brushes against her arm—a tree bough, covered with snow. Lucy looks down and she sees she is standing in snow. Ahead, a lamp gleams golden, and from afar she hears the sound of approaching sleigh bells. She's in another world.

"When you and I write, we put one foot in front of the next. We are playing hide-and-go-seek. We hear someone approaching, worry that we'll be found, and slip into the closet. One thing—the sound of footsteps—leads to another.

"And sometimes in the sequence of these actions and reactions, we take a step that transports us to another world. In the stories we are writing this month, we aren't transported to a magical kingdom, but in just as magical a fashion we may well burrow into a coat closet and find ourselves startled by the brush of a tree bough, by something from another time or place, something that signifies that suddenly we are in another space in the world of yesterday, or of tomorrow."

This is, of course, an elaborate way to teach children that they can break out of the confines of sequential time when they write narratives. My detour will be suitable for some classes of children, but it could confuse others. Use your professional judgment, then, to revise this session (and every one) so that it will work well for your children. As you weigh your choices, it may help to know that the reason I rope The Lion, the Witch and the Wardrobe into this lesson is that I want children to realize that there can be a very concrete, physical, embodied quality to the memories and fantasies we tuck into a personal narrative.

❖ **Name the teaching point.**

"Today I want to teach you that authors sometimes make characters in personal narratives travel through time and place. They often do this to highlight the meaning they most want to show, and do it by imagining future events or remembering past events that connect to what their story is really about."

TEACHING

Model how you imagine the possibilities for adding scenes from the past and future in your own story.

"Let's revisit my story about Luka. Remember how I edited one page to show that my sister was there to comfort me when Luka died? Here's how my story goes so far." I gestured toward the story on the chart paper. "As we read over this story, let's think about whether there's a place where we can jump back or jump forward in time in ways that pop out my relationship with my sister.

> "Luka, stop it!" I yelled as he ran into my legs. "Silly dog!" I huffed. He had too much energy for his own good. He looked up cheerfully, tongue hanging recklessly out of the side of his mouth. Then he bounded down the field, all his muscles rippling. "Why do I have to take him for his walks?" I grouched silently, shivering in the cold wind, and thinking of my warm bed.
>
> It was then that I heard the sounds. There was a screech, a thud and a whine so full of pain that my heart stopped beating.
>
> "What . . . Where . . . Where's Luka?" I didn't know my older sister was running through the field behind me until I heard her panic-filled voice. I turned to look at her but found I couldn't answer. Together we ran till we were beside the furry body that had curled into itself, now heaving gently.
>
> "Luka?" I heard my voice break as I knelt beside him. His eyes had never looked like this, glazed with shock, as if he couldn't see me at all. My sister, too, was talking—softly. Her face as she bent close to Luka was white. "It's ok . . . It's ok . . . It's going to be ok," she murmured. Her hand came up to hold my shoulder and I realized it was me, not Luka, that she was trying to comfort.
>
> Later, I took off my warm jacket and wrapped his stiffening body in it and together, my sister and I carried him back across the field that he had run through so joyfully that morning. I stopped near one of the big rocks that Luka and I had often sat on. My sister looked at me in confusion. "Here," I told her simply, gesturing to the ground beside the rocks. She didn't ask me any questions, just nodded and mumbled, "I'll get the shovel."

"Hmm, I'm just not sure," I said. "Tell your partner what you might do." They did—briefly. "Writers, I think I have an idea. See if you can learn from how I do this. I was thinking we could jump ahead and imagine life in the days ahead, without Luka. I could tell about getting a new puppy, for example. That might be a solution to the no-dog problem, so it's an option. *But*, that's not what this story is really about. This story is about me and my sister.

"So I'm thinking I could put in a place where I suddenly remember back to my sister's role when we first got Luka. That would push forward my meaning that my sister is there for me. Let me try this in the last scene of my story since that's really when my mind was flooded with thoughts." I reread this:

> Later, I took off my warm jacket and wrapped his stiffening body in it and together, my sister and I carried him back across the field that he had run through so joyfully that morning. I stopped near one of the big rocks that Luka and I had often sat on. My sister looked at me in confusion. "Here," I told her simply, gesturing to the ground beside the rocks. She didn't ask me any questions, just nodded and mumbled, "I'll get the shovel."

I picked up my marker and added this:

> As she walked off, my mind drifted back to the time we'd first seen Luka at the shelter—how he'd pushed his wet nose through the cage, into my small hand. Still too little for sentences then, I had just smiled and said, "Doggie." It was my sister who'd called out, "Hey dad, we found the one."

I voiced over as I wrote. "That flashback shows how even when we were much younger, my sister was there for me, finding me the perfect dog. Now let me return to the present time, to standing with my sister by the rock.

> The sound of shoveling snapped me out of my thoughts. My sister was bent over the spot I'd indicated, digging a hole. I reached out and hugged her from behind. I could feel her body shake. "Thanks," I mumbled into her ear, as we cried together.

"Do you see how I did that? I took this one tiny moment, getting ready to bury Luka, and added a flashback. But I didn't just add any old flashback. I first asked myself what I wanted to show in this part, and added in a memory that would help show that. Then I carried that feeling, that meaning back into the present scene."

ACTIVE ENGAGEMENT

Channel students to study a piece of writing, noticing when the author jumps forward in time.

"Let me show you an example of a writer who wrote a story of something that actually involved just about five minutes of real time. In this story, the narrator thinks *ahead*, imagining what will happen in the future. Be ready to notice when this happens in the story and show me a quick thumbs-up. Then we'll do another quick thumbs-up when she returns (like children in Narnia return) to the very real sequence of events. Are you ready?

"Listen," I said, and I pointed to the chart paper as I read aloud. "At this moment, a father is telling his daughter that her grandfather has just passed away. Be ready to put a thumb up when you hear the story jump to the future."

I have chosen to use a mentor text in the active engagement, helping children to identify the moment when an author switches forward or backward in time. This mentor text will serve as a guide for the students as they return to their seats and attempt to do similar work. You might decide to instead have children practice off of their own pieces. If you take this route, ask children to first remind themselves of their overall meaning, and then think about a flashback or flash-forward that could illustrate that meaning for readers.

Your abuelito is dead, Papa says early one morning in my room. Está muerto, and then as if he just heard the news himself, crumples like a coat and cries, my brave Papa cries. I have never seen my Papa cry and don't know what to do.

I know he will have to go away, that he will take a plane to Mexico, all the uncles and aunts will be there, and they will have a black-and-white photo taken in front of the tomb with flowers shaped like spears in a white vase because this is how they send the dead away in that country.

Across the room, many children gave the thumbs-up signal. "Yup," I nodded, "She is with her dad, hearing her grandfather died and whoop, suddenly she is in Mexico, days ahead, at the funeral. Let's read that part again. Be ready to put another thumb up when she jumps back to regular time, back with her father on this one day." I continued reading, rereading the flash-forward.

I know he will have to go away, that he will take a plane to Mexico, all the uncles and aunts will be there, and they will have a black-and-white photo taken in front of the tomb with flowers shaped like spears in a white vase because this is how they send the dead away in that country.

Because I am the oldest, my father has told me first, and now it is my turn to tell the others. I will have to explain why we can't play. I will have to tell them to be quiet today.

My Papa, his thick hands and thick shoes, who wakes up tired in the dark, who combs his hair with water, drinks his coffee, and is gone before we wake, today is sitting on my bed.

Again, children signaled that now the narrator was clearly back in her room, her dad sitting on her bed.

And I think if my own Papa died what would I do. I hold my Papa in my arms. I hold and hold and hold him.

"So Sandra Cisneros jumped forward, picturing what will happen soon when her father goes to Mexico for the funeral and then comes back to real time, sitting by her dad and thinking about how she'll have to tell her siblings about their grandfather." I showed them the following timeline.

- ✓ "Your grandfather died."
- ✓ My papa cries.
- ✓ I think of what will happen.
  - ✓ He'll fly to Mexico.
  - ✓ The relatives will come together.
  - ✓ They'll take pictures by the grave.
- ✓ I think of how I'll have to tell the other kids.
- ✓ My Papa is sitting on my bed.
- ✓ I realize he could die and hug him.

This excerpt is from Sandra Cisneros' The House on Mango Street. This entire book is a compilation of entries, any one of which is well-worth close study. You may also want to secure Jean Little's Hey World, Here I Am, as that book is the other most valuable collection of short published narratives.

Then, looking back on the timeline of actual events, I said, "Do you see that the actual events only involve a few minutes?"

LINK

Remind children that as writers, they need to draw on their entire repertoire of strategies to accomplish whatever it is they want to do.

"Writers, whenever you are writing a narrative, remember that you have the option of having your narrator or main character either imagine a future event or recall a past event. Today, you have lots of options. You could check for true and honest details in your writing, make sure that all parts of your story connect to what you are really trying to say, play with the pacing of your story and even work to revise your story arc.

"Then too, you want readers to dream the dream of your story. And you want readers to grasp what the story is trying to tell, to show. So as you reread, stop and ask, 'Is this what I really wanted to show? Is this what's most true and honest about my story?' Let the lens of truth be your guide for revision. Let's get started." I added the newest bullet to our "Techniques for Raising the Level of Narrative Writing" chart.

> • Incorporate scenes from the past or future to highlight the significance of your story.

Patching Together the Truth to Tell a Poignant Story

AS YOUNG WRITERS COMPOSE TRUE STORIES, often their tendency is to stick doggedly to a moment they've experienced, telling exactly what happened, as they recall it, right down to the most insignificant detail. While you've taught students to speed up during less important parts of a story, and to slow down and linger during more important ones, you may not have let your class in on an important fact that professional writers know: writing a compelling true story sometimes means altering what really happened.

MID-WORKSHOP TEACHING   Using Flashbacks to Convey the Main Feeling

"Writers, what I'm noticing as I confer with you is that many of you are finding that when you want to build up the feeling that you had in a story, to really make readers feel what you were feeling, it helps to tuck just a tiny bit of time travel into your draft. For example, Jane had been writing about when she stayed for a week at her friend Clarissa's house, and suddenly experienced a pang of homesickness and worry. In her first version of her narrative, she just *told* about that. She wrote:

> "I do this every year," and I smiled to myself, thinking it would be a wonderful time. I looked down the hill at the rest of the Catskills and thought, "This is a beautiful house." But then in the night I felt a rush of pain in my stomach. Tears built up in my eyes, until they paused at the brim of my lower eyelids, then the tears suddenly flowed down my cheeks like small rivers. "I don't know what to do . . . I miss my family . . . I need them!" I sobbed. Then I imagined them in a car accident and cried even more.

"Jane decided she could actually go into her mind and tell about what she imagined could happen to her parents, so she wrote this:

> A terrible feeling came over me and took control of my mind. Words appeared in my mind and turned into worries. I saw my dad driving the car and my mom beside him. I saw a deer jump in the road. I saw the car bang into the rail and flip over. "What if my parents get into a car accident!" I thought.

"Then Jane returned to the sequence of her story events, writing this:

> I was shaking. And my insides didn't know what to do. I called my mom and she told me that it's okay, that I should calm down . . .

"She's finishing the story now. I think Jane can teach all of us that one way to build up the main feeling that we want to convey in a story is to consider detailing what exactly we remember or worry will happen or hope for. She's also reminded us of another important lesson—that writers use paragraphs to show changes in time. This is especially important when we're jumping forward or backward in time." I pointed to the "time" bullet on our paragraphing chart.

Make a New Paragraph to Signal

- A very important part that needs space around it
- A new event
- A new time
- A new place
- A new character speaking

The story needs to be true with a capital *t*, even if the author takes poetic license so it is not true with a small *t*. What's important is that the truth of the experience—the meaning of the moment—comes through.

You may want to pull a small group of writers whose stories tend to go on endlessly, often beginning long before things get interesting, and ending up bogged down in unneccesary details. Say to this group, "Writers, I pulled you together because I've noticed you doing something similar that is getting in the way of your writing. You are telling the stories of your lives with such precise attention to exactly how they happened that what makes these moments worth telling—what makes them powerful—is getting lost. I have a secret to share with you that professional writers know. To tell a story that holds a reader's attention—one that the reader doesn't want to put down—sometimes means letting go of some of the real-life happenings. In fact, sometimes when you leave out parts of the story, or swap in a different beginning or middle or ending, you end up telling a more powerful story.

"Let me tell you a little story to help you understand what I mean. My aunt makes quilts. But she isn't interested in making any old quilts—she only makes quilts that mean something to her, or to the person she will give them to. One time, she decided to make a quilt in memory of my grandfather, her father. But again, she didn't want to make it with any old pieces of fabric . . . she wanted to make the quilt out of items that were meaningful. So she went in search of pieces of fabric that *said something* about my grandfather and his life. She found some of my grandpa's old T-shirts, ones he had worn so many times that they were nubby and tattered. She found his favorite pajama bottoms—the ones he'd wear when he'd pull his grandchildren onto his lap, the whole giant heap of us, and tell stories. She even found some patches and other material from when he was in the Army. She took little pieces of all these items and more, and she sewed them together into a beautiful quilt. That quilt represents my grandfather and his life better than any one of those items ever could.

"You might be wondering: What in the world does quilting have to do with writing? The truth is, a lot. Yes, personal narrative writers recount true experiences. Yes, they tell a moment from beginning to end with truth and honesty. But they also do a little patching in of details. They add a little of this and a little of that and they sew it all together to make a beautiful narrative. In fact, I have a secret to tell you. The day that Luka died was actually a warm, summer day. The part about having to take him out for a walk in the cold is true—it just happened at another time. But I needed the cold weather to show just how miserable I was about walking Luka. I sewed two experiences together—walking Luka in the freezing cold and Luka being hit by a car—to help my reader better understand the real truth behind the moment: That I felt guilty for not always appreciating Luka the way I should have."

You might then say, "Remember how yesterday I suggested that you may want to take a part of one of your drafts and add it into another draft? When you recreate memories on paper, you can do that, too. You can take a part of one moment and place it into your story about another moment. The only rule is that it has to fit with what you are really trying to say!"

I got children working quickly, asking them to think through what they wanted to show, and the moments they could patch together to show it.

Rena, who was writing about helping her mom with the Thanksgiving feast, decided she'd add in a part about spilling the cranberry sauce all over the floor and how her mom said, with a smile on her face, "You know you're a real cook when you've made a big mess!" In fact, this was something Rena's mom had said to her another time, when she spilled some milk while preparing cereal, but that small detail helped Rena make her point: that no matter what mistakes Rena makes, her mom always helps her feel good about herself.

Writing Flash-Forwards

Share an example of a student's writing that shows moving to a new scene at a new time, making sure that it strengthens the writer's overall intent.

"Writers, many of you are moving backward and forward in time, and your pieces are becoming richer as a result. Listen to Caleb's first draft (See Figure 10–1):

> I looked up. Shelves upon shelves of mitts stared back down at me. The air conditioner made me feel like a snowstorm was forming in my intestine. I had tried on more than ten mitts and was about to give up. Finally I found one. It was perfect.

"But then Caleb thought, 'What am I trying to show in my story?' and he wrote a note to himself: "I want the reader to know that my mitt is special to me." He again wrote about shopping at Sports Authority, but this time he shifted between telling about shopping and telling about what he imagines himself doing with the glove in the future. He moves forward in time. Listen." As I read aloud, I emphasized the parts that revealed Caleb's intentions by shifting to an imagined future (see Figure 10–2).

> I pulled the soft, leathery mitt from the shelf. I slid it onto my left hand. I imagined myself fielding thousands of grounders and swiftly throwing them to the first baseman. I imagined leaping over the center field fence and watching the white streak land in it, the mitt. I slid it off, held it in my hands and started turning it, the mitt, reading all the labels: "Mizano, max flex, 12.5 inches." "Then I slipped it on again and the tingling sensation started again. I imagined me, nabbing a runner at the plate. I imagined the headlines of a sports section in 2020, "Madison's fielding scorches fans!!"

Got My MITT

I looked up Shelves upon
shelves upon shelves of mitts
stared back down at me.
The air contitoner made me feel
like a snow storm was forming
in my intestine I had tried on
more than 10 mitts on and
was about to give up.
Finally I found one. It was
perfect.

FIG. 10–1 Caleb's first draft

I pulled the soft, leathery
Mitt from the shelf.
I slid it on to my left hand
I imagined myself fielding thousands
of grounders and swiftly
throwing them to the first
baseman. I Imagined leaping
over the centerfield fence
and watching the white streak
land in it, the mitt
I slid it off, held it in my
hands and started turning it the
mitt, reading all the labels; Mizano
Max flex, 12.5 inches. Then I
slipped it on again and the
tingling sensation started again.
I imaganed me nabbing a runner
at the plate. I imagined the
Head lines of a sports section
in 2020 "Madisons fielding
scorches fans!!

FIG. 10–2 Caleb's draft, rewritten to include flash-forwards

"Caleb's story is so much more powerful now that he's added these flash-forwards. Before, it was hard to tell what his story was really about, what he really wanted to say. But now his flash-forwards make it clear to his readers how significant choosing his mitt was to him. Remember to keep in mind what your story is about and add scenes from the past or future that show this meaning to your reader."

SESSION 10 HOMEWORK

USING PAST MEMORIES TO EMPHASIZE MEANING

Tonight, please work some more on your draft, you might add a scene from the past or future to emphasize the significant part of your writing. Here's an example from Juliana to again show you what I mean.

Juliana is writing about meeting her dad, Chris, for the first time at a restaurant. But she interrupts the story with this memory to emphasize how much this meeting matters to her and to give some backstory.

> I remember that when I was in preschool, I asked my mom if I had a daddy. She said, "No, not everyone has one." She reminded me that Alexandre in my class didn't have a daddy and that her own daddy died when she was a teenager.
>
> Then when I was in kindergarten my friend asked how come I didn't have a father. "I just don't," I said. He said I had to have a father, everyone had one. I went home and told my mom that Joseph said there was no such thing as not having a father.
>
> She said that Joseph was right. Everyone had a father because a mother couldn't make a baby all by herself. But not everyone had a daddy. A daddy was someone who stayed with them and took care of them. My father was a man named Chris who lived in South Africa. He helped make the baby but did not want to be a daddy. Our family was just me and her with no daddy.

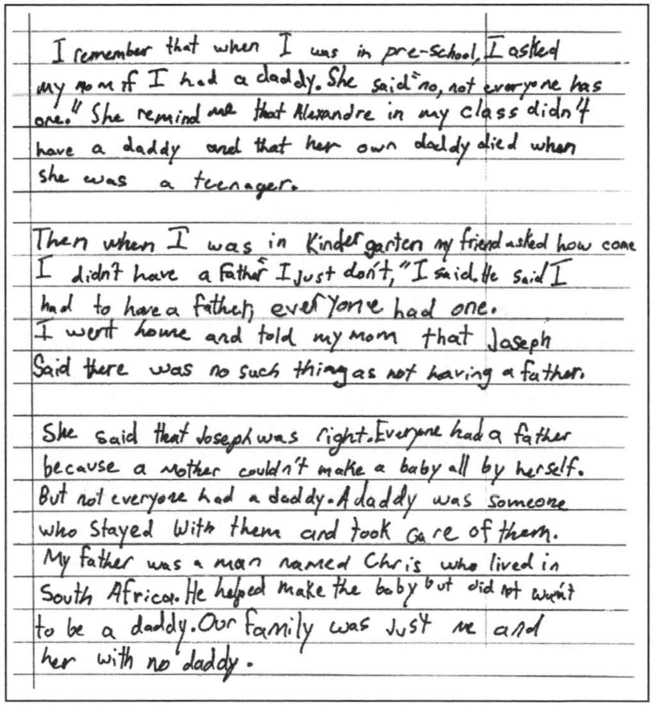
I remember that when I was in pre-school, I asked my mom if I had a daddy. She said "no, not everyone has one." She remind me that Alexandre in my class didn't have a daddy and that her own daddy died when she was a teenager.

Then when I was in Kindergarten my friend asked how come I didn't have a father I just don't," I said. He said I had to have a father, everyone had one. I went home and told my mom that Joseph Said there was no such thing as not having a father.

She said that Joseph was right. Everyone had a father because a mother couldn't make a baby all by herself. But not everyone had a daddy. A daddy was someone who stayed with them and took care of them. My father was a man named Chris who lived in South Africa. He helped make the baby but did not want to be a daddy. Our family was just me and her with no daddy.

FIG. 10–3 Juliana

Juliana uses *I remember* as a starting point for her flashback, and this flashback leads up to and gives importance to the story that she is writing. See if tonight you can try a flashback or a flash forward. If that isn't what your draft needs, try some other significant revision.

Ending Stories

IN THIS SESSION, you'll teach children a final revision strategy: that writers don't just end stories; they resolve problems, learn lessons, and make changes to end them in a way that ties back to the big meaning of their story.

GETTING READY

✔ The ending from *Charlotte's Web* by E. B. White (1990), on chart paper or an overhead

✔ Your ongoing writing on chart paper, with one ending ready to be revised in front of students (see Teaching)

✔ Each child's draft, with them in the meeting area for the lesson and the share (see Active Engagement and Share)

✔ "Techniques for Raising the Level of Narrative Writing" chart (see Link)

COMMON CORE STATE STANDARDS: W.5.3.a,e; W.5.5, RL.5.2, SL.5.1, L.5.1, L.5.2, L.5.3

O NE OF THE EXTRAORDINARY THINGS about the teaching of writing is this: almost any lesson I can possibly teach is equally applicable to a six-year-old and a sixty-year-old. The challenges of writing well are enduring ones.

Whether writers are six or sixty, the challenge to end a story well is an important one. Abby Oxenhorn, a kindergarten teacher and coauthor of *Small Moments* (2003) found that while teaching the small moment unit she finally resorted to laying down the law for her youngsters. "You are not allowed to end your story 'and then we went to bed'!" she said. Five-year-old Emma responded by ending her story about a ride on the Ferris wheel by saying, "And we lived happily ever after." Soon that ending, too, was on the off-limits list. Of course, Abby and I were secretly thrilled that even these littlest writers knew that stories need something special at the end.

"One of the extraordinary things about teaching writing is that any lesson is equally applicable to a six-year-old and a sixty-year-old."

You may not need to lay down the law as Abby did, saying, "No fair ending your story with 'then we went to bed' or 'we lived happily ever after,'" but you will need to decide how to nudge children to take on the challenge to write a good ending. Teach them that endings can be a place to fashion a new insight, develop a new thought, resolve an issue, or learn a lesson. Because the truth is that when we consider ways to end our stories, we are also inventing ways to resolve our problems. This is life work at its richest!

Ending Stories

CONNECTION

Explain that endings allow us to bring out meaning and leave readers with a final message.

"Writers, you are reaching the end of the second bend and putting the final touches on your pieces. I thought a lot about the work you've been doing in this bend—thinking about meaning and structure—and realized that endings are the last words you leave with your reader, and they have the power to bring your whole story together, to bring your whole message to light. I recently reread *Charlotte's Web* by E. B. White and remembered why I had loved it growing up. It's full of all sorts of lessons, about friendship and being the best versions of ourselves. But it wasn't until I got to the end of *Charlotte's Web* that I saw another big truth." I revealed an excerpt from *Charlotte's Web* to the children and began reading aloud.

> *Wilbur never forgot Charlotte. Although he loved her children and grandchildren dearly, none of the new spiders ever quite took her place in his heart. She was in a class by herself. It is not often that someone comes along who is a true friend and a good writer. Charlotte was both.*

"I read this final line again and again. I realized, at this moment, something I think E. B. White wanted his readers to know: that even though good things come along in life, like new friends and happy times, they never quite fill the old holes we have in our hearts. White's ending made me go back and rethink the book in an entirely different way."

❖ **Name the teaching point.**

"Today I want to teach you that like E. B. White, you can write an ending that leaves your reader with something big at the end. Writers think back to what they most wanted or struggled for in their stories and ask, 'What is it I want to say to my readers about this struggle—this journey?' Then they write an ending that shows this."

The example I choose is a bit of a spoiler for a class of children who have never read Charlotte's Web. If this is the case, you might choose another example (perhaps from a class read-aloud or a well-known picture book). Any ending that leaves readers with something new to think about will fit the bill!

TEACHING

Tell children that writers draft possible endings and do so by asking themselves a series of questions meant to elicit the story's real meaning.

"What I want to tell you today is that just as writers often take time to draft and revise different leads for our stories, so, too, they need to draft and revise alternate endings. But when they think about how they'll end their stories, they don't think right away about whether they'll end their stories with dialogue or with a small action or with a thought. Instead, they think first: 'What is my story really, really about? What was I reaching toward in my story? And what is it I want to say to my readers about this struggle, this journey?'

"For example, let me pull out the story I've been working on. On the outside, it seems like a story about discovering my dog Luka had died and feeling guilty about not being so nice to him earlier, but I want to remind myself what it is *really* about. Then I can consider possible endings that will help share what I want my readers to know about my struggle—my journey." I uncovered the draft of my story on a chart. "What did I most want to show in this story? Well, back when I was redrafting, I realized that what this moment is really about is realizing how much of a constant source of support my sister is to me. When I'm overcome with guilt and sadness that my dog has died, she is both reassuring and strong. I tried to show some of this through my flashback, remembering back to an earlier memory of my sister, when we first got Luka—how she advocated for the dog that I liked, when I was too little to voice this myself. Then the story returns to the present moment, at the rock where we plan to bury Luka, and my sister and I share a moment.

"But I'm noticing my story sort of drops off after that." I reread the next part of my story to the children, showing them how sudden the ending is. "It's like, poof, we start crying and that's it.

> Later, I took off my warm jacket and wrapped his stiffening body in it and together, my sister and I carried him back across the field that he had run through so joyfully that morning. I stopped near one of the big rocks that Luka and I had often sat on. My sister looked at me in confusion. "Here," I told her simply, gesturing to the ground beside the rocks. She didn't ask me any questions, just nodded and mumbled, "I'll get the shovel."
>
> As she walked off, my mind drifted back to the first time we'd first seen Luka, at the shelter—how he'd pushed his wet nose through the cage, into my small hand. Still too little for sentences then, I had just smiled and said, "Doggie." It was my sister who'd called out, "Hey dad, we found the one."
>
> The sound of shoveling snapped me out of my thoughts. My sister was bent over the spot I'd indicated, digging a hole. I reached out and hugged her from behind. I could feel her body shake. "Thanks," I mumbled into her ear, as we both cried.

"Do you see how sudden and sort of disappointing that is? I build up to this big moment where my sister and I grieve together, and then it ends. What is it I want to show here?" I made a show of really thinking, looking between my

In this minilesson, I am going to use my own writing to demonstrate how I go about considering and drafting alternate endings. I could instead have decided to use a mentor text. "Papa Who Wakes Up Tired in the Dark" would have been a good choice. If I wanted to use this text, I'd need to imagine what Sandra Cisneros probably did in order to arrive at her ending. I might, for example, tell children that she may have considered ending her story, "I ran off to tell my sister that our abuelito had died." Then I could say, "But she probably thought, 'Wait, this isn't really a story about the narrator and her sister,'" leading her back toward the ending she arrives at.

story and the marker in my hand. "I don't think this ending shows just how grateful I was for my big sister in this moment, and just how close to her I felt. My ending here doesn't fully convey this to my readers—it doesn't help them understand what my story is really about. I definitely need to make some changes if I want to leave my readers with something big at the end." I picked up my pen and began writing, crossing out the words "as we both cried."

> "Thanks," I mumbled into her ear. She reached up and put her hand over mine and I could feel, again, how she was trying to comfort me, even as she cried. "I wasn't very nice to Luka this morning," I confessed. Tears of shame stung my eyes. Suddenly, my sister had me in a tight hug. "It's okay," she murmured into my hair. "Luka knew you loved him."

"Do you see how I did that? How I thought back to what was most important about this moment and made sure that my ending really showed that meaning to my reader? I showed how even when when I expose something ungenerous about myself, my sister is there for me."

ACTIVE ENGAGEMENT

Ask children to revise their endings the same way.

"So, let's try. Take out your drafts and start by reminding yourself what it is really, really about. What were you wanting or struggling with in your story? When you're ready, turn and talk to your partner about how you might revise your ending to show the heart of your story—to reinforce what your story is really, truly about."

I listened in as children talked.

Takeshi said to Jake, "I think my story kind of drops off. It's like you can't even tell what I wanted. And that's so important to my story."

"Yeah," Jake said, "I think I did the same thing."

"What's your story really about so you can show it at the end?" Jake asked Takeshi.

"I guess that when I thought about it the other day I wanted to show that everything stays the same in my neighborhood. The deli man and the people sitting outside on the sidewalk. And I like it because I always know what I'll see." said Takeshi.

Jake coached Takeshi, helping him to brainstorm an ending. "So maybe you can end with something that shows everything will be the same. You could say 'See you tomorrow' at the deli, or something like that?"

"I like that idea," Takeshi said. "I'll work on it."

I gave them a thumbs-up and moved on.

One of the Common Core State Standards' expectations for fifth graders is that they need to be able to write endings that relate back to the central meanings in a story.

Don't worry if children don't grasp the full complexity of today's teaching. Endings are something professional writers struggle with every day, and one minilesson will not be sufficient to teach children all they need to know about the art of ending a story. Do expect, however, that this lesson leaves children thinking about their endings, rather than letting a series of actions dictate some finite place where their story must end.

LINK

Recall the teaching points, then remind writers of the repetoire of choices they can draw upon today and send them off.

"Writers, what you just saw me do, and what you began to do yourself, is a powerful revision strategy. Whenever you're revising your stories you can work on the endings—first reminding yourselves what you most want to show in your story and then using actions and thoughts and details and dialogue to show that meaning to your reader.

"Remember, you already know so much about revision, and today, like most days in writing workshop, needn't be a day where you only do what you learned in the minilesson. Take a moment and turn to your partner. List two or three *other* things you might do to revise today." I gave them a moment to do this and then reconvened the class. "Let's add this revision strategy to our chart and not waste a minute!"

Techniques for Raising the Level of Narrative Writing

- Dream the dream of the story and then write in a way that allows readers to experience the moment along with you.
- Revise using all you know about storytelling, not summarizing.
- Use all you know about grammar, spelling, and punctuation to edit as you write.
- Tell the story from **inside** it.
- Use details that are true to the event and that ring true.
- Use tools like the Narrative Writing Checklist to ask, "In what ways does my writing measure up? In what ways do I need to improve?" Then, revise your work to make it stronger.
- Ask: "What is my story really about?" and then write to bring forth that meaning.
- Bring out the story structure.
- Elaborate on important parts—parts that relate to what your story is really about.
- Incorporate scenes from the past or future to highlight the significance of your story.
- Don't simply end stories! Resolve problems, teach lessons, or make changes that tie back to the big meaning of your story.

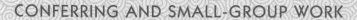
Supporting Revision

A S YOUR STUDENTS WRITE TODAY, many of them will focus on revising their endings so as to bring out meaning. You may want to coach into this work a bit, especially those who are still struggling to understand the day's lesson. Another way to explain this business of ending stories in powerful ways is this: endings *tie up* loose ends. So in a story about someone wanting something, the writer might ask herself, "In the end, does my character get what she wants? Why does this matter?" and in a story about someone struggling with something, the writer asks, "How is the struggle resolved? Does my character overcome the challenge or not? Why does this matter?" Notice that the emphaisis is still on meaning—however, the questions provide a little framework that allows the writer to conceptualize a resolution in ways that are significant.

Some writers say that a good story ending mirrors its beginning. This may be too complex for your struggling writers, but it is worth sharing with your advanced writers. You might pull aside a small strategy group today and demonstrate how you introduce an image or a phrase in a story's beginning that you then revisit at the end. Of course, not all stories work this way, and you will want to be clear that this is just one literary device that writers sometimes employ. The key to using this device effectively is choosing something meaningful to mirror. That is, you wouldn't mirror an uneccessary detail, but rather, one that holds significance; in my Luka story, for example, I might add the words "It's okay" to my beginning (later, my sister says these words to me twice, out of reassurance) perhaps in another context ("It's not okay to go out at the crack of dawn, Luka! Go away," I said, pushing him out of my face.), or I could begin and end with Luka's eager face or our special rock, if I wanted instead to spotlight something about my dog or our relationship, rather than my sister.

(continues)

MID-WORKSHOP TEACHING   **Focusing Story Endings**

"Writers, can I have your eyes? Rie is stuck on an ending. Let's see if we can help her. Remember Rie's story from earlier in our unit? She's writing about how she let her dad convince her to go surfing this summer even though she didn't want to—and she was so happy that she did, because she realized afterward that she could do anything. The most important point in her story is when she's actually up on her board—surfing.

"Let's say that Rie is going to end her story where she walks out of the water with her dad to have some lunch. In her first draft, the story ends with her thinking about the mac n' cheese that she's going to eat soon, but Rie realizes that feels like a whole new story. She knows it will throw her writing out of focus.

"Who can help Rie write an ending? So far she's written, 'My dad and I walked out of the water. "I've got mac'n'cheese, guys!" my mom yelled from under the umbrella.' Can anyone help? Turn and brainstorm some possibilities with the person next to you!"

Soon Rie had a plethora of suggestions. "Maybe when she's walking out of the water she could be thinking to herself, 'Wow, I'm so glad Dad got me to do that. Who knew I could surf?'" said Aalia. Robert chimed in, "Or maybe when she walks out she could be talking to her dad, saying what a great time she had and how glad she is that he pushed her to learn surfing." Once Rie had a few more suggestions, I sent the writers back to help themselves as they had helped Rie.

Meanwhile, of course, you won't want students to forgo other revision strategies as they work today, and so you may also decide to confer with students to find out the work that they are doing. You might remind them that just as a good ending spotlights a story's meaning, so too, do other parts in the story. As writers revise, they can ask themselves, "What is this story really about?" and then check to be sure they've brought that out throughout the story. They could tweak a story's beginning to be sure it invites the reader in—and packs a punch. They might run a story, or a part of a story, by a partner to be sure it reads the way they intended, or review the class's personal narrative checklist, or their own personal goal sheet to find things they haven't yet done. That is, there are many ways to revise and at this stage students should be working diligently to try out one thing, then another, then another, taking charge of their choices as writers, and aiming for their pieces to be as powerful and meaningful as they can be.

Sharing Powerful Endings

Gather children in a circle and tell them they will each have the opportunity to share their endings, forming a class poem of sorts.

"Writers, I don't know about you, but oftentimes when I write something powerful, I find it hard to keep it to myself. It's so good, so beautiful, that I *need* to share it. Is anyone feeling that way today?" Hands shot into the air as students begged for a chance to read aloud. I gestured for children to put their hands down. "Today, you are each going to have a chance to share a few lines from your ending. Read it over now in your head and prepare for how you will read it. You'll want to use your best storytelling voices."

I gave the children a moment to prepare and then called for their attention. "We'll start right over here with John. He'll read his ending, and then Takuma will go. We won't clap or say anything in between. We'll go around the circle and let your writing do the talking, forming a class poem of sorts." John began, and each child read his or her line in turn, starting with these:

"Never again, I mouthed to myself. Not a chance."

"I reached out and grabbed Gail's hand. She smiled at me and we rode the rest of the way in silence."

"Sometimes baseball is all you need."

"I'm sure my mom doesn't know why I'm squeezing her, but the feeling is so warm, she doesn't care. What I have is special. She squeezes me tighter. Special."

"I saw it coming before it hit me. Then, darkness."

"Wow, writers, the power of your endings is impressive. I am proud! You should be, too."

WRITING AND REWRITING LEADS AND ENDINGS

Some of you have written an ending you feel quite proud of today. Others of you are still reaching for the words to end your story in the "perfect" way. This is something published authors struggle with again and again, often drafting twenty or thirty endings before choosing the one that is best. Tonight, continue to explore a few different ways your ending might go, even if you feel you've already found the "right" one.

You might also spend some time thinking about your lead. Does it set readers up to understand what is going to be most important in your story? Does it grab your reader's attention and begin right at the start of the action? I'm sending you home with a copy of our chart, "Strategies for Elaborating on Important Parts," because often these strategies can help us to strengthen our leads and endings, as well.

Strategies for Elaborating on Important Parts

- Slow down the action, telling it bit-by-bit
- Add dialogue
- Give details
- Show small actions
- Add internal thinking

Putting On the Final Touches

 ear Teachers,

Today is the day when you'll help children move to final revisions and editing. In preparation for this lesson, you'll want to make sure that children have an abundance of tools within their reach. Students should be able to easily reference the teaching charts you've used throughout the unit. Of course they'll each need a copy of their Narrative Writing Checklist. You'll also want students using the Questions to Ask Yourself as You Edit Checklist you gave them earlier in the unit, and perhaps even the mentor texts they have studied thus far, such as samples of your mentor writing, student exemplars, and "Goosebumps." You will remind children that writers draw on *all* the tools they have as they put the final touches on their writing.

MINILESSON

We suggest you begin with a minilesson that reminds students that writers draw on tools. With the tools from the unit in hand, explain that writers draw on all these resources to finish their writing. You could talk about the way that checklists remind many professionals of all that they know how to do. Anesthesiologists use them, as do pilots.

You will probably want to demonstrate making a plan for how you will use these various resources to self-assess, revise, and edit your work. We recommend teaching writers to use one tool at a time, studying their work through that lens, and making revisions before moving on to another.

So, for instance, you might begin by looking at your piece of writing through the lens of structure, checking to make sure you have met each of the Grade 5 Common Core State Standards on the Narrative Writing Checklist and circling or highlighting those that you need to work on. Then, show students that you go back to your draft and see if there are ways that in these final moments, you can address items on the checklist that you still need to address.

COMMON CORE STATE STANDARDS: W.5.3, W.5.5, RL.5.2, SL.5.1, L.5.1, L.5.2, L.5.3

You might demonstrate a portion of the checklist you have not studied closely together prior to now. For instance, you could channel children to watch as you assess and revise by considering structure.

Ask children, with the help of their partners, to see how their own work measures up against the fifth-grade standards. After identifying a few goals and places for revisions, they'll be ready to begin working when they return to their seats.

CONFERRING AND SMALL-GROUP WORK

Before today's session, you'll want to look closely at your students' work, forming groups around common needs. You might, for instance, decide to convene a small group of writers who are writing in staccato sentences, using few subordinate phrases and transition words. You could remind these writers that it often helps to tuck into a sentence the answers to questions 'Where? When? How? Why?' A sentence 'I went to the park' becomes 'Late last night when the sky was almost pitch black, I went to the park, the one down the street from me.' Children can then mirror writing as a technique for exploring sentence-combining strategies. You might also pull another group who is struggling with leads or endings, and teach them a few concrete strategies for writing these effectively. Plan to teach children ways to raise the level of their work, but also help them feel ready to set this piece aside and begin anew tomorrow.

SHARE

It may come as a surprise that tomorrow you begin Bend III, and the children begin new pieces. Why wouldn't they publish these stories first, you might ask? The answer is twofold. First, you are teaching your young writers to cycle through the writing process faster and faster, raising the level of their work at each step; taking a day to copy over their writing will bring that process to a grinding halt. Second, you will teach writers a whole new set of strategies in Bend III and their pieces are sure to be far more powerful than what they have drafted this time around.

Narrative Writing Checklist

	Grade 5	NOT YET	STARTING TO	YES!	Grade 6	NOT YET	STARTING TO	YES!
	Structure				**Structure**			
Overall	I wrote a story of an important moment. It read like a story, even though it might be a true account.	☐	☐	☐	I wrote a story that had tension, resolution, and realistic characters and conveyed an idea or lesson.	☐	☐	☐
Lead	I wrote a beginning in which I not only showed what was happening and where, but also gave some clues to what would later become a problem for the main character.	☐	☐	☐	I wrote a beginning in which I not only set the plot or story in motion, but also hinted at the larger meaning the story would convey.	☐	☐	☐
Transitions	I used transitional phrases to show passage of time in complicated ways, perhaps by showing things happening at the same time (*meanwhile, at the same time*) or flashback and flash-forward (*early that morning, three hours later*).	☐	☐	☐	I used transitional phrases to connect what happened to why it happened, such as *If I hadn't . . . , I might not have . . . , because of . . . , although . . . ,* and *little did I know that . . . .*	☐	☐	☐
Ending	I wrote an ending that connected to the main part of the story. The character said, did, or realized something at the end that came from what happened in the story.	☐	☐	☐	I wrote an ending that connected to what the story was really about.	☐	☐	☐
	I gave readers a sense of closure.				I gave readers a sense of closure by showing a new realization or insight or a change in a character or narrator.			
Organization	I used paragraphs to separate different parts or time of the story and to show when a new character was speaking. Some parts of the story were longer and more developed than others.	☐	☐	☐	I used paragraphs purposefully, perhaps to show time or setting changes, new parts of the story, or to create suspense for readers. I created a sequence of events that was clear.	☐	☐	☐

You'll want to make today celebratory. Think about how you'd best like to celebrate their achievements. It will be important for children to share their piece with someone, so you might ask them to read their piece aloud in small groups. Perhaps you'll find a small token to give each of them—a flashy new pencil, an inspiring quote to paste into their writers' notebooks, or even a special read-aloud to celebrate. We recommend helping children to showcase the growth they've made by asking them to compare their first, not-so-powerful entries to this final draft. You might decide to dedicate a bulletin board to this, asking each child to hang the two pieces side by side with a note about what they have learned to do as a writer.

Make this day special for your students. Help them feel proud of all they've accomplished. And rally their energy for the next round of writing!

Reading with a Writer's Eye

IN THIS SESSION, you'll teach students that one way writers make writing powerful is by emulating narrative writing they admire.

GETTING READY

✔ Children need to have listened on an earlier day to you reading aloud "Eleven" by Sandra Cisneros. Now you need a marked-up text of "Eleven" with the powerful parts of the story circled in red (see Teaching)

✔ Chart paper to create the chart, "Lessons from Mentor Narratives" (see Teaching)

✔ Excerpt from "Eleven" copied onto chart paper (see Teaching)

✔ A copy of "Eleven" for each student to annotate during the workshop. Students will begin doing this in the minilesson so it's ideal, but not necessary, for them to have the text, a pen, and something to write against while in the meeting area.

COMMON CORE STATE STANDARDS: W.5.3.b,d; W.5.5, W.5.9.a, RL.5.2, RL.5.10, RFS.5.4, SL.5.1, SL.5.6, L.5.1, L.5.2, L.5.3

T HIS SESSION LAUNCHES THE THIRD AND FINAL BEND IN THIS UNIT. As you progress through all the units across this year, you'll come to expect that the work students are asked to do in each successive bend becomes more demanding. In this bend, for example, when students return to gathering entries prior to choosing one to develop into a major piece of writing, you'll note that you don't provide them with strategies for generating ideas for narrative writing but instead merely remind them that they already know many such strategies. Although you devoted two minilessons in bend one to teaching students that in order to write narratives, they need to climb into the shoes of the character (in this case, themselves from another time and place) and almost experience the episode as they write, today's mid-workshop revisits that emphasis. This

"We can apprentice ourselves to the works and words of other writers."

is an especially challenging and critical concept. As the bend continues to unfold, your students will progress through the writing process as they did in the prior bend, but this time you convey expectations that as they are progressing through the writing process they meanwhile are focusing on ways to lift the level of their work. Your teaching, then, supports students' transferring and drawing upon skills they developed earlier, while your focus is on new work. The new work centers especially on reading-writing connections, and on using a study of mentor texts—and in particular, of Sandra Cisneros' "Eleven"—to lift the level of student writing.

It is hard to emphasize enough the importance of reading-writing connections. In the old days, people became better at doing things by becoming apprentices. If you wanted to be a lawyer, you spent time with another lawyer, studying carefully and learning from seeing that lawyer in action. If you wanted to become a tailor, you apprenticed yourself to another tailor, observing the way that tailor measured material twice and cut once so as not to waste one scrap of cloth. Being an apprentice was a step on the road to becoming a master craftsman. Think of yourself as a student teacher and how much you learned from apprenticing yourself to watching the work of a master teacher so that you could one day become one yourself.

Writers are lucky enough to have the ability to apprentice themselves to masters at any time. Our masters are all of the written words of other authors who have come before us. We can apprentice ourselves to the works and words of other writers. Looking carefully and observing other writers in action, we can say, "Oh, there, I see how that detail sets it all up" or "That ending—I've read it at least ten times, trying to figure out how she did that." As William Faulkner reminds us: "Read, read, read. Read everything—trash, classics, good and bad, and see how they do it. Just like a carpenter who works as an apprentice and studies the master. Read! You'll absorb it. Then write."

Reading With a Writer's Eye

CONNECTION

Use a metaphor to explain that insiders see differently, learning not only from the products others have made but also inferring and learning from the processes behind those products.

"Writers, when I walk through an art gallery, I see people looking at paintings and saying, 'Oh, that would be lovely over the fireplace,' or 'Oh! I like this one, reminds me of the sunset during our vacation on the shore.' That's how the general public looks at art.

"But an artist walking through an art gallery thinks differently. 'Hmm...!' he'll be thinking. 'That's an interesting technique with dry paint and wet paint. It looks like the paint has been spread out with a comb to create the illusion of this fence. And what a clever thing to do, using this purple for the shadows—it brings out the light in the rest of the painting . . . I must try this.' He won't just copy the subject of a painting—he'll steal a technique. Pablo Picasso said, 'Good artists copy, great artists steal.'"

It's the same when I walk by people's gardens. I won't just say, "How pretty!" like anyone else might. I love gardening, so I will note, "Hmm..., they've grafted this rose to make such an unusual color. Must take a photo and graft with the same colors to see if I get the same result."

❖ **Name the teaching point.**

"Today I want to teach you that writers look at other people's writing differently. Like all readers, they let the writing affect them but then they also look behind the meaning to note, 'What is the clever trick this writer has done to affect the reader this way? Must try this.'"

TEACHING

Show children that when they want to make a good piece of writing, it often helps to find a mentor text and read a bit of it asking, "What did the writer do that I could try?"

"During our read-aloud time yesterday, I read you Sandra Cisneros's 'Eleven' and it affected us powerfully as readers, filled us with a knowing sympathy for the narrator. When a story has that kind of power, writers pause and admire the craft asking, 'What has this writer done to affect me this way? I must try it in my own writing.'"

I held up my marked text of 'Eleven' for the class to see. "See these parts circled in red—I marked the most powerful parts of 'Eleven,' parts that felt powerful and well-written.

When someone asked the great poet Robert Frost, "How can I learn to write?" Frost said, "Read Anna Karenena, read Anna Karenena, read Anna Karenena." He could have said, "Read 'Eleven,' read 'Eleven,' read 'Eleven,'" The point is that to learn from a text, we need to not only read it, but to reread it, reread it, reread it. This is the point you'll hope to make through today's minilesson.

"'Eleven' is such a powerfully written piece that I'm almost a student of this piece of writing. I've reread it and reread it and almost memorized the most beautifully written parts. Let me read one of those parts aloud, and ask that question that writers ask all the time: 'What has she done that I could try?'

> "Whose is this?" Mrs. Price says, and she holds the red sweater up in the air for all the class to see. "Whose? It's been sitting in the coatroom for a month."
>
> "Not mine," says everybody, "Not me."
>
> "It has to belong to somebody," Mrs. Price keeps saying, but nobody can remember.

"Writers, when I try to think what Cisneros has done that I could try, the first thing I see is that she's included the exact words that a character is saying—we already know that's a quality of good narrative writing. But when I study mentor texts, I don't just ask, 'What has the author done?,' I also ask, 'How has she done it?'

"Hmm.... What I am noticing is that she's written this in a way that shows Mrs. Price's intonation, her mood. I'm getting the idea, just from the way she talks, that Mrs. Price is arrogant and disdainful.

"Isn't that interesting? Sandra Cisneros never comes right out and tells us what kind of person Mrs. Price is, but she has her talk in a way that gives us a hint, anyhow." I mimicked Mrs. Price's talk, making my voice nasal and contemptuous. '*Whose is this? Whose? It's been sitting in the coatroom for a month.*' Then, I made my voice nasal again, '*It has to belong to somebody.*' Can you picture the kind of person Mrs. Price is, just by reading her words aloud?"

Name what the author has done in such a way that her skill can be transferred to another text——and then do so. Show how the same technique could be used in a different text or two.

"So Cisneros doesn't just use the words that a character could have said to advance the story, she gets her characters to talk in ways that reveal what kind of person the character is. Imagine if your kind old grandfather had found this sweater, what might he have said?" Making my voice kindly and gruff, I said, "Anyone lose a sweater? I'm worried it might be one of yours. Wouldn't want you getting chilly without it. I'll leave it on this table.

"As a writer, I'm noting that I might use this move that Cisneros uses. In my own stories, I too can use the words that a character could have said to reveal the person's tone and personality." Moving to the empty chart I wrote out the first bullet as follows:

Lessons from Mentor Narratives

- Writers create the words a person could have said, doing this in ways that reveal the character as a person.

You are hoping that your students will admire the craft in "Eleven" as you did. Be sure to read these lines aloud especially well. Be Mrs. Price, returning from the coat room, the offensive sweater dangling from her fingertips. When I read, "Whose is this?" my face is pinched, my body arched back a bit from the sweater.

Teachers, you could have highlighted one of an umpteen number of Cisneros's narrative qualities. This is one that is easy to spot at the very start of the narrative portion of "Eleven," and it is one we imagine youngsters would enjoy emulating.

Debrief. Name what you have demonstrated in a way that is transferable to other texts and other days.

"Do you see, I reread 'Eleven' and asked, 'What are things this author has done that I could try too?' I'm going to gather a collection of lessons from 'Eleven,' and then I'll try to write differently because of what I've learned."

ACTIVE ENGAGEMENT

Suggest children read like writers, noting parts of the text that feel powerful. Ask them to note what exactly the author has done.

"Let's study more of 'Eleven.' I'm going to skip past the part where the narrator thinks, 'Not mine, not mine.' I'll read a part that comes a bit later. Try to listen in a way that lets you feel the power of the story, and then later we can reread the part we're studying, and you'll have a chance to ask, 'What has Sandra done that I can do?'"

I read aloud:

> *Maybe because I'm skinny, maybe because she doesn't like me, that stupid Sylvia Saldivar says, "I think it belongs to Rachel." An ugly sweater like that all raggedy and old, but Mrs. Price believes her. Mrs Price takes the sweater and puts it right on my desk, but when I open my mouth nothing comes out.*

> *"That's not, I don't, you're not . . . Not mine." I finally say in a little voice that was maybe me when I was four.*

I skipped to a descriptive part slightly further down, a part that I knew would be easier for children to mine for qualities of good narrative writing.

> *Not mine, not mine, not mine, but Mrs. Price is already turning to page thirty-two, and math problem number four. I don't know why but all of a sudden I'm feeling sick inside, like the part of me that's three wants to come out of my eyes, only I squeeze them shut tight and bite down on my teeth real hard and try to remember today I am eleven, eleven. Mama is making a cake for me for tonight, and when Papa comes home everybody will sing Happy birthday, happy birthday to you.*

I stopped reading and gestured toward the printed copy of the text on chart paper, and said, "Let's study this closely." The children pulled out their personal copies of the text. Then I said, "What has Cisneros done in her text that you could do in yours?" The room grew silent, and I reread selected snippets as I mulled over the question.

After giving children long enough to generate a few ideas, I said "Tell your partner what you noticed."

As children talked, I listened for a few observations to highlight.

If you have bought the collection of texts that accompanies these units, you'll see that you have a copy of "Eleven" in that pack—If you have enough copies, you'll be able to give these to children. If you don't have a way to give children copies, then they won't be able to annotate their own individual copies.

The focus of this minilesson is a big part of the Common Core. The reading standards 4, 5, and 6 ask for readers to read, noticing the way in which a text was written thinking about the authorial decisions, and analyzing the relationship between craft and meaning.

Ask children to report on their findings, and then add their observations to the class chart.

After a minute, I nodded at one child to repeat what I'd just overheard him saying. Miles said, "She does that thing again of showing what a character is like, but this time she tells you *why* someone does what she does. Sandra says, 'Maybe because I'm skinny, maybe she doesn't like me . . .' so everyone knows that Sylvia is really mean."

"So what is it that Cisneros has done that you could do?" I pressed.

I wasn't sure I saw what Miles meant, and wasn't sure he'd settled on a transferable quality. He clarified. "She shows why people do things."

Joey added, "And she tells what her voice is like. When she says that she sounded like she was four, she explains the voice she used."

Ori added, "And it was the voice she used when she was talking to herself. I don't usually think about the voice when I talk to myself but it's good she does."

LINK

Reiterate the teaching point and send children off to study mentor texts.

"So, writers, today we launch a new part of our unit, and our goal will be to write the kinds of stories that make people stop in their tracks! We learned today that writers can read first as readers, trying to experience the story, and then as writers, seeing what you can figure out about writing. Chefs might taste a great apple tart and then think, 'What was the recipe?' Seamstresses might turn a particularly interesting dress inside out to study the seams, thinking, 'What pattern made this?' Hockey players might rewind video of a pro player and watch every move asking, 'How does he do that so well?' In the same way, writers read the work of other authors, asking, 'How did she write this? What did this author do that I could try?'

"Read over 'Eleven' again during the first part of today's workshop. At first you will probably notice mostly what we've learned so far in this unit about strong narrative writing—things from our chart. As you look closer, though, you'll find new things to try. Use everything you know about close reading and see what you can uncover! List the things you can try in your notebook, because about half way through the workshop, you'll switch back to being writers, collecting entries using the new techniques you've learned from studying mentor texts."

Lessons from Mentor Narratives

- Writers create the words a person could have said, doing this in ways that reveal the character as a person.
- Writers give reasons to explain the way a character acts.
- Writers show thinking by telling the exact words and the tone a character uses when thinking— like a dialogue with one's self.

You may decide to also give children another personal narrative or two that they can study. If you decide to do so, you may draw on the other benchmark texts for fifth-grade narrative writing, or other published narratives.

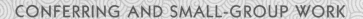

Helping Children See More as They Study Mentor Texts

TODAY PREPARE TO GASP AT THE PORTIONS OF "ELEVEN" that your children notice, and to do so in a way that draws them into close, analytic reading. If a child points in a half-hearted way to a section of the text as you circulate, pretend the child has just jumped up and down with excitement over the words and that you are joining in.

"Oh my gosh!" you'll say. "You are right. This is so powerful, isn't it?" Then read that section aloud. Read it like it's worth a million dollars. Don't question the child's judgment, and for now don't interrogate the child to get him or her to produce a defense for the selection. At least at first, don't even analyze the text to unpack the writing techniques that it illustrates. Instead, begin by reading the passage deeply and well. This will help children to also read in such a way that the passage can make a difference to them. Read the selection aloud so that the hairs on the back of your neck prickle. Read it slowly. Gasp at it. Read it again.

Then after you have joined the child in reading that section, model how a reader sometimes turns back to name the effect the passage created. Speak in true words, naming what the passage did for you. Avoid hackneyed phrases like "made a picture in my mind." Instead say something like, "When I read this, I realized I have done the exact same thing." Or you might say, "This part gave me a hollow feeling. The words are so stark. 'Not mine. Not mine. Not mine.' It sounds like amen or good-bye."

Encourage the child to say what he is thinking or feeling or noticing. Help draw words out of the child through gestures and body language; listen, nod, respond in ways that say, "Yes, yes, I know what you mean, say more." Don't worry today about whether your conferences follow the usual architecture of conferences or whether you are explicitly teaching anything. You will teach *implicitly* today. You'll help children immerse themselves in the sort of text you hope they will soon write—and meanwhile, you will create a drumroll for a new cycle of writing that essentially asks kids to go back and do what they did before, only better.

MID-WORKSHOP TEACHING   Channel Kids to Write

"Writers, can I stop your reading for a bit? You may not have finished annotating 'Eleven,' but it is important to save lots of time for going back to your notebook and writing more entries, because in another few days you'll again choose a seed idea. During our celebration at the end of our second bend, each of you had a chance to share your writing. I hope that having an audience gave you a glimpse of what it feels like to be a published author. With yesterday still fresh in your mind, turn and tell your partner one thing that having a real audience made you realize.

"I've heard a few of you saying that it was nice when your writing made your audience laugh. Or when you could feel people nodding with empathy or on the edges of their seats. Writers yearn to write in ways that make people stop in their tracks. So from this day on, remember that you are writing to make readers stop in their tracks.

"With yesterday fresh in your mind, take out your notebooks and get started writing some new entries that will eventually lead to your final publication from this unit. You know strategies for generating ideas." I gestured to the chart.

"But remember—the reason that 'Eleven' is so powerful is because Cisneros first dreamed the dream of the story. That is why she can make her readers visualize each detail, feel each scratch and hiccup, hear the exact inflection in the words a character utters. You want to dream the dream of the story before you get started—and then use some of the techniques you see in these mentor narratives. Get started writing!"

Revising Entries and Setting Assignments

Remind children to review and revise their entries.

Writers, some of you have been looking at the clock and sensing that writing time is running out. I can see a few of you are cutting to the chase in your entries, ending them quickly because time is running out. The good news is that you have time tonight to continue working on your entry—and that is important because as fifth-graders, you need to get accustomed to writing longer entries from the get go. Your entries should usually be about a page and a half in length—not always, of course, but often. So right now, think about what you are going to do tonight, make some marginal notes to remind yourself of goals for this evening's writing, and take a few minutes to finish whatever you are working on without cutting things short." I gave them a minute to work and then called for their attention again.

"You might also look over the new writing you've done today, quickly, and think, 'Is this as powerful as it can be?' 'Is my intended meaning coming out? My dream of the story?' 'Did I hope to do something that isn't yet reflected here?' Then, bring out a trick or two from up your sleeve! If you need a reminder, quickly glance at any of the charts we've made during this unit. Then jot on a Post-it note one or two revisions you'll make tonight. Then, turn and tell your partner what you'll work on tonight.

"And remember, whenever you are looking to strengthen yourself as a writer, you can study writing you admire, ask 'What has this author done that I might try, too?' and then try it!" (See Figure 13–1.)

> I stepped on Riverside Park's biggest hill. I grasped my purple sled. I could see my friend Logan and my little sister, Camilla, getting ready too. I was so excited because today was the first snow of the year.
>
> Camilla climbed onto the sled with me. I was like I was a grown up, like 13 or 14 or even older, because Camilla was following my lead.
>
> I was about to make my slide but I was thinking about sledding down the hill and didn't look around. But I was not scared because I had ridden other hills, but not as big. My sled started down the hill. Then I noticed a human shape. It was a man and his kid and I couldn't control my sled. I was headed right for them. My parents said "Watch Out!" but it was too late. I lost all my excitement. I was an inch close to the man. Then I felt my sled rub against his coat as I came to a complete stop.
>
> I saw the man's half angly, half alarmed face. I saw the kid's innocent face. I heard the man yell, "who's watching you!" as I felt Camilla's hand touch my neck. I ran as fast as I could to my mother and Logan who said, "It's OK," but I did not feel OK. I felt like a little kid that was about 3 years old. I felt like I was going backwards in life, from 9 to 3. I felt so grown up and now I was just a scared little kid.

FIG. 13–1 Francesca writes, inspired by "Eleven"

REVISING FROM THE GET-GO

Writers, you will give yourself an assignment for tonight. I'm sure that part of what you do will involve trying out the the tricks you've seen authors use—their craft techniques—to explore ways you, too, might make your text more powerful. But here's the thing: you already have lots of little tricks up your own sleeves when it comes to writing. And here's some advice: don't wait until the end to think not just about *what* you'll say but also about *how* you'll say it.

When you're writing an entry, you're wise to write quickly, getting the words and the story down onto the page. But as you write in a rush, you can also be revising. This doesn't mean pausing for long stretches to agonize over this word or that image. Instead, it means that you bring out your tricks as you go. You write for a stretch, then quickly reread and think, "That's a long section of description. I bet I could break it up with some thinking or a reaction my character has to being in this new place. Maybe she even does something to explore it." Or "The tension isn't really coming out in this part, and this is where things really start to build in intensity for my character. I'm going to add in just a few details to show that." Then you do whatever you notice your work might need and you keep going. This sort of revision, which professional writers call "front end" revision, is actually often easier than the kind that comes at the end of a piece because it allows a writer to work more deliberately while the piece is still in its early stages of coming to be something. In the early stages of writing, a story is malleable—that means flexible, moldable—like a piece of clay, and so is your thinking about the piece. Later, when you declare a piece of writing "done," it can be harder to jump back in and make big changes—even when you know those will improve the piece.

So tonight, write with revision in mind!

Session 14

Taking Writing to the Workbench

AS THE SAYING GOES, "Practice makes perfect." We know that in order to develop one's skills, it is critical to practice. That is why we've created abundant opportunities in this one unit of study for young people to practice narrative craft. Think of how many whole drafts your students have written just over the last few weeks. They wrote many entries that first week, then wrote several whole drafts of what became their first published piece, revising those, and now they are drafting entries for what will become their next published piece. That's a lot of practice!

But here's the thing. The saying should not be "Practice makes perfect." Many people develop a certain level of proficiency and then plateau. What makes the difference is mindful, goal driven work. The saying should be: "*Perfect practice makes perfect.*" Because it is deliberate practice that makes the difference, it is critical for learners to receive feedback (or to generate their own feedback through self-critique) and then to crystallize goals, and work resolutely and deliberatively toward those goals.

In this session, you let students know that writer's notebooks can be used as workbenches, with writers tackling identified goals and writing not entirely new whole drafts, but new portions of drafts. Perhaps one student wants to develop her characters more completely. She may decide to draft alternate visual details she could provide to bring the person to life. She does this for one character, jotting a few alternate ways to do this. Then she revisits the mentor text, gets some more specific help from the examples within that text, and again tries this work. She does it for one character in her current entry, then for another. She goes back to her published piece, and brings her new-found skills to that piece, despite the fact that it had already been pronounced done.

Of course, while students "workbench" their entries, they also write new ones. Because all these alternatives are open to all the children in the class, if you step back to scan the room, you'll find youngsters are engaged in a remarkably diverse array of activities. That is as it should be, in this last bend in a fifth-grade unit on narrative writing. After all, this is the start of your year—but you can also think of this as the eleventh month of last year!

IN THIS SESSION, you'll teach students that writers don't just use their writer's notebooks to gather entries; they also use their writer's notebooks as a place to try new things and to work hard at the writing goals they've set for themselves.

GETTING READY

✔ An excerpt from "Eleven" for you to read aloud that highlights a craft move you will be emulating (see Teaching)

✔ An enlarged section of your story on chart paper or an overhead with which you will model revising (see Teaching)

✔ The previous session's chart, "Lessons from Mentor Narratives" (see Teaching)

✔ Students should bring their mentor texts from the last session and their notebooks to the meeting area (see Active Engagement).

COMMON CORE STATE STANDARDS: W.5.3.b,d; W.5.5, W.5.9.a, RL.5.2, RL.5.10, SL.5.1, L.5.1, L.5.2, L.5.3

Taking Writing to the Workbench

CONNECTION

Establish a shared foundation of knowledge about the writing process by asking children to voice their expectations for how this upcoming bend—and how the writing process—is apt to go.

"Writers, you are in fifth grade. You already know a lot about the writing process. So tell me, what will you do today? Yesterday you wrote a quick entry. How's today going to go in the writing workshop, and tomorrow?"

The children called out that they'd write another entry today, another tomorrow, then pick their seed idea.

"And if you aren't sure what to write about in all those entries, where will you get help?" I asked, adding, "Point to your source of help for coming up with story ideas." The children pointed to the chart, "Strategies for Generating Narrative Writing."

I nodded, and said, "Nice work. You've got the process of writing in your bones, and that's good. You can flow along—generating entries, choosing one, imagining the story, and writing it strong and long."

Set children up to expect that today's session will not be business as usual.

"But now I'm going to do something that people describe as 'throwing a wrench in your process.' Can you figure out what that phrase means?" I repeated it: "I'm going to throw a wrench in your process."

Anna asked, "Give us another tool, another strategy, only it's a wrench?"

"You're sort of onto it, but it is a more disruptive image than that. Imagine a big machine with all these gears, humming along, all the wheels turning, and then suddenly I throw a big metal wrench into the machinery. Can you picture how that new tool makes everything go haywire for a bit? That's what throwing a wrench into the process means. Another way of putting it is this: 'I'm going to mess with your process.' Just when you thought you had the writing process down pat, I'm going to mess things up. You ready?"

◆ COACHING

Today's minilesson covers a lot of ground, so do this teaching quickly, maintaining a very lively pace. Expect your connection to take a minute. When you ask a question of the whole class, let a child or two answer, and then keep going. If they don't grasp what you are asking, it's entirely fine to chime in yourself. The point of today's connection is not to assess your students' understanding of the writing process—there are better ways to do that. Instead, your point is to consolidate what the class knows so that you can push off from that into new terrain.

This is an unusual way to signal "Listen Up." But that's what you are saying. "Draw in close. Get ready."

❖ **Name the teaching point.**

"Today I want to teach you that in order to learn from a mentor text, you can't just read the text and hope it rubs off on you. You have to work at it. And to do that, it helps to use your writer's notebook not just as a place to gather entries, but as a workbench where you work on making your writing do specific things."

TEACHING

Rally your students to invest themselves in self-initiating skill-building exercises within their writer's notebooks, where they drill themselves on alternate ways to achieve a goal.

"Some people think of 'work' . . . and especially of 'hard work' as a negative thing. Some people think that the best writers are people who write easily, that they are people for whom great writing just rolls out. But the truth is that in every field, the people who become pros are people who work at it. Albert Einstein—the genius mathematician—has described the reasons for his success, saying ' . . . it's not that I'm so smart, it's just that I stay with problems longer.' And Michael Jordan, one of the greatest basketball players ever, was cut from his high school team because he wasn't good enough. But he didn't just pout and whine. No way. He worked. Morning, noon, and night. He was always the first one on the basketball court and the last one off the court. He wasn't good at the jump shot so day after day, he went onto the court and practiced jump shots for hours.

"It's the same way if you want to get a part in a play. You don't just put the script under your pillow and sleep on it. You read those lines so many times you can recite them by heart. You ask your mother to listen while you read them, and your dog. You rent a video of the play and watch it, stopping the video a hundred times to study what the person whose part you are playing has done.

"Yesterday, you each found parts of 'Eleven' that you admired, and wrote an entry in which you tried to lift the level of your writing. That was a solid *first* step. But if you *really* want your writing to get better, you can't just look at 'Eleven,' underline parts of it, write marginal notes like 'Great details.' Instead you need to deliberately practice writing in ways that you admire."

Tell students that they can think of their notebook as a workbench.

"To do that, think of your notebook as a workbench, and think of yourself as someone who is trying to make something. You bang away at it . . . then you pull back, look it over, thinking, 'How do I like this?' And then . . . here's the key thing: you try it again, *differently, better.*

"And if you decide you're not all that skilled at something—like Michael Jordan wasn't skilled at jump shots—you find ways to get coaching and you practice all the more. If you're not yet successful at making characters come to life through dialogue, you work on that in lots of places in your entry, and you go back to earlier entries too, and work on dialogue in them, too. Just like the gym became a place where Michael Jordan worked on his jump shots, your notebook becomes filled with your efforts to do that one thing better, better, better, over and over."

This session aims to build students' sense of self efficacy, their confidence that they have in themselves that which is needed to make learning happen. We know students with a high sense of self efficacy see hard tasks as challenges rather than as something to be avoided, and see failures as chances to learn. We know that teaching can be designed to cultivate a sense of self efficacy.

Demonstrate how you might bring your own writing to the workbench and improve it by taking lessons from a mentor text.

"Let me show you what I mean by showing you a bit of my writer's notebook, where I 'workbench' something that I caught Sandra Cisneros doing in 'Eleven.'" I pointed to the last bullet on the chart "Lessons from Mentor Narratives" and read it aloud: "'Writers can reveal internal thinking by talking aloud in their own head—like a dialogue with one's self.' Remember what Sandra did in 'Eleven?'" I quickly read some sentences from "Eleven" that contained the specific craft move I would be emulating:

> *Not mine, not mine, not mine, but Mrs. Price is already turning to page thirty-two . . . .*

"I'm going to bring my Luka story to the workbench, and work at trying to talk aloud in my head in the way that Cisneros has her characters do." I mounted an enlarged section of the now-familiar Luka story onto the board for students to look at.

> "Luka?" I heard my voice break as I knelt beside him. His eyes had never looked like this, glazed with shock, as if he couldn't see me at all.

Teachers, it will be far more efficient to mount one specific portion of the story rather than the entire narrative—to showcase the specific part you're working on. This portion of the minilesson should illuminate for you the way in which you can return to a single familiar text over and over, using that one text to teach a score of lessons.

I picked up a marker and attempted a first stab at this work. I added:

> You can't die, Luka. No, no, no! Luka, are you okay?

I leaned back from the chart, surveying my work. "I've added some internal thinking, but it feels like too much. I'm not sure it's right. Let me try again."

I stared at the entry, visibly thinking, and then picked up a marker and added the lines:

> Open your eyes, Luka. You can't die.

Don't make this look easy for students. You want to reinforce the idea that writers try, then try again, until their writing is just right.

Then, I read aloud the next sentence and added another line.

> My sister, too, was talking—softly. Her face as she bent close to Luka was white. "It's ok . . . It's ok . . . It's going to be ok," she murmured. He's not okay. He's not okay! Why is he twitching like that?

Debrief, explaining how, exactly, you used the strategy from the mentor narrative in your own story.

"Writers, did you see how I used Sandra Cisneros's trick of making the person—in this story, it's me when I was a kid—talk in-the-mind? That is like the narrator did in 'Eleven'? I say, 'Open your eyes, Luka. You can't die' and it's almost like I'm willing Luka to live, using all my force and energy to keep him from dying. 'Open your eyes, Luka. You can't die.'"

I hope you see that I'm holding onto hope in this part of the story; I still believe that if I channel all my power to this cause, I can make things better again.

"But then my voice changes. I am frantic and bewildered when I shout out, to no one in particular, almost screaming: "He's not okay. He's not okay! Why is he twitching like that?"

"I'm not *telling* the reader how I feel . . . but I hope the way I create inner dialogue for those parts of the story shows how I feel. Now I'm going to work on doing this same thing in other places in my text."

ACTIVE ENGAGEMENT

Ask children to locate a powerful excerpt in the mentor text, to notice more about it, and then to bring that craft move to the "workbench" of their notebook.

"Writers, look back at your mentor text and pick out one or more spots where you found powerful writing. In the margin, jot down more that you notice the writer has done to create that power, that particular effect on the reader. You'll be annotating the text.

"Now, put this annotated text before you like a carpenter might pin up a picture of the bird house he aspires to make. Look at the entry you began yesterday. Some of you may be halfway through this, some of you may be done. Bring this entry to your workbench and see if you could use the strategy you've studied from the mentor text in your own writing. Do that now."

I circulated as I watched children work.

I crouched near Miles, curious to see what he had chosen to workbench. Miles had drawn a big circle around the following portion of his story, about the day he presented his father with his Father's Day gift.

> The point was covered with soft meadow grass, sprinkled with tiny wild flowers. I watched Dad take in this precious bit of the world and knew I had given him the right gift. Then from its hiding place I pulled out a fishing rod and laid it in Dad's hands.

"I want to show how grown-up this moment felt," Miles said. "Sandra Cisneros tells a lot about her characters by the words she uses. I want to do that also." As I watched Miles work, I saw him cross the words *pulled out* and replace them with *drew forth*. Leaning back to survey his work, he then added a bit of dialogue to the end of the passage, as he speaks to his father: "You deserve the honor of being first." Last but not least, he added the word *triumphantly* to his description of how he laid the rod in his father's hands.

One of the things to notice here is that in this section of the mentor text, I don't just bring out my feelings. Instead, those feelings evolve. It is as if there is a timeline to those feelings, a progression. Children tend to write as if a feeling is all-present, or absent.

This is as good a time as any to add the word annotate *to your writers' vocabularies. In fact, annotating mentor texts for specific craft moves is a long-term habit you'll want children to develop as they learn to read like writers.*

FIG. 14–1 Miles takes part of his story to the workbench.

LINK

Recap what you hope the minilesson has conveyed about using notebooks as workbenches and about reading-writing connections.

"Writers, early in this minilesson I asked you to think about how your writing process was apt to unfurl from writing entries, to selecting a seed idea, to drafting, revising. I suggested that today I was going to throw a wrench in your system.

"I'm hoping that you are coming from this session with a new image for what you can do in your writer's notebook. I'm hoping that from this day on, you realize that instead of collecting entry after entry in your writer's notebook, you can also use your notebook as a workbench, and deliberately practice some techniques in the notebook—just as Michael Jordan deliberately practiced his jump shots.

"And more than this, I hope you understand that if you want to learn from a mentor text, you can't just read the text and hope it rubs off on you. Instead, you need to actually work at learning from that person.

"Right now, will you think about the work you need to do today? As always, you have lots of choices. I expect some of you will use your notebook as a workbench and take some time to try something from our chart—or something else you noticed when studying 'Eleven.' I expect others of you will be finishing one entry or writing another. And even though I've thrown a wrench in your process, I know that you are all the kinds of writers who will keep yourselves moving through the process in a way that feels best for you. Today, as you work, you will likely also want to think about which entry might become your seed idea. You might find that the entry you take to your workbench becomes your new favorite and the one you want to take through the writing process. That is, you might find that making a mess of your thinking actually allows for you to come to some new, better ideas.

"If you need some reminders about ways 'Eleven' can improve your writing, draw on the items on our chart."

Lessons from Mentor Narratives

- Writers create the words a person could have said, doing this in ways that reveal the character as a person.
- Writers give reasons to explain the way a character acts.
- Writers show thinking by telling the exact words and the tone a character uses when thinking—like a dialogue with one's self.

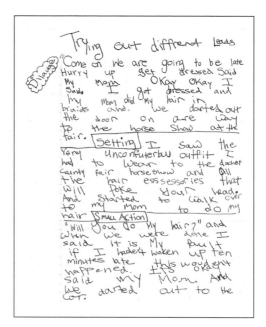

FIG. 14–2 Silas takes his lead to the workbench

Working with Determination Toward Goals

YOUR CONFERENCES AND SMALL GROUPS TODAY will prop kids up to work with purpose and determination toward concrete goals they selected for themselves during the active engagement section of the minilesson. Part of your role in this will be to cheer kids on; you'll carry around the mantra, "Try again, try again, try again" like a banner as you move from child to child, group to group. Meanwhile, it will be equally important that you steer students toward specific resources, including charts, books, other kids in the room, and of course their own backpack of resources, as they put that mantra to test.

As you confer with individual students or pull small groups, convey that using specific craft techniques with precision is essential to creating writing that will compel readers. Emphasize that readers, like writers, have choices. If readers don't connect with a character or feel engaged by a storyline, they can easily put down the book and pick up another. It's up to writers, then, to write deliberately, purposefully, drawing on all that they know about craft to write in ways that make the reader want to stick with their story.

If you pull a small group today, you might ask that they bring their notebooks with them to the carpet and begin applying whatever they marked in the mentor text to their own writing. Emphasize that they will be trying this out in lots of spots, doing it again and again and again, just as Michael Jordan did hundreds of jump shots in order to get them right.

As children work, walk around, peering over their shoulders and point out what you are noticing. Say things like, "I don't see it yet," and, "Can you show me how that's like what you marked in 'Eleven'? It's not clear to me."

After the group has written four or five lines, say, "Stop. Draw a line under the work you just did. Now, you're going to try it again, in another part of your writing, or in another way. This is hard work. Ask yourself, 'How will I make this even better?'"

Again, circle around as children work and this time, push them a little bit more. You might pull up next to a child and say, "Is this really your best? What do you think? I think you can do better. Look—right here in your published piece, you tried out this same strategy and it worked so well. I don't see that in here. I know you can do better than this."

You might say to the whole group, "You all have a strong grasp of what good writing looks like, and I'm not sure you're heeding that as you write entries. It's as if you're thinking about the sequence of the events in your story, but not about how the telling of those events should be crafted. Remember, to hold a reader's attention, to get that reader to keep reading your story, rather than giving it up for another, you have to pay attention not just to *what* you write but to *how* you write. So as you try this again, think more, craft purposefully. Ask yourself, 'Am I writing in a way that I will get my reader to want to keep going?' If you're stuck—maybe you're not sure how that might work in an entry, look around the room. All around you are resources. There are passages in books you can reread, charts of reminders, other students whose work you can reference—and whose techniques you can try out in your own writing." *(continues)*

MID-WORKSHOP TEACHING   Try and Try Again

"Writers, remember that taking something to the workbench is *not* easy work. Have you ever heard the saying 'Rome wasn't built in a day'? It means that all good things take time, practice, and dedication. So if you find your momentum fading, give yourself a little boost. Tell yourself that you can do better. Ask yourself, 'How will I make this even better?' Then, draw a line under the work you just did and try it again, in another way.

"Don't forget to use our chart, 'Techniques for Raising the Level of Narrative Writing,' as you work to make your writing better."

(continues)

Techniques for Raising the Level of Narrative Writing

- Dream the dream of the story and then write in a way that allows readers to experience the moment along with you.
- Revise using all you know about storytelling, not summarizing.
- Use all you know about grammar, spelling, and punctuation to edit as you write.
- Tell the story from **inside** it.
- Use details that are true to the event and that ring true.
- Use tools like the Narrative Writing Checklist to ask, "In what ways does my writing measure up? In what ways do I need to improve?" Then, revise your work to make it stronger.
- Ask: "What is my story really about?" and then write to bring forth that meaning.
- Bring out the story structure.
- Elaborate on important parts—parts that relate to what your story is really about.
- Incorporate scenes from the past or future to highlight the significance of your story.
- Don't simply end stories! Resolve problems, teach lessons, or makes changes that tie back to the big meaning of your story.
- Take your story to the workbench.

You might even ask kids if they've ever heard of the game "Steal the Old Man's Pack," a game in which players must, in a systematic way, grab other players' cards to win. Tell them that they can reach over, take another kid's notebook, steal a beginning—or

middle or end. Tell them that writers do that all the time. They actively copy techniques other writers have used to great effect. Then say, "Look, Max! Abigail has started the way you want to start. Borrow her notebook. Steal that beginning. Write off it."

Of course, to avoid having kids simply reach over and grab one another's notebooks, you may want to balance this suggestion with a proposal that each child in the group consider what he or she does well—and what he or she is trying to learn to do. Kids can then teach each other, swapping notebooks and techniques. In this way, you also set students up to feel like experts, even as they are working on something they may be struggling to perfect. Say to kids, "Use each other's talents. Amelia is such a great crafter of opening lines. She could help anyone who is struggling to write a good lead. And Sabrina is a master of show, not tell. Any of you who could use a little coaching in that, ask her what she's got."

You may need to remind children to use the very source they first turned to during the minilesson: Sandra Cisneros. Say something like, "Look at Sandra. She is sitting right next to us, on the carpet, and you're not using her. If you have to pretend you are talking to her, have someone read a bit of her text out loud and then say, 'I like the way you are . . .' and then try it in your own writing."

However you decide to run small groups or conferences today, in order for this concrete goal setting and repeat practice to feel like more than a one-day exercise, and more like a routine to add to the repertoire of things writers do to get better, you may want to have children put their goals up on an oversized checklist. Say something like, "As a community, we all want to make sure we're holding ourselves accountable to the goals we're setting. So when you feel like you've tried out your goal enough times that you want to

FIG. 14–3 Illana sets goals and works toward them

share what you did, show someone in the group, and then put your goal Post-it on the enlarged checklist I just hung up on the wall." (See Figure 14–4 in the Share.)

Writers Set Up Their Tools

Point out that many students don't have their tools—checklists, mentor texts, goal sheets—around them as they write. When working at a workbench, one needs tools to be on hand.

"Earlier, we talked about your writer's notebook as a workbench, as a place to use all your tools, trying things one way, then another way, until you get it right.

"But earlier, when I watched you working, I noticed many of you didn't have your tools on hand. One of the defining features of a workbench is that the tools are all nearby. If you're working on getting better as a writer—not just producing the same ol' same ol' stuff, then you need tools!

"So writers, like you, I'm writing entries—and I want these entries to be a lot better than the entries I wrote earlier this year. I'm not just going to pick up my pen, think up a story, and then let my pen fly, hoping for the best. Instead, I'm going to take the time to set myself up so that this piece of writing is apt to be the best I've ever done in my whole life.

"The first thing I get out is the Narrative Writing Checklist. I'm going to make sure that I'm holding myself accountable to *all* these goals, so I'll put the checklist right beside me as I write. I'll also have my goals beside me.

"Then the next thing I'm going to have out as I write is my final draft from earlier in the unit. Starting tomorrow you'll set to work on developing a new piece that you will publish and you will want to make sure it is the best piece of your life. So, will you be thinking about what seed idea you'll choose? Tonight you'll have a chance to write one last entry before you choose your best one. Then make your decision about your best entry and come into class tomorrow with your seed idea marked with a paper clip so you'll be ready to dive into working."

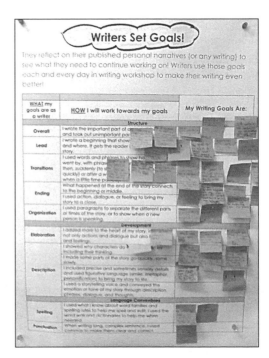

FIG. 14–4   One classroom's goal-setting chart

ONE LAST ENTRY

Writers, sometimes, in order to do your best work, it is helpful to set up a place where you can do your very best writing, and then to let your pen fly! Tonight, write an entry. But try, this time, to go straight to the very most important topic, to the most poignant moment, and get it onto the page. Tomorrow you'll be choosing another seed idea, so this is your last chance to get another contender into the mix.

When you write, use all the tools that you have for writing to write a new, better-than-best entry. You will definitely want to have "Eleven" by your side, your Narrative Writing Checklist, and your previously published piece so you can draw on everything you know about writing narratives well and then push yourself to extend that.

After you write this entry, read over all your entries—including the ones you gathered at the start of the year, and choose your seed idea. Put a paper clip on that entry so we can start tomorrow by working with it.

138

Stretching Out the Tension

I N "ELEVEN," SANDRA CISNEROS pulls many beautiful writing moves out of her sleeve. We've read this story with graduate students and with ten-year-olds, and each time, students see something in it that entrances them. One reason we particularly love the text is that its writing craft is so visible. There is a kind of exaggerated quality to the dialogue—Mrs. Price is so very arrogant, and there is an equally exaggerated quality to the character's emotions—the misery young Rachel feels is so despairing, so physical in its portrayal. It is this exaggeration that makes the story so gripping, and that also reveals some of its craft to young writers.

Donald Murray once wrote: "Writing is a craft before it is an art; writing may appear magic, but it is our responsibility to take our students backstage to watch the pigeons being tucked up the magician's sleeve." In the first sessions of this bend, writers had the opportunity to study and experiment with the particular bits of Sandra Cisneros's story that most struck them. Often those bits are the dialogue and the sensory detail—the way characters feel emotions in their bodies. They can practically feel Rachel's mortification. They find themselves wanting to jump up and push the disgusting sweater away. While they may not have written this way in their own drafts (yet), they recognize the effect of heated dialogue and strong emotion and thus are well positioned to try out this craft as writers.

There is another move that Sandra Cisneros makes that could be transformational for your writers. She structures the red sweater portion of the text as a story, not as a chronicle of events. She's a storyteller, not a diary writer. A storyteller knows how to control tension, to maintain a sense of building emotion, to not release, too soon, that sense of uncertainty, of "what will happen." Even if, in life, the story you are telling happened in the blink of an eye, a storyteller will stretch it out, have the problem get worse and worse in small ways, giving the character and the reader more time to react. Interestingly, in *Blink*, Malcolm Gladwell (2007) shares how first responders—policemen, EMTs, firemen, those men and women who arrive when trouble arises, throw themselves into the moment so thoroughly that they often describe a sense of "slowing down." That is, they describe being able to see a sequence of actions, sense many details, and make many decisions, all in what is really

IN THIS SESSION, you'll teach students that writers think carefully about how to structure their stories. One way they think about structure is to stretch out the problem, telling it bit by bit.

GETTING READY

✔ Each child's writer's notebook, with them in the meeting area for the lesson with a seed idea identified with a paper clip (see Connection)

✔ Narrative Writing Checklist, Grades 5 and 6 (see Link)

COMMON CORE STATE STANDARDS: W.5.3, W.5.4, W.5.5, RL.5.1, RL.5.5, SL.5.1, SL.5.2s, SL.5.4, L.5.1, L.5.2, L.5.3

the blink of an eye. It's why they are in these jobs and we are not. It's the same with elite athletes—in *Consider the Lobster*, David Foster Wallace (2007) shares how pro tennis players see the ball, consider their swing, make a lot of decisions, all in a single moment. Not all of us will learn to live that way—but we can learn to story-tell that way, to slow down the problem, to insert multiple moments of strain or pressure. In "Eleven," the sweater isn't just given to Rachel. First it is held up, then it is put on her desk, then she has to put it on. For Rachel, and the reader, it is an unbearable period, as the problem gets worse and worse.

> *"Even if the story you are telling happened in the blink of an eye, a storyteller will stretch it out, have the problem get worse and worse in small ways, giving the character and the reader more time to react."*

In this session, then, you'll lead your writers to consider advanced storytelling structure as they begin planning then drafting. Drafting, where they really put their story to paper, is a perfect moment to consider stretching out the trouble, telling it bit by bit, with each bit getting a bit worse. When drafting personal narratives especially, it's important to write as a storyteller, not a diarist. Stretching out the trouble, along with the craft that students have already studied so intently, should help your students write as writers, with the merciless attention to detail, the crafting of tiny moments, that make stories so compelling.

Stretching Out the Tension

CONNECTION

Convene writers in the meeting area and give them a vision for the week ahead.

"Writers, when you come to the meeting area, bring your notebook, which should have a paper clip marking your seed idea. So writers, you've got a seed idea—and in five days, you'll need to have taken yourself through the writing process—to have drafted probably more than one draft, revised, edited, and be ready to publish. By the end of the workshop on the fifth day, I expect your fully revised and edited draft to be ready for publication that night. That way we'll be ready for what will be a grand celebration of not only this bend, but this unit.

People benefit from clear expectations, from knowing the big picture.

Call to mind a familiar scene from a story or film where the trouble is stretched out in an episodic, bit-by-bit, ever-getting-worse manner.

"So today, I know you'll be drafting—and you know a lot about how to write a draft really, really well. Will you list across your fingers four things you will want to remember to do as you write your first draft?" I listed across my fingers as the kids did as well.

"Now, writers, I'm going to teach you about one more thing you can keep in mind as you write your draft today. Have you ever seen a sad or scary movie where there is one part that you can't forget?" I looked around at the nods and shudders from some.

I chose this moment from Titanic *because I knew my avid nonfiction readers had devoured books about it, and that other children had both seen the film and read versions of the story. Choosing an example that you think is current and accessible to your children helps you refer to storytelling craft in multiple media and shows your students that every kind of "text" can be a mentor text. If you look up "Titanic Sinking Scene" on YouTube, you could also choose to show this scene, which is approximately fifty seconds in length and pretty unforgettable.*

"I have too . . . in particular I'm thinking about the end of *Titanic*. I know the boat is going to sink, we all do, but it's still so painstakingly horrible to watch. First it fills with water, one floor, after another, after another. Then it tips upwards, almost in slow motion, so that it is perpendicular to the water. Finally, the ship and its passengers slide down into the sea." I used my hands to illustrate the sequence. "There is something unbearable about that sequence of events and how it slowly gets worse and worse—unbearable and beautiful. You can't forget it, right?

"Writers, I think this could be very important to you as you begin planning and drafting. Will you keep in mind the notion that you can structure your story so that the problem builds, and tension builds, just as they do in *Titanic*? You've been thinking about the craft that writers use—now it might be important to think about what they do with structure as well."

The teaching section of this session will look closely at "Eleven" again, and so you want to move directly from your connection into teaching, leaving time to unpack the structure of the text there.

❖ **Name the teaching point.**

"Writers, today I want to teach you that when writers set out to draft, they think about structure and they make an effort to structure their story, not 'how it happened in real life,' but as a compelling story. It's often helpful to call to mind how writers we admire slow down the problem in their writing, telling it bit by bit to make it a more compelling story."

TEACHING

Share your process as you tackle structure by first thinking about how an author you admire structures a story. Emphasize that authors don't just chronicle what happened, they craft a compelling story.

"I'm thinking this means you have to stop thinking about 'exactly how the story happened.' Instead you have to think like writers, and think 'How do I want to this story to go?' It's like you have to take off the hat that is you remembering, and put on your writers' hat.

"Let's give this a try together. So, first, let's think about how Sandra Cisneros tells the story of the red sweater. I'm picturing the story in my mind. Are you doing the same?" I waited for nods.

"Let's pay attention now to how she structures 'Eleven'—and specifically to how Sandra Cisneros stretches out the problem. Remember that the *Titanic* doesn't just 'sink,' and in the same way Sandra Cisneros doesn't just 'put the sweater on Rachel.' You know the story—think about the sequence of events that happen with the sweater. When you have those clearly in your mind, put a thumbs-up." I waited a moment for thumbs to go up. "Quick, turn and tell your partner, across your fingers, how events unfold with the sweater. I'll listen in.

"Writers, I heard you retell what happened with the sweater. First, Mrs. Price held up the sweater, and it was described in detail as something disgusting. What happened next?"

"Mrs. Price holds it up in front of the whole class," Rie began, "nobody said that it was theirs."

Caleb's hand shot up. "Then Sylvia said that it was Rachel's!"

I gestured for Takuma to pick up where Caleb left off. "And then Mrs. Price puts the gross sweater on Rachel's desk and Rachel tries to tell her to stop but she can't say anything. No words come out."

The class continued on with their detailed recounting, each adding more to the details of Rachel's horrendous ordeal. When we had finished, I asked, "Does that capture the sequence of events?" I looked around for nods.

"Well, writers, one thing that seems clear now is how Cisneros made it so that what happened with the sweater kept getting worse and worse. She didn't begin with Rachel having to put it on. Instead, she created a series of escalating bits with the sweater, a step-by-step retelling of Rachel's experience, and at each step Rachel got more upset."

You will want to have a copy of "Eleven" in hand—or at least a few, powerful sections.

As children retell the various parts of the sweater incident, be sure to encourage them to remember each and every detail that occurs. You can ask children to return to the text itself, rereading to capture the nuanced way Cisneros stretches out this one moment. If possible, help children notice the tiny, minute ways Cisneros builds tension—Rachel's open mouth and ensuing silence, the way she ever-so-carefully pushes the sweater to the corner of her desk. These are the details that grab us by the collar and leave us suspended, waiting for more.

Model for students how, like Sandra Cisneros, you can build rising tension in your own story.

"I think you can do this too. You just have to plan your stories more deliberately—you have to make sure that you don't go to the worst part of the problem too fast.

"I'll give it a go, so we can see how tricky this is. You know my story. I was planning on drafting it in these parts," I held up a finger for each as I spoke. "First, Luka and I were walking. Second, the part where Luka ran ahead and I heard those awful sounds. Third, there's the part where we picked him up, and he was already dying. Fourth, finally, at the end, would be the part where we decide where to bury him."

I said these parts again over my fingers. "We're walking . . . Luka gets hit . . . holding Luka . . . finding a spot to bury him."

Slow down your demonstration, thinking aloud in front of the children, emphasizing how you'll plan out the parts of your story so they will build, with the trouble getting worse and worse.

I looked up at the ceiling as if thinking, then, still looking a bit over the kids' heads, thinking aloud, I started musing. "I guess, if I were to structure my story like Sandra Cisneros does, building lots of tension as a storyteller, I'd have to tell the problem in bits, and also have my emotions build. Let's see," I paused, visibly thinking. "Maybe it starts with Luka running towards the road. I could watch him, and maybe whisper to myself, 'Be careful, boy.' Then, maybe I catch sight of an oncoming car, speeding quickly down the road. I could glance at Luka, then at the car, then at Luka again. There could be some beeping, and the car slamming on its brakes. Then maybe there is a clear thud, and that's when things get worse—and where my emotions get more serious, too."

I looked up at the students again. "Writers, I have to tell you, I would have just told my story the way it happened—and it felt as if it happened so fast—had we not talked about this. But now I'm wearing my 'writer's hat,' thinking about what Cisneros did with 'Eleven,' and this helps me plan all these tiny bad moments with Luka, like Sandra had with her sweater. I'll plan to have the problem and my emotions slowly get worse so that the story isn't over too quickly."

Share particular insights gained from trying this work.

"Writers, after trying this myself I'm realizing two things. One is, I'll have to escalate—that means build up—parts of my story. I'll have to build from the part where Luka runs off to the part where he gets hit. The second thing—I'll have to be careful to not make the first bit of the problem so bad that it can't get worse. I'll have to think across the parts, like a writer, as I'm drafting."

Notice how I quickly transfer the work we saw Sandra Cisneros doing to my own story, modeling with my own story before asking the children to transfer the strategy to their own writing.

Don't be tempted to "dumb down" the language you use when teaching children. Exposing students to a variety of sophisticated language is the best way to ensure that these words become part of their vocabulary, as well.

ACTIVE ENGAGEMENT

Channel students to think of the parts of their stories and then plan out how the problem will escalate across these parts. Invite them to rehearse with their partners, a now-familiar method.

"Let's give you a chance to plan how you'll structure the problem in your drafts as well. Think about the parts of your story—plan out the parts, like I did, on your fingers or in your mind. When you have those parts clear, give a thumbs-up."

I waited a moment for thumbs to go up. "Now, think just about the problem in your story. How could you stretch out the problem so that the tension escalates and builds? How will your problem get worse and worse? Use your partner to rehearse a bit, right now, the way you know how."

Francesca turned to her partner, Sabrina, and began to rehearse. Holding one finger up, she said: "First I grabbed my purple sled and my sister, Camilla." Then, raising her second finger, she continued. "I felt snowy fog rush through my hair like a cloud pushing me." She continued on, raising a finger for each new part of her story. "I wasn't scared. Then my sled started to move. It moved an inch. Then it was moving very fast. I spotted a man at the bottom of the hill." She continued to story-tell and I moved on to listen in on other partnerships.

LINK

Remind writers the time frame for their piece of writing, of their options for today, and then send them off to work.

"Writers, you have a ton of work today so I know you are raring to go off and get started. Likely many of you will be making quick plans and then drafting and others of you might still feel that you want to spend some time developing your stories. What I want to remind you of is that your piece is due in five days. You might use the Narrative Writing Checklist to help remind yourself of the goals you're aspiring towards. Today is your first full workshop to dive into the process; I expect—and you should expect—that you'll be working very hard."

Using Leveled Student Writing to Pinpoint Next Steps

A S YOU CONFER AND LEAD SMALL GROUPS, you'll often want to carry the fifth-grade leveled student writing samples for narrative with you, as well as the checklist. When you read over a youngster's work and listen to the description of what he's doing, part of what you will be doing is thinking, "Where is this child in the learning progression of narrative writing?"

I was drawn to Emily's desk because after writing a quick entry, she immediately set to work jotting marginal notes, checking the draft, and so forth. (See Figure 15–1.)

(continues)

> The Horses Eyes
>
> ② Emily   9/17   10/29   Box A out!
>
> *Info* he were riding bikes in the golf course in our hotel in Lancaster, Pennsilvania, then I saw some horses. I stood there for a minute just staring. One horse started to walk up to the fence it's eyes twinkled, I think was the leader because then another horse came with the same type of sparkely eyes, and then after another horses kept on coming to the fence about an inch away from me. Then there was 10 horses all with sparkety eyes staring at me. They stood there waiting and then when we started to leave they were still waiting. Then we rode away and 5 minutes later my dad saw an apple tree and we both had the urge to feed the horses.

FIG. 15–1   Emily annotates her writing.

MID-WORKSHOP TEACHING
Secondary Characters' Emotions Can Also Escalate

"Writers, I noticed Francesca looking back intently at 'Eleven' as you were drafting, and I asked her what was particularly catching her attention. What she said relates to our new ideas about how stories escalate, or build up in tension.

"Francesca was looking at the bits of 'Eleven' where Mrs. Price responds to Rachel and what she does with the sweater. Francesca noticed that it's not just that Rachel gets more and more upset. Mrs. Price gets more and more upset also. At first she just seems annoyed, then she gets loud, then listen to these lines. This is when Rachel pushes the sweater to the edge of the desk:

> "Rachel," Mrs. Price says. She says it like she's getting mad.
> "You put that sweater on right now and no more nonsense."

"Writers, this is almost like Mrs. Price has her own mountain of emotions or her own arc. First she is annoyed, then is more upset and almost a little frantic, right? If you drew a big mountain, you could see how her emotions escalated until the middle and then they started to quiet down. She has a full arc of emotion.

"So, in her draft, Francesca is planning not only for how her trouble will get worse, and how her own emotions will get more intense, but also how the other characters' emotions will get more intense, too. If you are looking to really build tension, you might try the trick Francesca discovered, as well. You might quickly return to your plans and look them over to think about the arcs of your characters—not just your major, but also your secondary."

When I asked Emily to explain why she'd jotted marginal notes such as "First see horses," "about the leader horse," and "scene changes," she explained that she really liked the entry and wanted to rewrite it rather than collecting another entry and she figured she needed to break it into paragraphs, expanding each one. Therefore, the section of the text that said "about the leader horse" was a place where she'd write more about the leader horse, and so on.

I sat, perplexed, for a moment because I was thrilled that Emily had taken the idea of annotating the entry seriously, and I was glad she was spending time planning her next draft. When she told me she planned to elaborate on the next draft, I was even more pleased—the checklist had made her writing more purposeful. I knew I would congratulate her on this. But on the other hand, I didn't sense the revisions she was planning would yield a more effective story.

The good thing was that because I had the fifth-grade checklist and two benchmark pieces of writing, I was able to scan them and come up with what I sensed was the point Emily needed to tackle. Her story was a chronicle of an event. She and her dad saw horses in a field, the horses approached them, Emily and her dad drove on remembering the horses. But this wasn't yet a story. In part, she needed to figure out what the story was really about. Was this a father-daughter story? A story about Emily wanting a pet?

I pointed out to Emily that she didn't just need to extend her lead and her ending. She needed to figure out what the story was really about and then make the whole story build onto that. In the checklist, the lead and ending both need to relate to what will be a problem for the main character. I left her with benchmark texts and with the suggestion to continue planning that all-important next draft.

Check That Each Character Has an Arc

Gather the writers at the meeting area and show them a way to check that each character has an arc that will lead to a satisfying conclusion.

"Writers, I've been watching you all diving into planning and drafting and I want to give you a tip that a real professional writer once gave me about structuring my story. Sarah Weeks, who is the author of books like *Pie* and *So B. It*, which you all love, taught me that every character needs to have an arc in the story. So here's what she does before she writes. She takes a big piece of rope and lays it out on the floor like this in the shape of a mountain. Then she takes index cards or Post-its and she writes the major events of the story and makes sure the story is structured with plenty of rising tension and a stretched out climax. But then she also takes index cards and she jots down the different emotions the main character will experience through the course of the story and she uses the rope arc to check that those emotions naturally build and escalate and then resolve. Then, she does that for each character.

"Sarah says that an arc is one of the most key aspects of a story and that without a strong, full arc, the story just won't work. Making sure each character has an arc is a way for readers to go on a journey with the people in your story, and experience their emotions and feel satisfied at the conclusion. That tiny detail at the end of 'Eleven,' when Mrs. Price pretends like everything is okay, completes her character arc. We know that her emotions have died down and she may even feel slightly embarrassed. And Rachel's arc is completed too—we know that she feels so much younger than her eleven years and is devastated by what has happened to her—a sad ending but satisfying because that's the only real way the arc could be completed."

Set writers up to check that each of the people in their stories has a strong arc.

"So right now, many of you have planned and are elbows deep in drafting, but I want to tell you that it is important to pull back and check the arc of your story throughout your drafting, not just when you start. So right now, will you see if you can sketch out an arc for the main characters in your story and make sure that your plan will lead that character on a journey with a satisfying conclusion for the reader? If you have time, do this for a secondary character, too."

In the fall of 2012, Sarah Weeks taught a writing class at Teachers College and this is when she showed us this interesting method of planning.

REVISING STORY ARCS

During today's share, each of you checked to make sure that your main character goes on a journey and comes to some sort of resolution at the end. Some of you tried this with a secondary character too. Many of you realized that some of your characters were missing strong, full arcs, and that because of this, the story just isn't working.

Tonight, take time to revise based on what you noticed today. If a character is missing something in his or her story arc—a moment of tension, a satisfying ending—add that in. Be sure that each of your characters takes a journey in your story.

If you finish this work quickly, begin revising your piece in other ways. Step back, reread your piece, and be a critical reader. Ask, "What is this piece of writing missing? What part feels weak to me?" and then use your backpack of revision strategies to make it better.

Catching the Action or Image that Produced the Emotion

OFTEN, IN A FIRST ATTEMPT to balance action and dialogue, children sprinkle the external plotline of a story with dashes of thought. They might write "I did this, then I thought this." And while they are right to work toward this balance, what is missing is the true connection between the external action and the internal story. In essence, we must teach children to capture the exact action that made them react the way they did.

It isn't the easiest thing for a child to pull out a piece of paper, catch a tiny moment from the burst of his life and put it down. "Write as if you were a movie camera," John Gardner says. "The trick is to get it down precisely . . . what you really noticed." But it isn't easy, even for Hemingway.

For Hemingway, he called it a problem of *depiction*. While writing, he'd ask "What was the precise action that produced, evoked, my emotion?" And he'd wake in the night searching for that real sequence of action and response. "Waking in the night," he writes, "I tried to remember what it was that seemed just out of my remembering and that was the thing that I had really seen . . . ."

It is worth teaching children this work that all the best narrative writers struggle—and then manage—to do: "and, finally, remembering all around it, I got it. When he [the matador] stood up, his face white and dirty and the silk of his breeches opened from waist to knee, it was the dirtiness of the rented breeches, the dirtiness of his slit underwear and the clean, clean, unbearably clean whiteness of the thigh bone that I had seen, and it was that which was important."

Authors of all ages will struggle to get it right, to make the writing be true to life, to catch that very specific detail of the clean, clean, unbearably clean whiteness of the thigh bone. An image that stark carries its own emotional weight. It produced an emotion when the writer originally saw it. When Hemingway reveals it to the reader, it has equal power to evoke emotion.

This is a big lesson in narrative craft: perfected by Hemingway to Cisneros and all the great writers in between. Narrators tell a story bit by bit—and by now your students have

IN THIS SESSION, you'll teach students that writers think about which actions or images happened before they felt or thought something, and then they write those exact actions or images on the page to evoke the same emotions or thoughts in readers.

GETTING READY

✔ Excerpts from "Eleven" prepared for the overhead or on chart paper (see Teaching)

✔ An additional excerpt from "Eleven" that will be used to teach similes (see Conferring and Small-Group Work)

✔ Your story to share on the overhead (see Teaching, Mid-Workshop Teaching, and Share)

✔ An additional excerpt from "Eleven" that will be used to teach repeating images (see Mid-Workshop Teaching) and metaphor (see Share)

COMMON CORE STATE STANDARDS: W.5.3.b,d; W.5.5, RL.5.1, RL.5.3, SL.5.1, L.5.1, L.5.2, L.5.3, L.5.5.a

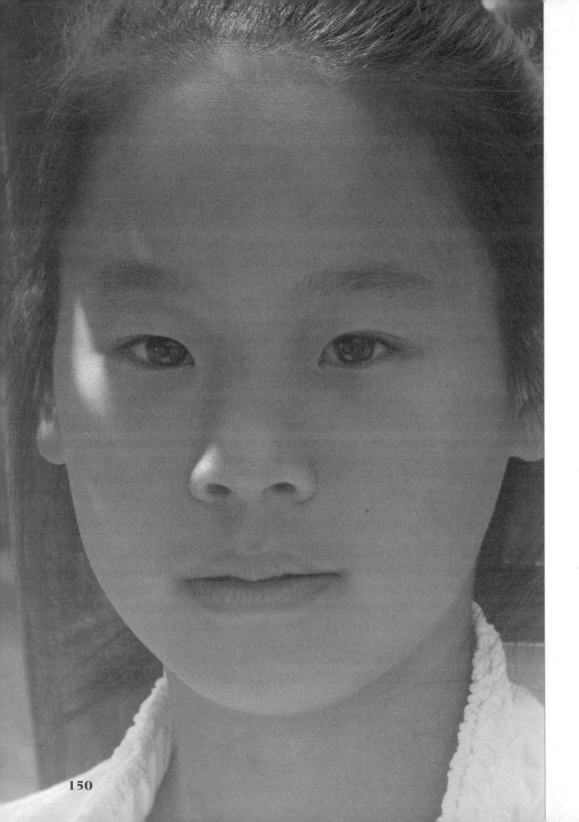

learned to do this. Narrators balance action with thought—and your students have learned to do this, too. Now there is one next step to teach your students. True narrative craft captures on the page the exact image, the exact action—that minute twitch or hushed word or the wafting smell—that provoked the emotional oomph. The writer must dig into his own truest memories (and his imagination) to find that finite detail or split second that yanked so hard at his own heartstring. And then, rifling through the assortment of language in his head, the writer lays this twitch—this stark image—bare on the page, for the reader.

"Write as if you were a movie camera."

And so Rachel doesn't need to explain what she felt about the ugly sweater on her desk. The image of it shoved to the "tippy-tip corner of her desk" till it's "hanging all over the edge like a waterfall" makes the reader shift uncomfortably away from the offensive thing. She doesn't need hollow adjectives to describe a sweater that smells like cottage cheese. She doesn't need to explain that she is trying not to cry. Her action—squeezing her eyes shut tight and biting down on her teeth real hard—reaches out and clenches the reader's own heart.

The work of this lesson is to teach your writers to take cues from "Eleven," and dig into their own memory of the precise action or image that stirred them, and to put this faithfully, in its most precisely honest form, on the paper.

Catching the Action or Image that Produced the Emotion

CONNECTION

Share two brief writing samples with children, one that summarizes an action and another that plays this action out with images that evoke emotion.

"Writers, I want to share a revision I recently made in a true story I was writing. I won't share the whole story, just the tiny revision. Are you ready? This was my original draft:

> I was fishing. I cast out. I held the fishing rod still. After a long while I caught a fish. I loosened the hook from its mouth. My heart soared, and I thought, "I did it." But later I wondered why I had done it.

"The next draft went like this."

> I was fishing. I cast out. I held the fishing rod still. Then I felt the tiniest of tugs. "That's it: a fish!" I thought. "I did it." After I had loosened the hook from its mouth, I held the sunny in my hand, its gills breathing in and out, its mouth opening and closing ever so slightly. "Why did I do this?" I thought.

Invite students to compare the two writing samples and decide which is more effective.

"Could you turn to your partner and discuss, for a bit, what I was trying to do in my latest revision?"

The children talked, and predictably they mentioned that the last version was more detailed. After a moment, I stepped in. "I hear many of you saying that the second sentence has more detail. But writers, what I want you to notice is that I haven't added any ol' detail. I have added the exact detail that prompted me to have the thoughts that I include. And it is that—the exact detail, then the thought, the reaction—that makes a story ring true. 'I held the sunny in my hand, it's gills breathing in and out....'"

This is an unusual connection. Break stride. It's another way to signal to your children, "Listen up."

I've chosen to begin by spotlighting an example of what I will teach children to do today. I hope to give them a clear, coherent vision for the work we'll be doing, and the ways in which they will revise their writing.

❧ Name the teaching point.

"Today I want to teach you that when writing a story, you aim to put the exact thing that you—or the character—did or saw before you thought something, felt something. As you write, you try to recall how it went. You ask, 'What was the exact sequence of actions?' Then you put that sequence onto the page so the reader can go through those actions too, and have those reactions."

Model noticing the way a published author uses true details to evoke emotion.

"Before we try to do this on our own, let's look at an excerpt from 'Eleven.' As I read this, ask yourself: Has Sandra Cisneros put the exact sequence of actions that led Rachel to have the thought, 'Not mine, not mine?'"

I began reading, beginning with the part where Mrs. Price places the red sweater on Rachel's desk.

> *But when the sick feeling goes away and I open my eyes, the red sweater's still sitting there like a big red mountain. I move the red sweater to the corner of my desk with my ruler. I move my pencil and books and eraser as far from it as possible. I even move my chair a little to the right. Not mine, not mine, not mine.*
>
> *In my head I'm thinking how long till lunch time, how long till I can take the red sweater and throw it over the steel yard fence, or leave it hanging on a parking meter, or bunch it up into a little ball and toss it in the alley.*

"Cisneros could have written it like this:

> *When the sick feeling goes away and I open my eyes, the red sweater's still sitting there like a big red mountain. I thought, "That's not my sweater," and I moved my things—my pencil, books, eraser, and chair—far away from the red sweater.*

"Writers, what I want to suggest is that Cisneros' version is worlds better, not just because it is more detailed, but because it has the exact sequence of how this went. It captures the actions in order. 'I move the red sweater to the corner of my desk with my ruler. I move my pencil and books and eraser as far from it as possible. I even move my chair.' These precise actions, these precise images, help the reader understand Rachel's response: 'Not mine. Not mine.' These deliberate images make us loathe the sweater just as Rachel does."

Model taking this strategy to your own writing, attempting to isolate the exact action or image that evoked your most powerful response.

"Will you help me take a look at my own writing? The moment that evoked the most emotion for me was the moment when I saw Luka lying there, after he had been hit by a car." I revealed a portion of my story on chart paper.

> It was then that I heard the sounds. There was a screech, a thud, and a whine so full of pain that my heart stopped beating.

This portion of Cisneros's writing is a perfect example of the strategy we hope to teach. Each sentence details an exact sequence of events and images that lead the main character, Rachel, to react the way she does. Cisneros does this so successfully, that we, as readers, find ourselves whispering 'Not mine, not mine,' as well.

I call this a nonexample—an example of what an author could have done had he or she not implemented a certain strategy. It can be helpful for children to see a 'bad' non-example, as it accentuates what you hope to highlight in the positive example.

Watch how this same text threads through the unit yet again.

"What . . . Where . . . Where's Luka?" I didn't know my older sister was running through the field behind me until I heard her panic-filled voice. I turned to look at her but found I couldn't answer. Together we ran till we were beside the furry body that had curled into itself, now heaving gently.

"Luka?" I heard my voice break as I knelt beside him.

"But what, exactly, led me to respond the way I did, to kneel beside him in horror and whisper, 'Luka?' Yes, it was the shock of seeing Luka lying there, curled into himself. But there was more." I looked out toward the room, visibly trying to recreate the moment in my mind. "I already included the part about his heaving chest." I looked back out towards the room, then suddenly turned back to the children, having found my answer. "It was his tongue," I said, almost as if to myself. "As he lay there, a tiny little bit of his tongue was sticking out. It was so little and pink, so vulnerable, and it reminded me of earlier that morning, when he ran about freely with his tongue hanging out!" I took a marker and began to add to my story.

Together we ran till we were beside the furry body that had curled into itself, now heaving gently. With each breath, a tiny, pink tip of tongue peeked through his lips—nothing like the tongue that had hung recklessly from his mouth moments earlier. "Luka?" I heard my voice break as I knelt beside him.

Debrief. Name what you hope children are learning.

"Do you see how I did that? As I wrote, I tried to recall the exact sequence of actions and images. I aimed to put the exact thing that I was seeing before I felt something. Then, I put that image onto the page so that the reader could experience it too, and have the same reactions as I did.

"Today I want to teach you that when writing a story, you aim to put the exact thing that you—or the character—did before you thought something, felt something. As you write, you try to recall how it went. You ask, 'What was was the exact sequence of actions?' Then you put that onto the page so the reader can go through those actions too, and have those reactions."

ACTIVE ENGAGEMENT

Set writers up to focus on a specific part of their story and call to mind some of the specific images associated with that part, considering the emotion they want to convey to the reader.

"Writers, right now will you open your notebook and look at those quick sketches of character arcs that you did yesterday? Choose one section of your piece that comes into your mind as important right now. In a minute, I'll ask you to close your eyes and step into that moment again. Think about an emotion that you want the reader to feel. I gave them a minute to think. "Okay, this time as you let the movie of that moment unfurl in your mind, make yourself feel the emotion you most want to convey. I gave them a long moment and began voicing over quietly to scaffold their thinking. "What smells, sights, sounds are there? Be precise." I gave them another moment. "Okay, writers turn and tell your partner that moment in a bit-by-bit way, conveying the actions or images that evoked that emotion. Partner 2, you'll tell your story, and Partner 1 will you listen and let Partner 2 know what feelings you were having as you were listening? Okay, turn and talk."

Convene writers and highlight examples that you think would benefit the whole class.

"Writers, let me gather you for a moment. I was just listening in as Sabera told her partner, Takuma, about the part in her story where she looks over the ledge of a boat and realizes she is too scared to jump into the water. But listen to Sabera's first version and see if you notice the same thing Takuma did." I read from Sabera's piece.

> I glanced over the side of the boat and into the crystal-clear water. I saw fish—yellow, green, rainbow—swimming by. "I can't do it. I won't go in the water!" I sad to my dad.

After reading this portion of Sabera's writing, I turned to the children. Takuma said, "I don't get it! The water sounds beautiful. It makes me want to go swimming right now." The children giggled. Sabera realized that Takuma had pointed out a problem in her writing—she had written with true, exact details, but she had not written about the actions or images that led her to fear going into the water. After talking a bit, Sabera realized that the fish didn't look beautiful to her at all—in fact, they looked scary. I said, "Today, Sabera's going to work on revising the details she includes about the fish, so that her reader understands the action and image (looking down into the water full of big fish) that led to her response."

LINK

Send writers off to continue to take themselves through the process, reminding them that they have four days left, (including today), to work.

"Writers, you have four days left, including today, to produce the best narratives of your life. Will you think about what you will do the minute you leave the rug? Visualize the exact image of what you will do first. Thumbs-up if you see yourself hard at work and know your first step today." Thumbs popped up immediately. "Writers, as you work keep reminding yourself of all you have learned to raise the craft and structure of your piece. Go!"

As children talk, listen carefully for examples that will be worth sharing with the class. You'll want to spotlight the work of a child or two that is successful with the work, but that perhaps tackles some predictable problems the writers in the class have been facing. In this way, you don't just share, but also teach.

Supporting Effective Use of Figurative Language

AS STUDENTS ATTEMPT TO CAPTURE IMAGES AND EMOTIONS, you may find that they sprinkle in figurative language, but that it doesn't reinforce their ideas. In this case, you'll want to teach them to identify the places where they have used similes, metaphors, or another form of figurative language, and channel them to ask themselves: How does this writing help to show what my story is really about? It is common for students to enjoy writing with figurative language. Once they are exposed to it through their reading or writing lives, it tends to show up everywhere.

On this particular day, I taught a small-group lesson that began, "Yesterday, Marlin and I were reading his personal narrative. There's a scene where he's sitting with his mom at the vet's office waiting to find out if his dog has survived surgery. He does such a great job helping us understand the depths of his sadness and worry. But when the nurse comes into the waiting room to tell him the news, he writes, 'I jumped from my chair like a Jack-in-the-Box.' As Marlin was reading this, he said, 'Wait! That sounds really happy, but I was actually still really worried.'

"Marlin did careful work, noticing that! He was using a simile, which was a cool thing to try, but he realized that it was not showing the idea he wanted to show. So, he decided to take it out unless he could find one that actually fit what he was trying to show."

To further support their use of figurative language, channel students to study mentor examples. For example, students can examine the description of Rachel crying in "Eleven," noticing the use of figurative language that this time all combines to show the growing overwhelming sadness Rachel feels. At first she cries, "animal noises coming uncontrollably out of her mouth," then it quiets into "shakes like hiccups." These are similes that are used by the author to strategically convey the main character's emotions.

MID-WORKSHOP TEACHING
Significant Images Recur Across a Piece

"Writers, can I have your eyes and attention? As you are working to create these precise, powerful images in your pieces, I want to teach you that when images recur across a piece, they take on more meaning.

"Think of how that red sweater comes up over and over and over in 'Eleven'— we know how important it is. And when images do recur across a piece, and become even more significant, they can also become symbolic and help to convey the larger meaning of the story.

"So let's look at my story for a minute." I displayed my story to the class. "That image of Luka bounding out of doors, happy and carefree." I pointed to the beginning of my story, and continued, "that image repeats in my story. It repeats because that moment is significant. That's the last time Luka is alive and it symbolizes his joy and his life. See how I refer to that moment again in little ways throughout the piece? Like here," I pointed to further down the page, "when we walk across the field that he had 'run through so joyfully that morning?' And here again at the end," I pointed, "when I remember that I wasn't very nice to Luka in the morning, I'm helping the reader to recall that moment again. As that image repeats, it conveys to the reader that I wished I'd been more grateful and enjoyed being in that moment with him, and it helps to forward my meaning. Another image that repeats is the image of his tongue. Hanging happily from his mouth, and then just a tiny speck as he lay on the road.

So, right now, will you look at the plan and arc of your story and think about a moment or an object that is significant? Think about ways that image could recur. Try it and you'll find that your story becomes more significant and also more cohesive. Okay, back to work!"

Creating Metaphorical Images

Gather writers and let them know that some images can be metaphorical. Look together at an example of this from "Eleven."

"Writers, can I have your eyes and attention? I want to remind you as you are working today that some of those precise, deliberate images and actions in your stories can be metaphorical. Let's think about some of the precise images Cisneros included in 'Eleven.'" I displayed a section of the text so the students could see the beginning. I tapped the fifth paragraph and underlined the words "Only today I wish I didn't have eleven years rattling inside of me like pennies in a tin Band-Aid box." "Think about that image. Rachel doesn't actually have pennies rattling inside of her, but Cisneros is using a simile to get us to see how Rachel feels about being eleven years old. Look at the choice of pennies and tin. Pennies and tin are not very valuable, and the sound of them rattling against each other is irritating and painful to the ears.

"So the whole phrase helps us to see that eleven years does not feel like much of anything good. Cisneros uses this figurative language because it evokes more emotion than if she had said, 'I still feel like a little kid.' In the same way that Sandra Cisneros lets us know that Rachel had eleven years rattling inside of her like pennies in a tin Band-Aid box or that she wants to be far away like a runaway balloon, like a tiny *o* in the sky, you can think metaphorically to create images that evoke emotions in your readers."

Demonstrate quickly coming up with a metaphorical image for your own story.

"So if I were to do this with my story about Luka, I might think about that image of Luka bounding down the field so happily, so innocently, not knowing what was coming. I might think to myself, 'What could I compare Luka to that would really get that point across to the reader and make the reader feel protective toward him?' I might say, 'Luka bounded down the field like a small child at play, all his muscles rippling.' Do you see how I'm comparing Luka to a child to get my readers to feel a certain way about him and to convey that image more precisely?"

Set writers up to think of metaphorical images for their own stories. Rally them to create a few of these.

"So right now, will you think about one of the images you have worked to create today? Will you consider how you might use figurative language such as a simile or a metaphor to help you to convey that image in a way that is even more precise? Open up your notebooks and jot some of these metaphorical images down. Try out a bunch." I gave them time to do this, watching as their heads bent over their writing.

Have writers share their best image with a partner.

"Okay, will you choose what you think is your best one and share that with a partner right now?"

I listened in as Sophie spoke. "I think the teddy bear in my story can be kind of like my relationship with Claudia. I want it to be like, I guess like a symbol that stands for our friendship. I need to work some on that, I think."

I moved on to Ori. "I think that when I'm describing how it felt to watch my parents fight, I want to show that it was like 'up and down, up and down.' It felt like being in a big storm. Or no, maybe it felt like being on one of those roller coasters (and with this, Ori gestured the up-hill then down-hill motions that roller coasters make). "It was definitely something like that."

Send writers off to continue to think about how to be precise in their work.

After a minute, I convened the students again. "Writers, your next step will be to look over your piece so far and think about where this metaphorical image can be tucked in. As you keep writing, you'll want to push yourself to keep finding the most precise way to convey the experiences and emotions in your piece to readers. Metaphorical thinking can help you to do that."

Every Character Plays a Role

IN THIS SESSION, you'll teach students that writers make sure every character has a role that connects to—and furthers—the larger meaning of their story.

GETTING READY

✔ Excerpt from "Eleven" (see Teaching)

✔ "Lessons from Mentor Narratives" chart (see Link)

✔ Each child's writing, in the meeting area (see Share)

THE TRUTH IS THAT I AM AN UNABASHED ENTHUSIAST for revision. I remember once, I was scheduled to speak to a large auditorium of teachers, and just before I began my speech, a messenger entered the room carrying the very first copy of my book, *The Art of Teaching Reading*. A teacher saw me holding—stroking—the brand-new book and murmured, "Imagine, you wrote *all those words!*"

I looked at her and said, "You don't know the half of it." When we redid our kitchen, the contractor brought one of those industrial trailers into our yard and parked it beside the house, filling it with debris. When I wrote that book—or any book since—I think I filled five industrial trailers with discarded drafts!

I *love* to revise. I put myself on the page the best that I can. I put all of me there—my experiences, my priorities, my knowledge, and my ignorance and biases too—and then I

> *"I love to revise. I put myself on the page the best that I can . . . and then I reread and see myself."*

reread and see myself. And then—glory be!—I get to fix myself up, to make myself into the kind of person I want to be. I revise to make myself (and my ideas) more clear, more generous, more informed, more helpful.

In life, I don't get a chance to recall my first-draft efforts: I say something, I do something, and my words and actions are out there in the world, creating waves of reactions. I can't call those actions and words back in order to make them wiser, better. But when I write, I get a chance to pull myself up by my bootstraps. When any one of us has done our very best, and can then stand on the shoulders of our best work in order to produce work that is better yet, this is a great treat.

COMMON CORE STATE STANDARDS: W.5.3, W.5.5, RL.5.2, RL.5.3, SL.5.1, L.5.1, L.5.2, L.5.3

By now your students are immersed in the revision process, considering their word choice and mulling over what images and objects really mean in their stories. You have taught them to push themselves to consider that the way in which they choose to describe actions, images, and so on creates an effect on the reader. Today you will raise the level of that work by letting students know that it is not only objects that are symbolic in stories. Characters, too, can be symbolic. Today you will help students learn that each person in a story plays a role. Which means that every character must be there for a reason. A mother cannot sneak in at the end if she was not there all along unless it is for good reason.

Characters help writers to convey larger messages and thus, they play roles. Students will be most used to this notion in fantasy, where the character archetypes are clear: the wise guide, the reluctant hero, the villain who craves power, and so on. Today you will help students to see that archetypes do not only exist in fantasy. You will involve them in considering the role that each character plays in the story, thinking how that character's role works to reveal the larger meaning.

Every Character Plays a Role

CONNECTION

Draw on a real-world example of how people "play roles" in each other's lives.

"Writers, I want to tell you a story. I had this friend once who wanted to throw a surprise party for another friend of ours. She asked me to help her and she promised we'd split the work, but as time passed, I ended up doing more and more of the work. I sent out invitations, went grocery shopping, bought decorations, ordered a cake—everything. 'I'll help you with the next part,' my friend kept promising. Only on the day of the party I had done everything. When the birthday guest came through the door, my friend yelled 'Surprise!' like she had planned the whole thing.

"Writers, that friend played a role in my life. She taught me that I needed to depend on myself and that others might let me down. She also taught me a lesson. Remember in the story *The Little Red Hen,* when nobody wants to help make the bread but everybody wants to eat the bread? Well, my friend was more of a 'I will help you eat this bread' kind of person, wasn't she? She was the kind of person who was always around for the good times but not for the work. That was the role she played in my life and it taught me to not wait around for others.

"I tell you this story because just like that friend played a role in my life and taught me important lessons, the secondary characters in your narratives play roles and influence you, the main character.

"There's a saying that everyone who comes into your life comes into it for a reason. Well, I don't know if that is true, but here's what I do know: everyone who comes into your story comes into it for a reason."

❖ **Name the teaching point.**

"So today I want to teach you that authors ensure that every character, main and secondary, plays a role in forwarding the larger meaning of a story."

Teachers, we are trying to build a community where students have common literary references to which to allude and thus common lenses through which to interpret stories they are reading, writing, and living. When I say my friend was a "I will help you eat this bread kind of person," I do so deliberately, wanting to plant the idea in students' minds that there are archetypal characters that appear in stories and in our everyday lives. I'm sure every one of you can easily think of the person in your life who's a "Little Red Hen" type!

TEACHING

Channel students to study the role of a secondary character in a mentor text.

"So right now, let's study how Sandra Cisneros put characters into 'Eleven' to play roles." I put up a copy of the story and studied it for a moment quietly. What about Mrs. Price, for example? What role does she play? Hmm . . . ." I continued to look at the story.

I zoomed in on the part of the story where Mrs. Price is most dominant, rereading the lines as if to myself. "Reread and think along with me," I said to the students.

> *"Whose is this?" Mrs. Price says, and she holds the red sweater up in the air for all the class to see. "Whose? It's been sitting in the coatroom for a month."*

I made Mrs. Price's words loud and jarring as I read.

> *"Not mine," says everybody. "Not me."*
>
> *"It has to belong to somebody," Mrs. Price keeps saying, but nobody can remember.*

I stopped, taking a moment to think. "So far, Sandra Cisneros has showed Mrs Price to be a very aggressive, sort of mean character. But what effect does that have on the story? On Rachel?" I looked back at the text as if pondering the question. "Well, Rachel says 'even if it belonged to me I wouldn't say so.' It's a bit like Mrs. Price's loudness makes Rachel more quiet."

I skipped a few lines, reading on a bit later in the text.

> *Today I wish I was one hundred and two instead of eleven because if I was one hundred and two I'd have known what to say when Mrs. Price put the red sweater on my desk. I would know how to tell her it wasn't mine instead of just sitting there with that look on my face and nothing coming out of my mouth.*

"This goes with what I was saying before. It's as if Rachel can't find her voice. She is silent, and Mrs. Price plays a big role in Rachel's silence."

I skipped to the last line of the story, after Mrs. Price had forced Rachel to put the sweater on.

> *I wish I was anything but eleven, because I want today to be far away already, far away like a runaway balloon, like a tiny o in the sky, so tiny-tiny you have to close your eyes to see it.*

"I'm wondering what role Mrs. Price plays in this story about Rachel feeling so small and so silent. Hmm . . . . You know, I think maybe Mrs. Price is here to make Rachel feel those ways. She's the bad guy in the story."

Debrief, naming out the replicable steps you took.

"I'm hoping you noticed what I just did. First, I looked for a character to study. Then, I reread, asking myself 'What role does this character play in the story's meaning?'"

Explain to children how you would transfer this strategy to your own writing.

"In my own story about Luka, I could do something similar. I'd focus in on a character, let's say Luka, and ask myself, 'What role do I want this character to play in my story? How will this character help forward what I am most trying to show?'

"I know that my story is about my sister, about how she is always there for me when things are tough. So really, Luka's role is to make things tough. I stretch out the pain and sadness of his death so that my reader knows just how hurt I am, how much guilt I feel. Then, my sister can swoop in and help me feel better. As a writer, I think I might want to work a bit harder to show how much I loved Luka, and then add a bit more to the part where my sister plays her big role—comforting me."

ACTIVE ENGAGEMENT

Ask students to consider their own secondary characters, the roles they play, and the ways they might further the meaning behind their stories.

"Think about your story now. What role do the secondary characters play in forwarding your big meaning? Is there still work you need to do in order to write more like Sandra Cisneros? Turn and talk to your partner."

I listened in as Zora discussed the role of the coffee patron in her story. "My story is really about how special my relationship is with my mom. The lady in the story laughs at us, like in this one part, (Zora began to read aloud):

> "Ha, Ha, Ha, He, He, Ho" the woman behind us in line obviously can't take it anymore, because she starts cracking up. She taps her palm up and down on the glass counter, laughing like she's at def-comedy-jam. She stomps her feet and nods her head. "You two are hilarious . . . you would be great on stage, my daughter is in high school and is always moody." I can't believe this woman had been listening to our conversation.

"When I think about this part of my story, I realize that I only saw that my mom was so important because that woman pointed it out. She said that we were 'special' later on, and then I started to believe her. So maybe I could change my story a little bit so that it is obvious that this lady taught me that my mom and I have a special relationship. Like, I could say a bit more about what she did that made me realize it."

After a minute or two, I called the children back together.

I am not just relying on the mentor text to do my teaching. I know that one of the hardest parts of learning is transference, and that it is important for me to model not only noticing a craft move in a text, but then attempting to use that craft move to raise the level of my own writing. Here, in the name of time, I do this work quickly and merely name out the work I'd do as a writer in my Luka story.

FIG. 17–1 Zora explores the role of character in her story.

LINK

Ask children to set goals for the period ahead, keeping in mind today's minilesson.

"Today, you have quite a bit of work to do. It is time to put the finishing touches on your pieces. Take a minute to prepare by thinking about what you'll work on today. I've added the most recent strategies to our chart, 'Lessons from Mentor Narratives.' When you have a clear mission for your writing work today, you can head off and get started."

As always, I try to reinforce the notion that children are the captains of their own writing process. Some of them will go off to strengthen the role of secondary characters in their stories, but others will have more pressing revision strategies to tend to. With links like this one, I hope to empower children to make their own choices.

Lessons from Mentor Narratives

- Writers create the words a person could have said, doing this in ways that reveal the character as a person.
- Writers give reasons to explain the way a character acts.
- Writers show thinking by telling the exact words and the tone a character uses when thinking—like a dialogue with one's self.
- Writers slow down the problem and stretch out the tension (for main and secondary characters).
- Writers capture the exact actions and images that lead to an emotional response.
- Writers ensure that secondary characters play a role in the story's overall meaning.

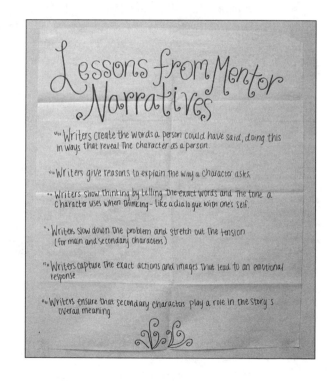

Supporting Final Revisions

A FRIEND OF MINE recently told me about the song her toddler learned in day-school. Apparently, at the end of each day, the teachers begin singing "The Clean-Up Song." The children chime in, singing along, and before long, little toddlers are running to and fro, tossing toys in bins and putting blocks on shelves. The teachers run after the little ones, helping them with their intended clean-up goals.

In some ways, today feels like a "Clean-Up Song" kind of day. This is not to say that the unit is over—children will still edit and prepare their pieces for publication—but today will be one of the last chances you have to run "to and fro," helping children with the largest of their intended revision goals.

Plan to meet with lots of children today, either in small groups or conferences, helping them to make final revisions and shore up the loose ends in their writing. If your students are beginning to feel like they're finished revising, you might add new fuel to their work by having them meet with a partner to discuss the revision decisions they've made. Students might prepare for their partnership talk by rereading their drafts and marking the crafting techniques they've used in their writing. When they meet with their partners, they can each discuss the work they've done and name how each technique somehow improved the quality of their writing. Then, they can lean on each other to make further revision plans. They might ask questions such as, "What work has my partner tried that I might try as well?" or "What have we learned that I've yet to apply to my writing?" You might emphasize that writers try to reimagine their writing, and sometimes the revision work they do pays off and sometimes it doesn't. What's important to remember when revising, however, is that stretching one's way of thinking will often lead to new discoveries.

You might also choose to begin focusing on mechanics today. In the upcoming session, you will remind your children that writers edit not only to make their work conventional and correct, but also to make it powerful. Before you go into tomorrow, spend just a little time thinking about ways you can help children understand that writers take great pleasure in making decisions about how we will use even the littlest marks on a page—a period, a comma, a parenthesis.

Pico Iyer says, "Punctuation then is a matter of care. Care for words, yes, but also, and the more important, for what words imply. Only a lover notices the small things: the way the afternoon light catches the nape of the neck, or how a strand of hair slips out from behind an ear, or the way a finger curls around a cup. And no one scans a letter so closely as a lover, searching for its small print, straining to hear its nuances, its gasps, its sighs and hesitations, poring over the secret messages that lie in every cadence. No iron can pierce the heart with such force as a period put at just the right place . . . . Punctuation, in fact, is a labor of love" (1996).

MID-WORKSHOP TEACHING   Using What You Know about Studying Characters in Books When Developing Your Own Character

"Writers, what you are creating is literature—no different than the literature we study in reading workshop—the stories written by authors like Lois Lowry and Patricia MacLachlan. When you think about the characters in the story you are writing, it can be helpful to use some of the strategies you use as a reader. Most importantly, you want to remember that as a reader, you often ask: 'What kind of person is this character?' and then gather details from the character's actions, words, and thoughts to support your idea. As a writer, you want to make sure that you are creating clear characters that readers can have ideas about. When you have a moment, step back from your story and pick a character. It might be yourself, it might be a secondary character. Ask, 'What kind of person is this character supposed to be?' and then check to make sure what the character says, does, and thinks fits with this intention."

You may want to rally a small group to study punctuating a picture book. Try one by Patricia Polacco or Tomie De Paola or Cynthia Rylant. Choose a book that children already know well. Those authors all use luscious punctuation. Take Hesse's *Come On, Rain* or Rylant's *Night in the Country*, perhaps. Open to any page with students, and study the punctuation that the author has used. Teach the children to ask, "Why did Rylant write with these dashes? With these short sentences and periods? With this exclamation point?" It is easiest to answer these questions if they also entertain the question, "How would this have been different had she punctuated this sentence differently?" Students can try rewriting the sentence they've just read, playing with another author's words, before turning to their own writing to fiddle and play with punctuation in similar ways.

Above all, leave children with a sense of closure today. Regardless of the state of their story and the large-scale revisions you may or may not be hoping for, allow them to relish in the process of putting "final touches" on their writing.

Developing Character Traits

Share an example of a student who meant to convey one set of character traits in her story, but realized that she didn't.

"Writers, many of you spent a bit of time studying the characters in your story today and realized that, wait, the person you were trying to portray was not necessarily the person you were showing!" Aalia, for instance, said that what she most wanted to show about herself in her story is the way she overcomes her shyness and fear. The external plotline shows this: she moves to a new school, prepares for the first day, and eventually makes a new friend. But really, Aalia didn't show us any of her internal characteristics. She realized that she didn't use words or thoughts or even tiny actions to show how scared and shy she was in the beginning, as she brushed her teeth and thought about the day ahead. And she didn't let the reader in on the fact that, as she stood in front of her new school's door, she had visions of running away, back to the safety of her warm bed."

Ask partners to study each other's characters.

"Right now, switch papers with your partner. Tell your partner what you most want to show about yourself as a person in this story. What ideas and theories should a reader have about you? Partners, read each other's writing with this in mind. Does the author give clues that let you in on the kind of person he or she really is? Do his or her actions and words and thoughts support what the author most wants to show? If not, you'll want to be ready to give your partner some suggestions so that he or she can make revisions tonight."

SESSION 17 HOMEWORK

REVISING WITH CHARACTER IN MIND

Each of you had a partner conference today and your partner gave you a few suggestions for the ways you might bring out the characteristics of the people in your story. Remember what you know as a reader—a person's actions, thoughts, and words can say a lot about them! Tonight, revise your stories to ensure that you are showing what you most hope to show about your characters, main and secondary. We know that Sandra Cisneros is a master of this—showing us that Rachel feels shy and voiceless and angry, without actually *telling* us that once! Be sure to bring your copy of "Eleven" home with you tonight so that you can study Cisneros' techniques before revising your own writing.

Session 18

Editing

The Power of Commas

W E ALL RESIST DOING WHAT WE'RE TOLD. Even if the truth is sound advice, good counsel, and the right thing to do, it's still irksome. Following rules too often and too carefully chafes.

It's not enough, then, for our students to see editing as simply a matter of following the rules of English grammar at every turn. In this session, I aim to present editing as an adventure, potentially full of exploration, discovery, and invention.

As I discussed in *A Guide to the Common Core Writing Workshop*, the book that opens this series of units, there are four methods for conveying a teaching point that I use over and over again in my minilessons: demonstration, telling and offering an example, guided practice, and inquiry. Of course, I also use combinations of these methods. The majority of minilessons I've laid out in this series so far have used the first three methods. In this session, I use the inquiry method of exploring a teaching point.

To use the inquiry method, I set up a situation in which children can explore a problem. In this case, I'll set the stage for kids to ask and try to answer the question, "How can commas help us in our writing?" Of course, this same basic minilesson can be used to help children start exploring any punctuation mark or any grammatical structure or any aspect of language. Just as children studied powerful published texts to think about techniques for writing well, so too can they study mentor texts to think about techniques for using commas—or any other meaning-making mark. Then, once they've determined some uses and effects of the comma, they can try doing the same thing in their own writing.

Three wonderful books that you can turn to for more about teaching conventional English grammar, including punctuation, are *A Fresh Approach to Teaching Punctuation*, by Janet Angelillo (2002), *The Power of Grammar*, by Mary Ehrenworth and Vicki Vinton (2005), and *Practical Punctuation*, by Dan Feigelson (2008).

IN THIS SESSION, you'll teach students that writers learn about punctuation—commas in particular—from writing they admire, to make their writing more exact.

GETTING READY

✔ Your chart of "Eleven" for use during the minilesson

✔ A chart with three columns labeled Examples of Commas in Mentor Texts, What Does the Comma Do?, and Using the Comma in My Own Writing (see Teaching)

✔ Each child's draft and copy of "Eleven," in the meeting area

✔ Each child's "Questions to Ask Yourself as You Edit" checklist, from Session 3

COMMON CORE STATE STANDARDS: W.5.3, W.5.5, W.5.9.a, RL.5.1, RFS.5.4, SL.5.1, L.5.1, L.5.2, L.5.3.a

Editing
The Power of Commas

CONNECTION

Remind children they will be cycling through the writing process again and again, each time learning new strategies for creating better writing.

"So, writers, many of you are now satisfied with the overall shape of your stories. You've made sure the important parts are developed, you've crafted your stories so that the details and leads and endings bring out what the moment is really about, and now you are ready to turn your attention to the detailed changes you could make, the final editing you could do to polish your story. Every time you go through the writing process, every time you make a piece of writing, you'll go through these steps, and you'll have an opportunity to learn new ways to make your writing stronger.

"The first time you got to this editing stage in this unit, you were thinking hard about paragraphing. The next time around you thought about that much sooner, and when you got to this stage you thought of an editing checklist. Now, you still have your 'Questions to Ask Yourself as You Edit' checklist, but I bet you can tell me that you do more and more of it before you even get to editing, right? So today, in addition to using paragraphs and using your 'Questions to Ask Yourself as You Edit' checklist, I want to teach you another way to gather information that can help you edit your writing. What I'm about to tell you is a method that writers use all the time.

"What writers know is that every single punctuation mark that exists in the world—like periods, commas, quotation marks, dashes—every single punctuation mark has hidden power. As a writer, you are allowed to use any punctuation mark you want, but if you want it to bring its hidden power to your own writing, and not just sit there doing nothing on the page, then you have to know that punctuation mark's secrets. And they all have secrets!"

✤ **Name the inquiry.**

"Whenever you want to learn a punctuation mark's secret, when you are ready to add its power to your writing, what you have to do is study that mark. You have to scrutinize it, examine it, study it with both your eyes and your whole mind to figure out what it does. Today what I want to teach you is this: you can figure out any punctuation mark's secrets by studying it in great writing."

One way you can tailor the difficulty of this minilesson is by compiling sets of examples of comma usage of varying levels of complexity. You might, for example, select examples of commas separating items in a list. On the other hand, you might select a set of unconventional comma uses, or omissions, as in the opening passages of Toni Morrison's The Bluest Eye.

TEACHING AND ACTIVE ENGAGEMENT

Explain that just as children learned to write in powerful ways by studying a mentor text, so too can they learn to use commas powerfully.

"In this unit, you've studied published writing to see what the author did, and then you tried those same things in your writing. Well, I told you then and I'll tell you now that you can use that same technique for learning just about anything about writing. We can do the same with punctuation marks! Today we'll study the comma. What would the writing be like without it? What message does the mark send to readers about the words? Does the mark change the sound or speed or importance of the words?

"Then, after we've figured out some of the secrets of commas, some of what their power is to change and frame words, you'll have a chance to put commas into your own writing, both things you've already written and things you've yet to write, and you'll try to bring that same power to your own writing."

Set children up to explore the comma with their partners.

"Okay, to study a punctuation mark, you'll need to read aloud parts of a text with the mark in them and think about it and talk about it. Remember, some of the questions you and your partner can think about are 'What would the writing be like without it? What message does the mark send to readers about the words? Does the mark change the sound or speed or importance of the words? Let's examine commas in our copies of 'Eleven,' which we all know well. Now take some time to copy this chart into your notebook, and then with your partner begin to fill it in."

Examples of Commas	What Does the Comma Do?	Using the Comma in My Writing

As children studied the texts, I moved about the meeting area, helping them to identify examples of commas and then grapple with the words to express what the comma does. "Sophie and Zora are reading sentences aloud," I said to the class. "This is helping them to hear what the comma does. Cameron and Caleb are working together to construct sentences with different kinds of commas!" As I listened in I began compiling a list on chart paper of comma uses that children had discovered. After a bit, I stopped them.

"So, children, let me stop you now, even though I know you haven't finished. The comma has many different powers, doesn't it? You are finding some of them; I heard you and copied a bit of what you noticed.

When you use the inquiry method to teach, you'll find that you always have the option to angle your teaching toward improving children's methods of inquiry or toward ensuring that children understand and can use the information they've derived. In this minilesson, I try to do both, but I emphasize the process of learning from mentor authors over the content of how to use commas. You may tip the balance in the other direction for your students.

Collect what you heard children say, compiling and presenting what you heard.

"This is some of what you said and some of how you filled in your chart:

Examples of Commas	What Does the Comma Do?	Using the Comma in My Writing
• "When you are eleven, you are also ten, and nine, and eight, and seven, and six, and five, and four...." ("Eleven")	• "Commas make you stack it all together."	• (Caleb) "I saw three, seven, a million mitts piled on the shelves."
• "That's not, I don't, you're not ... Not mine. I finally say." ("Eleven")	• "Commas mean 'stop' but not all the way."	• (Jake) "I hated her, but she was still my sister."
• "I take it off right away and give it to her, only Mrs. Price pretends like everything's okay." ("Eleven")	• "Commas mean that's one part of it, but there's another part coming up."	• (Sabera) "There was pink frosting, rainbow candles, and a plastic ballerina with a silver skirt."

Channel students to compare notes as they discuss what you laid out, and what it means for their writing.

"Turn to your partner again and talk about how these discoveries about commas are the same or different from what the two of you discovered when you studied 'Eleven' together.

"Now, take a look back at your own writing. Where might you try some of these techniques? You might start by circling a few lines you don't love, those you'd like to make better, and imagining the ways commas can help you do that. Are there sentences you can string together? Places where you've used commas but get the sense it isn't quite working?" As I spoke, I gestured for children to look back at their drafts.

LINK

Remind children of what they learned, both specifically and generally.

After a short period of talk, I signaled for children to turn back to me. "Today, so what you learned will stick, you need to try to make commas use their full power, not just sit there; you also need to keep noticing commas in the writing all around you—in your own writing, in your friend's writing, in your favorite books, on your milk carton at lunch, everywhere!

When you teach children by giving them materials to explore and learn from instead of simply waiting for them to find what you've told them to find, you won't know exactly what they are going to come up with. This means that you have to trust their intelligence and powers of observation to lead them to conclusions about what they are studying. You will have to decide for yourself how far to let children lead the study. If they come up with hypotheses about the functions of commas that you know from experience will be false or undependable, you have a choice to make. Will you ask them to test their hypothesis until they discover for themselves that it won't hold? Will you point to an example that will show them that it won't hold so they can test it quickly? Will you take the rule and treat it as correct until the class discovers the error? Each teaching path has its purposes, and you will have to choose the one you believe will be best for your class.

In this active engagement, I have highlighted discoveries from three sets of partners that will serve the class well although the "rules" are not yet honed to perfection. That will come. The other discoveries by other partnerships are still in the air, but by highlighting these three and offering children a chance to talk about how their observations relate to these, I hope our class knowledge will be consolidated. If any invented rules conflict with these statements, they are likely to come to light here, and we can decide as a class which to follow.

"So remember, we learned today that you can always, as a writer, study the work of an author you admire, and learn ways to make your own writing better—even in areas of conventions. Some of you might decide to continue on with your comma investigation a bit longer before turning to your own writing. You can continue to do this work in 'Eleven' or even try it in a book you are reading. Others of you still have plenty to do in your draft —remember, our celebration is just two days away!—and will be busy revising and editing, keeping in mind the lessons you've learned about commas.

"Take a moment and talk to your partner about the plan you have for your work today. Once you feel ready, you can head back to your writing spot and get started."

Studying Commas by Studying Mentor Authors

TODAY'S SESSION HAS BEEN ABOUT COMMAS, but in the larger sense it has been about teaching children that they can learn from authors if they study the writing they admire with a writing question in mind. If you decide to confer to support today's minilesson, you can either support children in learning from mentor texts or you can help them use commas with greater skill. Of course, one path does not necessarily exclude the other, but it may help you confer with greater clarity if you decide which is your primary goal in each conference. Which lesson will give the child a leg up at this moment in his writing development?

You may want to confer with several examples of comma uses from mentor texts at your fingertips. You could lay out a sentence and together puzzle over the comma use it demonstrates. Working through the process of discovery with the child and then helping him apply that discovery to his own writing provides the child with an extra bit of guided practice.

If the child has shown you that he knows how to learn from mentor texts and is now trying to apply that learning, to be more correct and pointed in his use of commas, then you will want to research his understanding of comma use by asking him questions and studying that use in his own writing. Alongside the child, you could ask "How is this comma affecting this sentence?"

If a child seems able to put commas into her writing after it is written, the next step can be to help her compose her drafts with commas, inserting them as she goes. If she already does that, the next step can be to help her write more complex sentences in her entries so that she needs more commas right from the start. The more automatic comma use is for the writer, in other words, the earlier in the writing process she is able to use commas, the more fully she can utilize their power. This concept of helping children use language and grammar automatically, earlier and earlier in the writing process so that they can reap its full power, is true for all conventions of our language—grammar, punctuation, vocabulary—all of our syntactic structures. We can create only what we can imagine, and learning the relationships and possibilities offered by grammar educates our imaginations.

MID-WORKSHOP TEACHING   Discovering Uses for Commas

"Can you all stop for a minute? I want to tell you what Khalid learned just now. He was studying the commas around him, and he noticed another power they have. He said, 'They go around words, to say "I'm gonna say more about it."' Do you know what he means? Here's the example he gave from his book:

> **To make words seem off to the side**
> It was cherry-flavored, my favorite.

"That's another power of commas that you can use if you need to in your own writing. Remember, if you want to know ways to get power out of every mark on your page, you can study great writing. I'll add this observation to our list! Okay, get back to your writing."

Sharing Our Best Comma Work

Ask children to share with their partners their most successful implementation of a comma from today's minilesson and plans for studying their next punctuation mark.

"Writers, please read though the writing work you did today, and show your partner the place where you think you used a comma very, very well. Talk with your partner about why you think that comma belongs there and how it's using its full power! If you didn't use a comma today, you can talk with your partner about where you chose not to put one where another writer might have chosen differently."

I glanced over John's shoulder, who was sharing his work with Francesca. "I tried a couple different ways to use commas," John said. "I realized I wasn't doing it right when I had people talking, like here," he said, pointing to the line, "'I'm off to the beach mother.' So I put commas in dialogue." John dragged his finger down his draft, visibly searching for another part. "Here. I also had this one part where it used to go, 'No. I suppose not.' But, I decided that I didn't want it to be a full stop for my reader. It's when my mom says something to me and I'm kind of thinking it over, so I want the word *no* to kind of go with the next part. So, I changed it to 'No, I suppose not.'" Pleased with the work John had done, I moved on to another partnership.

Takuma was talking to his partner Sabera, explaining that he had taken his short, sometimes choppy sentences and woven them together using commas. "Like here," he pointed to his draft enthusiastically. "Instead of writing short sentence—stop—short sentence—stop, I made it like this: 'He kicked AJ, so I got upset and pushed him back hard. "Leave them alone," I said, and then I stood next to AJ and tried to look big and tough.'"

I called the class back together. "Writers, so many of you have found uses for commas. You've drawn from the chart we created earlier, from what you noticed with your partner, and from your own, independent studies. Keep up the great work!"

REACHING FOR VOICE

One of the most important qualities of good writing is something people refer to as *voice*. Donald Graves suggests that voice is the imprint of the author, the sense that a real person is behind the words. He said children are more likely to write with this magical quality if they've first story-told or shared their draft aloud.

Tonight, read your draft aloud and listen for voice. Does this piece sound like it was written by you? Can you hear your own voice as your read it? If parts feel forced or awkward, it may be because you were writing in a way that is not your own. Maybe you were trying to sound like someone else or were trying to do something that does not fit with your writing style. Find these awkward places, practice other ways they might go aloud, and then rewrite them to bring out your voice.

More than anything else, your writing should be your own!

Session 19

Mechanics

Dear Teachers,

In the session before this one, you invited children to study mentor texts to discern the special powers that commas have to change meaning in various, subtle ways. For the next session, or anytime you see that there is a need for extra attention to conventions, you might take this minilesson's framework and use it to guide you in creating more minilessons about grammatical structures. Here are just a few examples of situations that might call for a minilesson like this one.

- If, in reading over children's shoulders, you see that children need to learn about punctuating correctly around parentheses, you could craft an inquiry minilesson around that subject. "What does punctuation look like near parentheses?"

- If you see that your writers seem trapped by row after row of declarative sentences, you might try offering a focus on clauses, or sentence structures.

- If your writers love exclamation points, and pepper their writing with them, try offering up the study of how others use them. They'll quickly discover their scarcity!

To structure a minilesson patterned after the previous session's lesson, then, you'll want to follow these steps:

1. **Assess children's writing and goals as writers.**
   To do this, you will want to first study children's writing to determine which kinds of mechanics instruction would be most likely to improve the quality of their writing. Are they writing with sentences of various lengths and structures? Are they comfortable using colons, semicolons, parentheses, and ellipses? Are they marking dialogue effectively? As you ask yourself each of these questions, you might also ask yourself if students are using these structures and marks for a purpose that matches their writing

COMMON CORE STATE STANDARDS: W.5.3, W.5.5, W.5.9.a, RFS.5.4, SL.5.1, L.5.1, L.5.2, L.5.3

intentions. If you see an enthusiasm for colons, for example, but you don't see students using them effectively, or if you see no colons in students' writing at all, colon use might well be a prime candidate for a minilesson's teaching point.

2. **Choose the teaching method.**

Once you have chosen the teaching point, as always, you have several methods of teaching from which to choose: demonstration, explain and give an example, guided practice, and inquiry. (Of course, a combination of these is also possible.) If yesterday's session went well and you want to emulate that structure, you'll choose inquiry.

3. **Assemble the texts containing the grammatical structure or punctuation mark you will be studying.**

Your next step is to assemble the material your students will study; for instance, you might go in search of passages or short texts that hold colons. Alternately, you could also leave the search for the materials, the search for texts that demonstrate colon use, to the students. This would take a bit longer than assembling them alone, but it would help children form a wide-awakeness to the texts in their lives. For now, they'd be looking everywhere for colons, then they'd be looking everywhere for semicolons, until eventually they would acquire the habit of noting punctuation use in texts!

You'll want to make sure that the texts students study are passages that contain at least a few examples of the punctuation mark, and are long enough to allow readers to feel the impact of the punctuation mark on the whole text, not just the isolated sentence. Punctuation marks' powers come not only from their specific effect on the sentences in which they are found, but also from the contrasts they present with other sentences and punctuation marks.

4. **Research examples to hypothesize about the particular effect on meaning the punctuation mark or grammatical structure has.**

Once the excerpts and short texts are assembled, the next step is to channel students to study the examples of usage and to make some generalizations about them. They generally do this in groups or partnerships and then compare notes, to make a class chart. (See Figure 19–1.)

5. **Take the newfound knowledge to writing and reading.**

Oftentimes, the charts you and your students create will start as long lists of very specific uses of a punctuation mark. Over time, you will want to edit the list down as a class, deleting incorrect assumptions, combining the observations that overlap, and making new rules that seem to apply nearly all the time. For instance, in a colon study, the class might hone a chart about colon use to two simple facts: colons are used to introduce and they are found after independent clauses.

At that point, the guidelines belong on an editing checklist. To keep the study of colon use (or whatever you choose to study) alive and well, you will want to celebrate and make public and open for discussion students' uses of these marks in their writing. At first, that colon use is bound to be a bit incorrect and a bit overdone—that's to be expected! With practice and feedback, though, children's use

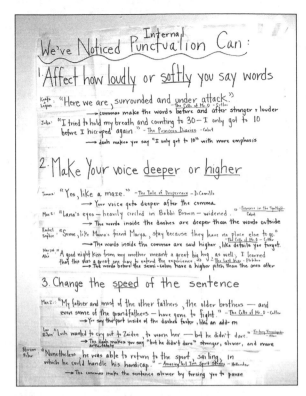

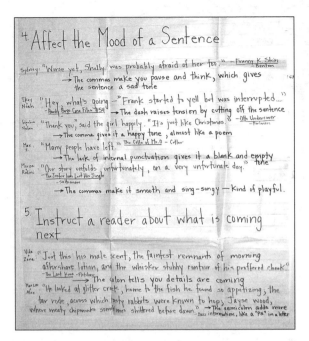

FIG. 19–1   A chart of student observations about internal punctuation

of the newfound structure or newfound mark will settle into its proper place among the other language skills and bits of information they are learning. As that knowledge settles, you will want to hold students accountable for using what they know about punctuation earlier and earlier in their writing process, reflecting that they've integrated knowledge of that mark's use.

Enjoy designing and teaching this session!
Lucy and Ali

Reading Aloud Your Writing
A Ceremony of Celebration

IN THIS SESSION, students will have an opportunity to share their writing with an audience, as writers strive to do. Children will read their pieces aloud, adding a chorus to give the occasion appropriate ceremony.

GETTING READY

✔ Prepare four children to read their writing or an excerpt from their writing to the whole group.

✔ Preassign each child to one of four groups.

✔ Prepare the rest of the children to read their writing or an excerpt from their writing to their small group.

✔ Set up the room to allow for all present to hear the first four children and then divide into four groups.

✔ Children need to have memorized a few lines of a poem, one they've written or found, to chant as a chorus; write this on a chart.

✔ Invite guests—parents, another class, teachers—as appropriate.

✔ Prepare refreshments.

✔ Provide baskets of note cards, enough for three or four per child. Set up in prominent places around the room.

I N THIS SESSION, children will read their writing to an audience of parents and each other. People will write letters in response to the writing.

I want to encourage you to take author celebrations very seriously. Just as authors create alternate worlds through stories, you, too, create alternative worlds through your teaching. When you teach, you create a counterculture within your classrooms. If you've done your job well, just as surely as Lucy and Edmund and Peter and Susan in *The Lion, the Witch and the Wardrobe* knew they were in another world, so too, the children who enter your room can sense that you have created a different kind of place. You teach by helping them know they are indispensable to a community of writers. You teach by helping them live in a place where words are cherished, where people lean in to listen deeply to each other's words and read words as if they have magical powers. You teach by helping children to regard each other as authors and to relish the different tones and textures, passions and purposes in each others' texts.

Of course, an author celebration is an extraordinary form of parent education too. These celebrations teach parents about what's happening at school and about qualities of good writing. Author celebrations also give parents another chance to learn about their own sons and daughters. I will not forget last June, at the final author celebration of the year, when a young boy who'd come into the year writing only the shallowest of sports stories read a piece aloud in which he'd written with a wide-open heart and with exquisite sensitivity and talent. His father came up to me and to his teacher afterwards, with eyes brimming, and said quietly, "I never thought he had it in him."

It is incredibly important to create a sense of occasion around these celebrations and to give children the extraordinary gift of knowing that their stories are reaching readers.

COMMON CORE STATE STANDARDS: W.5.3, RFS.5.4, SL.5.1, SL.5.6, L.5.1, L.5.2, L.5.3

Reading Aloud Your Writing

CELEBRATION

Welcome children and their family members. Explain that when we read stories, authors bring us into other worlds. And today, the writers in the class will read aloud, bringing all of us into other worlds.

"Writers, many of you have read or watched C. S. Lewis's *The Lion, the Witch and the Wardrobe.* You've seen Lucy enter that wardrobe, pushing past the coats, and then suddenly something cold brushes against her arm. It is a tree branch, covered with snow. She looks down and sees she is standing in snow and looks up and sees a lamppost, burning bright among the trees.

"In that story, as in every story that has ever been told, listeners are invited into a world. It is not just Lucy but all of us who push past the furry coats into the back of the wardrobe, and all of us feel something cold and find we are standing in snow. That is the magic of story. C. S. Lewis's story takes us into the land of Narnia, where four children are called upon to save the world.

"In this classroom, stories can also take us to other worlds: to the bustle of the sports store where Caleb finds the mitt, to the oceanside when Rie conquers her fears and goes surfing. Stories can take us to stand with Joey on the edge of the dock, looking into the murky water of the pond."

Explain the plan for today's author celebration. In this case, explain that after a few children read to the group, everyone will disperse to a corner to share writing in small groups.

"Today we'll hear four stories together as a community. And then you'll disperse to our story corners. (The young writers know their corners, and grown-ups, you can tag along.) In those corners, you'll read your pieces aloud."

Tell writers that after each reading, listeners will respond not by clapping but by reading a poem chorally.

"All weekend, I thought and thought, trying to decide how we could best respond to each other's writing. And I came to the decision that at this author's celebration, as at many graduations, weddings, anniversaries, we will share poetry. The poet Erica Jong once said, 'People think they can do without poetry. And they can. At least until they fall in love, lose a child or a parent or lose their way in the dark woods of life' (*In Their Own Voices: A Century of Recorded Poetry* 1997).

"So, after a writer reads, let's join in a choral reading of a poem. We've chosen a favorite that we can all read together. To start us off, will the four whole-class readers come and sit in the chairs here at the front of the room? I will read the poem, and then one reader will read. The room will be absolutely silent after Claudia reads (no clapping please), and then we'll all join in to say the refrain of the poem. Then Zora? Let's get started." The four children read their writing aloud, with the chorally read poem marking the silence between each reading.

Disperse the readers, reminding them to honor each other's writing with a choral reading.

"Let's disperse into our corners. Writers, you lead the way. Parents follow. Begin right away with one child reading, and remember to honor that reading with the choral reading."

After each child has a chance to read his or her piece aloud, ask listeners to write notes to the readers.

When everyone had read, I brought out the snacks and said, "For the next little while, every child will keep his or her narrative on hand. Get some food, and then would all of you—parents and children—circulate among each other, reading each other's stories? You'll see that I've left little note cards in baskets around the room. Please take the time to write responses to the writing you heard earlier today or to what you read now. Write responses that let writers know the parts that resonated for you, the way the writing made you feel. I've got a mailbox up here, and as you write a response, could you bring it up here? I'll distribute them later."

As parents circulated among the kids, I kept an eye on the responses, and from time to time made a point of steering a particular parent toward a child whose work wasn't being read. In this fashion, (and by adding my own notes), I checked that every child was receiving several writing "valentines."

Here is Zora's final personal narrative (see Figure 20–1).

Something Special
By Zora

"Jingle, Jingle, Jingle" the door chimes bang against each other as I pushed open the wooden door to Starbucks. My mom and I walk up to the counter.

"Nice to see you back here again Julie," said Paul.

He looked down at me, "Hi, Zora."

"Hi Paul." I moaned back. I shifted my eyes to the clock, 8:27. I'm not a morning person.

Paul hands us our drinks and smiles at me. "Chin up Zora." The he turns and walks off to the "Employees Only" room. As soon as he left, my mom took a few deep breaths and said, "Zora, why are you in such a dull mood?" I jump up and stare at my mom like she is a three-headed donkey

If you are looking for a poem to use, I especially recommend "Things," by Eloise Greenfield. "Things" ends with a child who "went to the kitchen/made me a poem." When using this as the refrain in a celebration of stories, we alter the word accordingly.

Compliment the class as a whole, but also use this as an occasion to seek individual children out, to look the child in the eyes, and to tell the child what you have noticed that he or she can do uniquely well. Does one child have the knack for writing with rhythm, for prose that makes readers read aloud so, so well? Tell the child that you see this. Does one child know how to speak the truth in words that are straight and true, words that go directly from the child's heart to the reader's heart? Tell the child this.

This ritual may seem unnecessary, but on the last day of Teachers College's summer institute, people read their writing aloud to each other and oftentimes listeners write notes in response. For decades now, I have seen teachers gather up those notes as if they were the love letters we'd desperately wanted. People have told me that, years later, they still keep those notes. I know what they mean because sometimes I, too, receive a note from a reader. After putting oneself on the line, as writers always do, it is a rather extraordinary thing for someone to write back and say, "Your words mattered."

that talks. I never noticed but my mom just doesn't understand. I have a lot of things on my mind. There's a lot to do when you're nine and three-and-a-half-quarters.

"I've been very busy lately mother." I finally respond in a highly sophisticated voice.

"Busy, huh?" my mom rolls her eyes and stares out at the watery gray sky. She squints her eyes and looks at the bright lipstick red off in the distance, the sun.

"No really," I say trying to regain her attention. "Tours for middleschool, afterschool, homework and school, mother, there are simply not enough hours in the day . . . ." My mom looks at me, like she is not quite believing what she is hearing. Her big brown eyes getting wider and wider with every word that comes hopping out my mouth. She looks completely amazed by the time I'm finishing my lecture. "That's why I'm feeling moody today . . . ."

"You, . . . moody? Every day I go to work, pay bills, I pay mortgage every month, come home, help with homework, cook dinner, and you're . . . you're . . . you're moody?" Her average spiel.

"Ha, Ha, Ha, He, He, Ho" the woman behind us in line obviously can't take it anymore, because she starts cracking up. She taps her palm up and down on the glass counter, laughing like she's at def-comedy-jam. She stomps her feet and nods her head. "You two are hilarious . . . you would be great on stage, my daughter is in highschool and is always moody." I can't believe this woman had been listening to our conversation.

"I never spend time with my daughter, you two have it all, you have something special." She smiles, bangs her hand against the glass tabletop a couple more times and her bracelets jingle and jump.

"Ha, not enough hours in the day!"

Then I got to thinking. I don't spend much time with my mom. She works five days a week. She gets home really late, and sometimes, I'm already in bed. But I push myself to stay up late, just to kiss her goodnight. I have never seen that lady in Starbucks before, never. But still out of nowhere she compliments me and my mom. She calls us special, and for a quick second, I don't believe her. How can a relationship be special if you barely see her? Half the kids in the world have one parent, no parents, or parents who can't afford them. Yeah it is great to have a mom that sees you all the time, but I don't have that type of mom. But I'm not complaining. I consider myself lucky, I have a mom, that's enough for me.

I wrap my arm around my mom's waist and squeeze, and she squeezes me back. I'm sure my mom doesn't know why I'm squeezing her, but the feeling is so warm, she doesn't care. What I have is special. She squeezes me tighter. Special.

Something Special

'Jingle, Jingle, Jingle' the door chimes bang against each other as I pushed open the wooden door to Starbucks. My mom and I walk up to the counter.
"Nice to see you back here again Julie," said Paul. He looked down at me, "Hi, Zora."
"Hi Paul." I moaned back. I shifted my eyes to the clock, 8:27. I'm not a morning person.
Paul hands us our drinks and smiles at me. "Chin up Zora." The he turns and walks off to the 'Employees Only' room. As soon as he left, my mom took a few deep breaths and said, "Zora, why are you in such a dull mood?" I jump up and stare at my mom like she is a three headed donkey that talks. I never noticed but my mom just doesn't understand. I have a lot of things on my mind. There's a lot to do when you're 9 and 3 and a half quarters.
"I've been very busy lately mother." I finally respond in a highly sophisticated voice.
"Busy, huh?" my mom rolls her eyes and stares out at the watery gray sky. She squints her eyes and looks at the bright lipstick red off in the distance, the sun.
"No really," I say trying to regain her attention. "Tours for middleschool, afterschool, homework and school, mother, there are simply not enough hours in the day..." My mom looks at me, like she is not quite believing what she is hearing. Her big brown eyes getting wider and wider with every word that comes hopping out my mouth. She looks completely amazed by the time I'm finishing my lecture. "That's why I'm feeling moody toda-..."
"You, ... moody? Every day I go to work, pay bills, I pay mortgage every month, come home, help with homework, cook dinner, and your... your... you're moody?" Her average spiel.
"Ha, Ha, Ha, He, He, Ho" the woman behind us in line obviously can't take it anymore, because she starts cracking up. She taps her palm up and down on the glass counter, laughing like she's at def-comedy-jam. She stomps her feet and nods her head. "You two are hilarious... you would be great on stage, my daughter is in highschool and is always moody-" I can't believe this woman had been listening to our conversation.
"I never spend time with my daughter, you two have it all, you have something special." She smiles, bangs her hand against the glass tabletop a couple more times and her bracelets jingle and jump.
"Ha, not enough hours in the day!"
Then I got to thinking. I don't spend much time with my mom. She works 5 days a week. She gets home really late, and sometimes, I'm already in bed. But I push myself to stay up late, just to kiss her goodnight. I have never seen that lady in Starbucks before, never. But still out of nowhere she compliments me and my mom. She calls us special, and for a quick second, I don't believe her. How can a relationship be special if you barely see her? Half the kids in the world have 1 parent, no parents, or parents who can't afford them. Yeah it is great to have a mom that sees you all the time, but I don't have that type of mom. But I'm not complaining. I consider myself lucky, I have a mom, that's enough for me.
I wrap my arm around my mom's waist and squeeze, and she squeezes me back. I'm sure my mom doesn't know why I'm squeezing her, but the feeling is so warm, she doesn't care. What I have is special. She squeezes me tighter. Special.

FIG. 20–1 Zora's final personal narrative

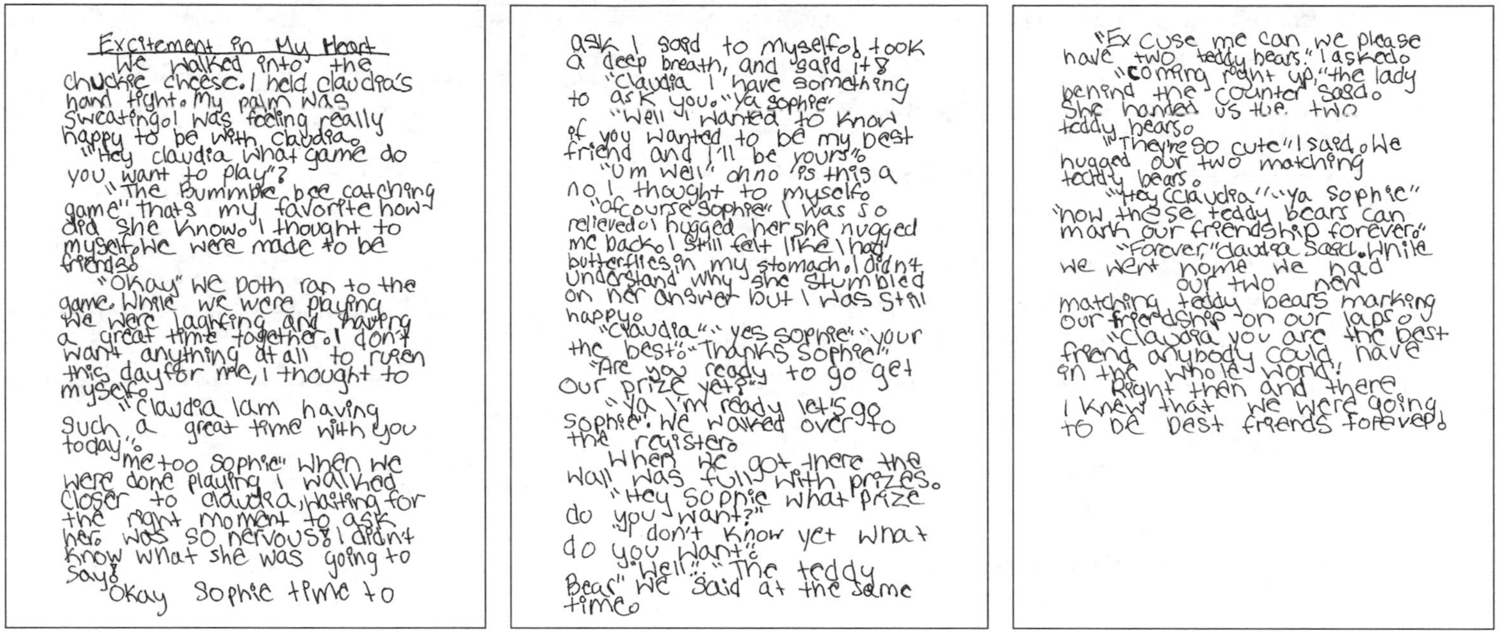

Excitement in My Heart

We walked into the Chuckie cheese. I held Claudia's hand tight. My palm was sweating. I was feeling really happy to be with Claudia.

"Hey Claudia what game do you want to play"?

"The bummble bee catching game" thats my favorite how did she know. I thought to myself, we were made to be friends.

"Okay" we both ran to the game. While we were playing we were laghing and having a great time together. I don't want anything at all to ruren this day for me, I thought to myself.

"Claudia I am having such a great time with you today".

"me too Sophie" When we were done playing I walked closer to Claudia, waiting for the right moment to ask her. I was so nervous. I didn't know what she was going to say.

"Okay Sophie time to ask I said to myself. I took a deep breath, and said it.

"Claudia I have something to ask you." "ya Sophie"

"Well I wanted to know if you wanted to be my best friend and I'll be yours."

"Um well" oh no is this a no. I thought to myself.

"ofcourse Sophie" I was so relieved. I hugged her she hugged me back. I still felt like I had butterflies in my stomach. I didn't understand why she stumbled on her answer but I was still happy.

"Claudia." "yes Sophie." "your the best." "Thanks Sophie."

"Are you ready to go get our prize yet?"

"Ya I'm ready let's go Sophie." We walked over to the register.

When we got there the wall was full with prizes.

"Hey Sophie what prize do you want?"

"I don't know yet what do you want."

"Well." "The teddy Bear" we said at the same time.

"Excuse me can we please have two teddy bears." I asked.

"coming right up," the lady behind the counter said. She handed us the two teddy bears.

"They're so cute" I said. We hugged our two matching teddy bears.

"Hey Claudia." "ya Sophie" "now these teddy bears can mark our friendship forever."

"Forever," Claudia said. While we went home we had our two new matching teddy bears marking our friendship on our laps.

"Claudia you are the best friend anybody could have in the whole world!

Right then and there I knew that we were going to be best friends forever.

FIG. 20–2 Sophie's final draft

GIFTS THAT COUNT

On Father'sday morning, I woke up in an Adirondaks campsite. I watched the beautiful red morning sun and thought about what I had planned for my Father's day present; a piece of land that had snatched my heart.

I tip-toed over to Dad's tent and unzipped it, waking Dad. I said, "Dad, let me show you your Fathers' day present."

"OK" he answered.

I Shepherd him between the two rows of trees, out into the Sun light, onto my point. The point was covered with soft meadow grass Sprinkled with tiny wild flowers. I watched Dad take in this precious bit of the world and knew I had given him the right gift. Then From its hiding place I drew forth a fishing rod and laid it triumphantly in Dad's hands. His eyes sparkled and I said "you deserve the honor of being first."

Dad nodded and cast. The line Sailed through the air.

We watched in Silence. We all waited; Dad, mom, Evan, and I. Dad held his breath, his fingers tense.

Suddenly the line jerked. A huge dark Shape struggled under the water. Dad Slowly brought it to the surface. We gasped. A huge bass... Suddenly, Snap! The String broke under tension and the monster fled to the bottom of the lake. So we Christened the point, 'Bass Point'. On that day, Evan and I gave the love of fishing to Dad.

FIG. 20–3 Miles's final draft

Running Away from Life

    I stepped out on Riverside Park's biggest hill. Today was the first snow of the year and I looked down and made a perfect boot print with my new, blue boots. I felt big standing at the top of the hill. I grasped my purple sled and Camilla, my little sister, climbed onto the sled with me. Camilla was following my lead and I felt like a grown up, like 13 or 14, or even older. I could feel the snowy fog sweep my hair like a cloud pushing me up high.

"Ready, Camilla?" I asked excitedly.

    I was not scared because I had sledded on other hills that were bigger. She didn't answer but I felt her arms tighten around my waist.

    My sled started to move an inch and then faster. I noticed a human shape on the hill. It was a man and his kid. I tried to control my sled but I couldn't because I was moving so fast.

    "Watch out!" my parents shouted. But it was too late. I lost all my excitement. I was getting closer to the man. Then I felt my sled rub against his coat as I came to a complete stop. I felt like a bird that had just missed hitting a tree.

    The man's half-angry, half-alarmed face stared at me. The little kid looked scared.

    "Who's watching you!?" he shouted as I felt Camilla's little warm hand touch my cold neck. I ran as fast as I could to my mother.

    "It's O.K.," she said. But I did not feel okay. I curled up on the blanket with hot chocolate. I felt like a little kid, like I was 3 years old.

    I lay in the cold snow and could hear distant voices yelling and playing. I felt like I had gone backward in life. I didn't feel 14 anymore.

    I know that not only one event in your life makes you grownup but this even was going to change the way that I thought of myself. I felt so grown up and now I was just a scared little kid running away from life.

FIG. 20–4   Francesca's final draft

Transferring Learning
Applying Narrative Writing Skills across the Curriculum

ear Teachers,

As you end this unit, you might find yourself asking, "What now?" You are no doubt preparing to launch into your next unit of study. As you prepare to move on, you'll also want to consider the ways in which you might keep narrative writing alive in your classroom.

Norman Webb's research reminds us to be sure young people are encouraged to engage in cognitively demanding work. One of the ways to be sure students are doing DOK Level 4 work—cognitively complex work—is to make sure you teach youngsters to transfer what they learn in one discipline to another. As part of this, you will probably want to help children imagine the ways in which the skills learned in this unit can be applied to other areas of learning, as well. After finishing this unit, we suggest that you hold a small meeting with your students that goes something like the following.

Begin by rallying writers to transfer and apply all they've learned.

"Once you know a strategy, it's yours for life," you might begin. "We've learned that skills and strategies are meant to be used again and again. They don't get old and they don't wear out." Tell a small story to exemplify this, describing a life skill you learned that can be transferred to different areas of learning for different purposes. For instance, you could say, "Who here has heard stories about when they first learned to walk? For me, it began in a little walker with wheels. I'd sit in the tiny, red seat, swing my legs to and fro, and roll away toward new adventures. Eventually, I learned to walk on my own. It took several months, but my little legs soon mastered it. Later, I learned to run, hop, jump, and skip, too." Continue on, helping children to realize the value of transference and constant application. "Wouldn't it be silly if the day I learned to walk I said, 'Well, now that I know how to do that I'm never going to do it again. Walking is old news. I'm onto bigger and better things!' Of course, that would be ridiculous. Instead, I use what I know about walking every day. I use it to rush across the street before the light turns red. I use it to stroll along the

COMMON CORE STATE STANDARDS: W.5.3, W.5.4, W.5.7, W.5.8, RL.5.2, RI.5.6, SL.5.1, L.5.1, L.5.2, L.5.3

river on warm evenings. I use it to hike up steep mountains and hop over rocks and thick, fallen branches in the woods." Continue on, telling students that what they've learned about writing personal narratives can serve them for their whole lives, as well. "In many ways, writing is the same. What you've learned in all your years of writing workshop, and especially this past month, can help you in social studies, science, math, reading, and even personal, life matters."

Start by teaching children to transfer explicitly.

You'll want to begin by teaching children to transfer skills explicitly, making sure all of your learners have the opportunity to grasp this important work. For instance, one teacher began by taking a chart from the turning-points lesson and helped children imagine how a strategy for generating writing can also be a strategy for generating *ideas* about characters. After modeling how to identify and then reflect on turning points in characters' lives, the teacher hung the chart and encouraged readers to add this to their repertoire of strategies for developing theories while reading (see Figure 21–1).

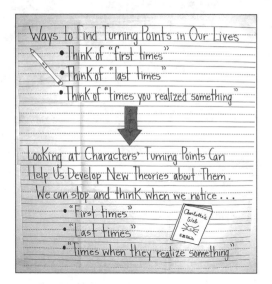

FIG. 21–1   One possible chart to support transference

Ways to Find Turning Points in Our Lives:

- Think of **first times.**
- Think of **last times.**
- Think of **times you realized something.**

Looking at Characters' Turning Points Can Help Us Develop Theories about Them. We Can Stop When We Notice:

- First times
- Last times
- Times when they realize something

This needn't only be a reading strategy, however. Allow yourself to imagine the other kinds of transference you hope for. Do you want children to use the strategies above to better understand historical figures? Do you want to teach children to reflect on their work and set personal goals in math? Do you want to teach children to research the life cycle of butterflies, using narrative writing to capture the insect's movement from birth to death? The possibilities are endless and will serve not only to reinforce children's narrative writing skills, but also to offer new access points from which to master new content.

Let go, allowing children to imagine the possibilities for transference and make choices of their own.

As children become accustomed to the idea of transferring skills across areas of learning, you'll want to give them opportunities to imagine some of these possibilities for themselves. After all, we know the highest cognitive demands come from work where children are asked to analyze a situation, evaluate their possibilities, and apply what they know independently You might tell children the intended outcome of their learning and allow them to devise their own plans for how they'll achieve that end point. For example, in one fifth-grade classroom, a teacher explained to students that they would have the opportunity to engage in their own independent research projects. Students were asked to use what they know about reading, research, and writing to convey the experiences of an escaped slave to the class. One student wrote a personal narrative from the perspective of a freed slave, using what he knew from writing workshop to convey the difficulties of having been a slave that escaped to freedom (see Figure 21–2).

The Black Snake Whip

Back in 1830 when I was a young boy, my life was so hard it made your life look as if it was heaven itself. All day I worked picking cotton until I could pick no more. But if I could pick no more out would come a black snake whip. Some saw that whip once a day, 'specially the old and sick.

That black snake whip had a 500 dollar price tag on it. Whenever that black snake whip came out, Master Smith said, "You see this tag? It says 500 dollars." And you've got to say "Yes, sir." And he would say "I make that much money in one day and if you don't do your share I make 480 dollars, you hear me?" And you've got to say "I do Mister Smith," Then he would give the whip to Sage the slave breaker. And that snake bit, hard.

On my 12th birthday my father told me to save up my free time so that he could give me his present. Every time I asked about it he would give me a mysterious smile—no more. After we had saved 6 hours of free time he took me into the forest and gave me my present. A bright red penny-knife. And during those 6 hours he taught me how to make a fire with 2 sticks and how to catch fish with nothing but my penny knife and some willow wood. Last of all he taught me how to find my way north. He told me that moss only grows on the north side of trees and he showed me the big dipper and the way to the north.

"There," he said "lies the promise land, but mind you, I won't let you run till you're 15."

And I did wait until I was 15. By then I knew everything I needed to know about survival so I wasn't about to let some slave catcher scare me.

So Saturday night, master's party night, I took off—not at full speed. I flitted from tree to tree, bush to bush, until I was at the woods. Then an owl hooted. I froze, but it was not the sound I was afraid to hear. Then I bolted into the woods. Then a cool wind blew against my face. And I relaxed.

In another classroom, children were asked to create a project as a culmination to their study of fractions. Jack, using his penchant for narrative writing, likened fractions to dragons as a way to illustrate their complex properties (see Figure 21–3).

FIG. 21–2 An excerpt from DJ's writing

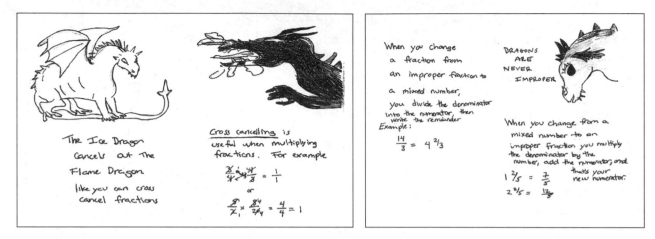
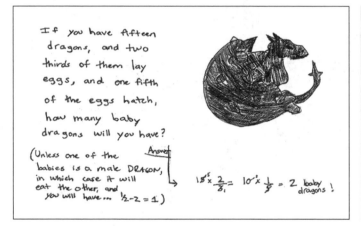

FIG. 21–3 Jack's book on fractions

In each of these examples, children gathered information from a variety of sources, synthesized that information, considered the desired outcome of their work (e.g., what the assignment called for), and applied what they knew about narrative writing to achieve that end goal.

Celebrate children's attempts to apply their learning across the curriculum.

More than anything, you'll want to celebrate as children attempt to carry learning from one area of the curriculum to another. Encourage this kind of thinking. You might wonder aloud during read-aloud, "Hmm…, the author seems to have stretched this part out. I wonder why. Let me think back to the work I do as a writer. Why might I stretch out a part of my story?" Then too, you'll want to exult in the moments when your students do this work on their own. "Class," you might say, "can I stop you for a moment? Sabera and

I were just talking about the reading she's doing in social studies. When she got to this one part, about the British taxes, she asked 'What is this really about?' She began to develop this theory about the Colonists, that for them it was less about the taxes and more about the fact that England wanted to control them in every way. Do you see the way she used a strategy from writing workshop, asking 'What is this really about?' to better understand history?"

In the end, we hope this work helps you foster independent, resourceful thinkers in your classroom while simultaneously reinforcing all they've learned this month.

Good Luck!
Lucy and Ali